The Creative Process

The Creative Process: Stories from the Arts and Sciences asks how celebrated works of art and breakthroughs in science came to be. What was the first inkling? What were the steps and missteps along the way? How was the process experienced by the creative person as it proceeded? And what are the implications for the psychology of the creative process?

Each chapter focuses on a specific creative endeavor, situating the work in the context of domain, culture, and historical era. Then it traces the development of the work—from what we know of its beginnings to its fulfillment. Qualitative materials—interviews, notebooks, diaries, sketches, drafts, and other writings—allow a story of the creative process as lived to emerge. The narratives exemplify established concepts in the psychology of creativity, propose broadening some, reveal the need for modification, and suggest new ones. Application of phenomenological frameworks illuminate the episodes in new ways as well. The case study approach proves again that each episode is unique, yet themes and variations come into view when the episodes are considered together in a final reflection.

From Darwin's theory to an unusual jazz sound, here are 11 fascinating stories of how specific works took shape. Psychologists, students interested in creativity, and all those intrigued by the process from any creative field will find this book essential reading.

Charlotte L. Doyle, psychology professor at Sarah Lawrence College, Bronxville, New York, is an avid explorer of the creative process. She has written articles and book chapters on her research, on the educational implications of creativity findings, and on theoretical considerations such as how the features of flow challenge theories of cognition. She is also author of several textbooks including *Explorations in Psychology* and, to her surprise, seven picture books for children.

The Creative Process
Stories from the Arts and Sciences

Charlotte L. Doyle

 Routledge
Taylor & Francis Group

NEW YORK AND LONDON

First published 2022
by Routledge
605 Third Avenue, New York, NY 10158

and by Routledge
2 Park Square, Milton Park, Abingdon, Oxon, OX14 4RN

Routledge is an imprint of the Taylor & Francis Group, an informa business

© 2022 Charlotte L. Doyle

Library of Congress Cataloging-in-Publication Data
A catalog record for this title has been requested

ISBN: 9780367856052 (hbk)
ISBN: 9780367856021 (pbk)
ISBN: 9781003013860 (ebk)

DOI: 10.4324/9781003013860

Typeset in Berling Roman
by Deanta Global Publishing Services, Chennai, India

For Margery and Ray

Contents

Acknowledgments   *ix*
Illustration Permissions and Credits   *xi*

Introduction   1

Part I: Classic Case Studies of Creative Episodes: Reflections and Extensions   **7**

1   How Poincaré Inspired Psychologists: Experiences in a
    Mathematics Contest   9

2   Darwin's Path to Evolution Theory: Changing Frameworks and
    Feelings   22

3   Picasso's *Guernica*: The Creative Process in Art as Visual Thinking   37

Part II: Creating as Navigating Among Different Psychological Worlds   **51**

4   Creating Novels and Short Stories: The Writing Realm and the
    Fiction World   53

5   Acting for the Stage: How Three Actors Created Their Roles   66

Part III: Focus on Intuition and Embodied Creating   **79**

6   Music by Biscardi: Letting the Hands Go Someplace   81

7   Sendak's Search: Finding and Taming the *Wild Things*   94

**Part IV: Writers as Phenomenologists: Discoveries from
Exploring the Inner Landscape** **107**

8   Tolstoy's *Anna Karenina:* From Condemnation to Understanding   109

9   Woolf's *To the Lighthouse:* Revelations from Streams of Consciousness 122

Part V: Creating Collaborations in Science and Art **135**

10   Blackburn and Company: Unraveling the Telomere Mysteries   137

11   Ron Carter's Nonet: Inventing and Developing a New Sound   150

Epilogue   *163*
Index   *171*

Acknowledgments

The power of learning about the creative process through a fine-grained study of single creative episodes came to me first from Rudolf Arnheim and his close look at Picasso's sketches for *Guernica*. Rudi later became a supportive mentor and friend. Howard Gruber's poring through Darwin's notebooks gave me a second example of the value of investigating the process through careful inquiry into a single episode. A third inspiration came from my late husband, playwright Jim Doyle, when I lived with his creative episodes as they emerged.

My own systematic inquiry into creative episodes came from interviews and I am enormously grateful to those who shared their worlds as their creative work took shape: writers Kathleen Hill, Mary LaChapelle, the late Jerome Badanes, and the late Grace Paley; actors Leon Addison Brown, James DeMarse and Lois Smith; music-makers Chester Biscardi and Ron Carter. Their generosity in disclosing their difficult, their pedestrian, and their sublime moments as their creative episodes evolved, was awe-inspiring.

The idea of writing a book was only a hazy idea in my mind until Marlena Sullivan visited my office to talk about trends in psychology and then asked me if I ever thought of writing a book. When I told her maybe, sometime in the future, she introduced me to Taylor & Francis and editor Ceri McLardy. Ceri followed up right away and stimulated me to think seriously about the possibility. And when I found words to embody my vague thoughts, she immediately grasped the kind of book I was thinking of writing, encouraged me, and has been exceptionally supportive throughout the writing process. I am grateful for her enthusiasm, flexibility, and understanding.

I thank Museo Reina Sofia and the Pablo Picasso Museum Paris for their comprehensive online displays of Picasso's work. Clara Nguyen, the archivist at the University of Connecticut in charge of the Sendak Collection, was exceptionally generous in making material from the collection available to me. Zhongtian Zhang, a talented microbiology researcher, sharpened the accuracy of the Elizabeth Blackburn chapter. Robert Blaisdell shared a pre-publication draft of his book on *Anna Karenina* before it was available to the public; I thank him for his kindness and for his insights.

Sarah Lawrence College, my academic home for many years, supported me with a semester of paid leave and a stipend for a faculty assistant; I thank President Cristle Collins Judd, Dean Kanwal Singh, Associate Dean Melissa Frazier, and the Faculty Advisory Committee on Appointments for making these possible. Jerrilynn Dodds, my friend and art historian extraordinaire, walked a naive and sometimes frazzled author through the process of acquiring figures with patience and grace. Philip Ording of the mathematics faculty helped me to understand the technicalities of Poincaré's contributions. Susan Guma, friend and for many years Sarah Lawrence Dean of Graduate Studies, suggested I interview Ron Carter and put me in contact with him. Carter Wilken, an outstanding former student, did all sorts of things cheerfully to help ready the manuscript ready for publication.

No book is published without the help of a production team. I am grateful to production editor Lauren Ellis and her team, project manager Lillian Woodall, the art department, and editorial assistant Shreya Bajpai for their shepherding the process from manuscript to book.

Writing a book can be lonely, especially sheltering at home alone during a pandemic. Family and friends kept up my spirits with regular contact via the internet. I am grateful to Jim Doyle Jr. and David Doyle, Bob Lackner and Janice Harris, Jim and Tomi Allison, Emily Devine and Jim Lee, Alan and Susan Guma, Ray Franklin, Pamela Pollack, Barbara Schecter, and Nemo, Lidia Li and baby James Zhang.

Nor did I feel alone in the writing itself. Margery Franklin was my intellectual companion every step of the way. Margery had been my colleague at Sarah Lawrence College and remains my mentor and my friend. Week by week, I shared what I was doing, discussed the problems that emerged, and communicated my uncertainties. Her sensitive listening, her deep and wide-ranging understanding of psychology, her wisdom, and her unending support were crucial as the writing of this book unfolded.

Illustration Permissions and Credits

Introduction

The story of creating a moving work in the arts or a groundbreaking discovery in science is fascinating in and of itself. The twists and turns along the way and the final triumphs are inspiring and can deepen understanding of the work. They are also important for psychology's study of the mind, examples of human functioning at its very best.

This book tells such stories. Some are of the making of works that are generally acknowledged as pioneering such as Maurice Sendak's *Where the Wild Things Are* and Picasso's *Guernica*. Others have been recognized by their colleagues but are not as well-known, such as the Blackburn and Greider work on telomeres and two works by composer Chester Biscardi.

Each chapter looks at a specific episode with an effort to find out how it was experienced by the creative person over time. Beginning with the initial seed, the chapter traces what we know of the lived experience as we follow the steps and missteps along the way to the project's final fulfillment—a narrative-phenomenological approach. Of course, experience as it was once lived can never be fully recovered. But it can be reconstructed from traces left behind. Darwin kept notebooks; Woolf wrote diaries and letters. Picasso drew sketches. Biscardi, bandleader Carter, and New York actors and writers agreed to interviews. Tolstoy left behind five drafts of *Anna Karenina* and letters; Poincaré wrote an essay on his own creative process and corresponded with other mathematicians. Biographies put the traces left behind in context with information about what else was happening in the creator's life in the midst of a creative project.

No one clue is a flawless path to the creative experience itself. Memory is not perfect whether recalled in an interview or written in a memoir. Journals and diaries are selective depending on how the diarist sees its purpose. Drafts and sketches reveal only part of the story. Here, a rich supply of clues support one another—diary material supporting drafts, interview material confirmed by other sources.

Psychologists look for insight into the creative process in many different ways. Laboratory researchers focus on what they see as elements or models of the process under controlled conditions. Theorists from psychoanalytic traditions apply concepts from psychoanalytic theory to deepen their understanding of creative episodes in terms that they find meaningful. Ward (2001), a distinguished laboratory researcher, has called for a convergent approach, one which draws on various approaches looking for convergence. Each chapter will explore the extent to which the stories confirm in context what these different approaches have offered and show how they interact

DOI: 10.4324/9781003013860-1

in particular creative episodes: concepts like field, heuristics, incubation, insight, flow, and processes outside the light of consciousness. At the same time the book will present what a narrative-phenomenological approach to case studies can add. Some traditional concepts will be enlarged: the concept of conceptual combination will be broadened into the idea of convergence of streams. The work of phenomenologist Alfred Schütz on psychological worlds, applied to the experience of creating, provides a new way of looking at incubation. In turn, exploration of the experience of creating points to extending the framework to include interactions among the different worlds.

The story of each creative episode is unique. Its uniqueness is part of its fascination. To follow it means going into detail in the substance of the creator's thinking. Thus along the way, we will learn about evolution theory, different approaches to theatrical acting, the microbiology of the caps of chromosomes, the many tasks of a bandleader. The very detail makes visible some features of the creative process. When all the stories in this book have been told, the epilogue will look at themes that speak to the range of experiences these particular episodes suggest.

The people whose stories are told in this book were chosen, in part, because extensive clues to their creative process as it unfolded were available to the author. They come from the last 250 years and from societies that have recognized traditions in the arts, mathematics, and the sciences—a limited range. Yet, the episodes described here reflect an amazing variety of experiences, material enough to intrigue psychologists, scholars, and all who seek to understand the human mind at work.

THE PLAN OF THE BOOK

The chapters are grouped under five themes. Once a theme and the concepts related to it are introduced, they thread their way through the rest of the book. The three chapters in Part I present classic case studies of the creative process and reflections on them. Chapter 1 highlights Poincaré's description of his creative experiences on the way of putting together his entry for a mathematics competition. Psychologist Wallas drew on Poincaré's material in putting together an influential four-stage account of the creative process which, in turn, inspired a great deal of research on creativity. A look back at Poincaré's description in the context of his life brings to the fore many of the concepts that have since emerged in psychology and so an opportunity to review some of the creativity domain's most relevant findings. Poincaré's description also points to ways in which his experience differed from laboratory studies and to the variety of ways the creative process may unfold.

Chapter 2 considers Darwin's creation of the theory of evolution through natural selection. It draws extensively on the insights of Howard Gruber who did a pioneering study of Darwin's notebooks in the period when Darwin was putting together his evolution theory. Gruber constructed a step-by-step account of Darwin's changing thinking and put forward concepts which capture features of Darwin's work, concepts which continue to provide tools for studying episodes of the creative process. The chapter supplements Gruber's presentation with help of primary sources and two excellent biographies in telling Darwin's story, sources that throw additional light on the emotional aspects of his creative experience.

Chapter 3 tells the story of Picasso's process in painting the mural *Guernica*. It, too, was the subject of a pioneering study of a creative episode, influential in art history as well as psychology. Rudolf Arnheim studied all the known preliminary sketches that Picasso preserved as well as photographs of various states of the mural. An artist as well as a psychologist, Arnheim saw images as conveying meaning in several different ways and showed how images give clues to visual thinking. Applying these concepts to Picasso's sketches and stages, Arnheim followed Picasso's thinking through the changes. The chapter adds the discovery of mural sketches made before the bombing of Guernica and considers how this enriches the understanding of Picasso's creative process. The chapter also introduces the term *avatar* to refer to an artist's representation of some distinctive features of a living person without portraying all of them.

Part II formally introduces Schütz's framework of psychological worlds as a way of capturing the experience of the creative process. Chapter 4 is based on qualitative interviews with four contemporary fiction writers. The similarity in their stories suggested a tentative account of their fiction writing. Among the interview highlights was a striking change in their descriptions. First they spoke about what they wanted or planned to do using the word *I*. Then they spoke of a flow that they experienced as the story appearing to them, their fingers writing without conscious control. As their writing unfolded, they told of being surprised by what the characters were doing and by unexpected events. Following Schütz, the writers had entered a mode of experience outside the everyday, a *fiction world*. His multiple reality framework provided tools for analyzing the features of the fiction world in contrast with those of an everyday world of action and a reflective *writing realm*.

Chapter 5 draws again on qualitative interviews, here with three actors telling the story of their creation of their characters in scripted plays. They too described several different modes of experience which pointed to three different psychological worlds: the everyday world, a reflective world in which they analyzed their roles, and a drama world in which they let go of conscious control and responded spontaneously to one another as their characters. The chapter extends the multiple realities framework as the actors' descriptions suggested the ways in which the different psychological worlds affected one another successively and simultaneously. For example, when the actors were on stage in the drama world, the everyday world was implicitly in the background with possible figure-ground reversals elicited by events such as prop malfunctions or cell phones going off.

Part III considers creative episodes that highlight the roles of intuition and embodied creation. Chapter 6 traces modern classical music composer Chester Biscardi's process as he created two different works. The two creative processes differed in the seeds that started the composing, the duration of the creative episode, and the degree to which structure was present at the start. Major aspects were the same: Composing had to be done at the piano with fingers on the keys—embodied composing in a music world. A body intuition told when a passage was right. If not, heuristics suggested variations to play till something did. Diary entries revealed the intrusion of everyday concerns about his identity as a composer during worktime and creative visitations amid other activities.

Intuitively, his hands led him to universal musical meaning with personal significance as well.

Chapter 7 follows Maurice Sendak's process as he wrote and illustrated the children's book *Where the Wild Things Are*. Sendak called the eight-year lag between an early version about wild horses and returning to the project "his apprenticeship." The chapter follows the changes from the wild horses draft, through wandering, free-associational drafts, to a final text in which every single word mattered. At times he played with possibilities, recognizing what felt intuitively right when it appeared in his writing and sketching—examples of embodied creation. Often it was the word or image that captured multiple meanings. The chapter also tells how "things" came to replace horses and why Sendak spoke of this book as "more myself" than any he created earlier.

Part IV tells of the creative processes of writers who, in a sense, became phenomenological psychologists, as they developed new literary forms to portray their characters' inner worlds. Chapter 8 traces the changes in drafts Tolstoy wrote for *Anna Karenina*. Early drafts saw an adulteress as unattractive and socially coarse, hurtful to her kind, sensitive, but awkward husband; the final book finds her beautiful, socially graceful, and intelligent, saddled with a cold, unattractive mate. The early drafts had a single plot, adultery. Later drafts had two major plots with a happy marriage as major counterpoint. The theme then broadened again, this time portraying how different characters lost and found meaning. Accompanying these changes and perhaps stimulating them was a change in writing style, most scenes now told from the perspective and feelings of one character or another as they encountered dramatic events. Form and content developed together, inextricably intertwined.

Chapter 9 presents Virginia Woolf's process as she was creating *To The Lighthouse*. Beginning with wanting to deal fictionally with her childhood, her first intention was to write a short story, then a novel based on her father. An unexpected fiction world flow brought her the structure for the book. Woolf's method for much of the book was one she had been developing, multiple streams of consciousness. As she wrote, she discovered that her mother's avatar was to take center stage. The character of a painter was one of several avatars in the book for Woolf herself and allowed her to describe her own experience of the creative process. Though Woolf's work was intermittently interrupted by physical and emotional illness, she persevered, and not only produced an important modernist novel but also brought relief from obsessions that had been haunting her for years. Her multiple stream of consciousness form was the key.

The chapters in Part V describe episodes in which someone envisioned and brought to fruition a creative episode that required collaborators. Chapter 10 is an exploration of the creative process in contemporary, laboratory science. Scientific method, as it is taught, is clear and objective: hypothesize, experiment, see if the hypothesis is confirmed—if not, start again. This chapter looks instead at the creative process as it was lived by Elizabeth Blackburn and her collaborators. When Blackburn was introduced to a quirky one-celled organism, *Tetrahymena thermophila*, she "fell in love." It was the ideal organism to study telomeres, the caps that prevented chromosomes from unraveling. She was curious about the structure of telomeres and found mystery in how they were formed. Working with a peer with different expertise and a determined graduate student who wouldn't give up, with the courage to risk a cockamamie experiment and an intuition that went against received wisdom, a series of experiments uncovered findings that thrilled the investigators and startled the field.

Chapter 11 takes us to the world of jazz, to bassist Ron Carter, and his invention of a new sound. He had always heard music reverberate in his head. From a background of first playing classical cello but moving to the jazz bass, he began hearing other sounds— melodies to compose, standards to arrange, a new instrument to invent. All this culminated in his hearing a sound like no other, one that integrated the strains of four classical cellos with the improvisatory playing of a jazz quintet—a nonet. He had to find the players, discover what they could do together, compose and arrange music for them, adapt the music to their musical strengths, win their respect and trust. The chapter tells how these multiple creative endeavors came to fruition in the performances of his nonet, each performance bringing surprises as it was created anew in the present.

The book concludes with an epilogue, reflections on some of the themes and variations that emerged when considering the previous creative episodes together.

So, to begin…

REFERENCE

Ward, T. B. (2001). Creative cognition, conceptual combination, and the creative writing of Stephen R. Donaldson. *American Psychologist, 56,* 350–354.

PART I

Classic Case Studies of Creative Episodes

Reflections and Extensions

CHAPTER 1

How Poincaré Inspired Psychologists

Experiences in a Mathematics Contest

Henri Poincaré was a mathematician, physicist, and mining engineer who became well-known in psychology. The reason is that Poincaré was not only entranced by mathematics; he was fascinated by the workings of the mind that result in mathematical discovery. His essay on mathematical invention included a detailed description of how he experienced a creative episode. That description began this way:

> It is time to penetrate more deeply and to see what goes on in the very soul of the mathematician. For this, I believe, I can do best by recalling memories of my own... I beg the reader's pardon; I am about to use some technical expressions... I shall say, for example, that I have found the demonstration of such a theorem under such circumstances. This theorem will have a barbarous name, unfamiliar to many, but that is unimportant; what is of interest for the psychologist is not the theorem but the circumstances.
>
> *(Poincaré, 1908/1910, p. 326)*

Poincaré's account of his creative episode, along with a brief introduction to his path in mathematics, the context of his creative work, and why it became famous in research psychology is this chapter's story. Along the way, his story illustrates many concepts that psychologists interested in creativity subsequently have put forward and suggests some new considerations.

POINCARÉ BEFORE ENTERING THE COMPETITION

Henri Poincaré (1854–1912) was born near-sighted and had a serious bout of diphtheria when he was five years old. It left him paralyzed for two months and with lifelong poor muscle coordination. He was unable to speak for months, but he invented a set of signs to communicate which worked especially well in "conversation" with his three-year-old

DOI: 10.4324/9781003013860-3

sister. The near-sightedness often meant he could not see the blackboard in school, but he developed a powerful visual imagination and an excellent visual memory, so he did very well in school—he was commended for the content of his writing in elementary school and for his quickness in learning mathematics in high school. Still, he was occasionally penalized in mathematics because he had problems drawing diagrams.

In 1870, France and Prussia were at war, and Prussian soldiers occupied the Poincaré home. Sixteen-year-old Poincaré took the opportunity to improve his German. That later became useful when he exchanged letters with a German mathematician. France lost that war to Prussia, but unlike some parts of Alsace-Lorraine, Poincaré's home city, Nancy, remained part of France.

Poincaré's problems in drawing diagrams kept him from going to the top French higher institution for mathematics and so he trained as a mining engineer instead. Yet he continued to work on mathematics with one of the professors at the School of Mines. As 1877 turned into 1878, when he was still at the mining school, he submitted a doctoral dissertation on differential equations to the mathematics faculty at the University of Paris. In it, among other inventions, Poincaré devised a new method for studying such equations. And though his doctoral committee chided him for submitting a dissertation with careless errors and the need for further explanation, they applauded the challenging questions he undertook to answer and the range of material. One supervisor, Darboux (quoted in Verhulst, 2012) wrote that Poincaré's work contained enough material for several good dissertations, that he thought intuitively, and that it would be easy to correct. Poincaré later explained his carelessness by telling Darboux that other ideas were occupying his mind. It was typical Poincaré. When he found a school subject boring, he tuned out, a habit that sometimes lowered his class standing. Fortunately, he was fascinated by most subjects he studied and had a stellar school record. In the case of his dissertation, he had already made his discoveries and now new questions had taken over his mind. Though we don't know much about them, those early thoughts may have been the beginnings of a new creative episode.

Why would Poincaré's mind wander when his task was to perfect his dissertation—an important step to launching his career? Psychologists have studied mind-wandering away from an assigned task (see Smallwood & Schooler, 2015). They asked, where does the mind of the mind-wanderer go? Research found that thoughts go to matters of self-relevance—ruminations and regrets, remembering and preparing for upcoming events, planning action for future goals—in general unresolved or unfinished business of importance to the mind-wanderer. We can surmise that Poincaré's thinking on his dissertation felt complete and the writing to be done seemed a trivial task. Once new questions came to him, finding a solution mattered.[1]

It is likely that a new problem beckoned to Poincaré, stealing his concentration from the task at hand. Psychologists contrast *intrinsic motivation* (that which comes from within) with *extrinsic motivation* (that which comes from outside incentives). They have shown that intrinsic rather than extrinsic motivation is more likely to lead to work judged to be creative (Amabile, 1996). Inventing in mathematics was intrinsically motivating for Poincaré. He was drawn to it like metal to a magnet. Yet, motivations are often mixed. A mathematics competition was announced a few months later and the money and the prestige provided additional extrinsic motivation.

THE PRIZE COMPETITION

In March 1878, the *Académie des Sciences* in Paris challenged mathematicians "To improve in some important way the theory of linear differential equations in a single independent variable." Lazarus Fuchs was a leading German mathematician and the author of the theory. Jeremy Gray (2013), a mathematician, mathematics historian, and Poincaré biographer, suggested that part of the reason for the choice of question was to spur French mathematicians to catch up and go beyond the subject of Fuchs's work. Though France lost the war, here was an opportunity to "win" something over Prussia (Gray, 2013). The creative episode takes place in the context of a particular culture and a specific time in its history (Wallace, 1985; Gruber, 1981).

The spur provided by a competition illustrates what psychologist Csikszentmihalyi (1996) pointed out: a person's creative process is always related to a *domain*, a culturally defined subject area, and a *field*, the people and institutions that provide opportunities and make decisions about whose work will become part of the domain. The schools and professors that educated Poincaré in mathematics were part of the field. And so was the *Académie*—an opportunity maker and gatekeeper for the domain of mathematics; its sponsoring the competition created opportunity and incentive for working on particular kinds of problems. Poincaré's (1908/1910) essay on the creative process in mathematics drew heavily on the experiences that resulted in his entry in the competition created by the field.

The word "entries" may be more appropriate than the word "entry." Poincaré submitted his first entry on March 22, 1880. But then, on May 28 he submitted a new one. Poincaré added an 80-page supplement on June 28. In September and December, he sent two more supplements to the contest judges. This was not the usual way of entering a competition (Gray, 2013).

Several sources of information help us to glimpse what happened. First of all, we have Poincaré's description of his experiences which refer to this period. Though memory almost 30 years later may be inaccurate, there is corroborating evidence. An exchange of letters between Poincaré and Fuchs support the essay. Gray and Walter (1997) found the originals of the various versions of the entries and traced their progress. Finally, Toulouse (1910), a psychologist who tested and interviewed Poincaré, wrote about Poincaré's usual routine. Here is one way of putting together the story based on these sources.

Toulouse (1910) reported that Poincaré generally followed the same schedule. He worked on mathematics in the morning between 10 am and 12 pm and again between 5 and 7 pm. He was a lecturer at the University of Caen at the time and perhaps he taught in the afternoons. Poincaré told Toulouse that he did not do mathematics later in the evening for fear it would keep him awake so he read instead.

Here's another piece of the puzzle: his first entry sent in March 1880, perhaps the problem that kept him from concentrating on the writing of his dissertation, was different from the subjects of his later submissions. Its area within the mathematics domain, real differential equations, was one less directly concerned with Fuchs's work than the entries he sent in next.

Conjecture: perhaps the event that spurred work on the May 28 entry was reading more of Fuchs's work during his evening reading sessions. Fuchs had theorized that for a certain class of differential equations to give a particular result, there were conditions, both necessary and sufficient, that have to be met. During his work periods, Poincaré started out to prove Fuchs's theory, but the events of one sleepless night led him elsewhere.

Poincaré himself pointed out above, his description is intriguing for psychology even though many, including this author, do not understand the mathematics involved. The excerpt below is the first of five we will consider. Just as writing a novel consists of different chapters, so Poincaré's contest entry came in a series of five related waves, five chapters in his creative episode.

The Road to a New Entry: Effortful Cognition, Heuristics, and Flow

This is how Poincaré described his first discovery related to Fuchs's work:

> For fifteen days I strove to prove that there could not be any functions like those I have since called Fuchsian functions. I was then very ignorant; every day I seated myself at my work table, stayed an hour or two, tried a great number of combinations and reached no results. One evening, contrary to my custom, I drank black coffee and could not sleep. Ideas rose in crowds; I felt them collide until pairs interlocked, so to speak, making a stable combination. By the next morning I had established the existence of a class of Fuchsian functions, those which come from the hypergeometric series; I had only to write out the results, which took but a few hours.
>
> *(Poincaré, 1908/1910, p. 326)*

This excerpt and the paragraphs that followed it became important to psychology because Graham Wallas (1926) used them to support the framework for the creative process he had been putting together, a framework psychologists have returned to again and again to support, add to, and modify (recently by Sadler-Wells, 2015; see also, Doyle, 2016). Wallas delineated four stages that resulted in what he called "the birth of an idea": (1) preparation: preparation of two kinds: concentrated, effortful work on a known problem, but also education in the domain of a problem; (2) incubation, a period of turning away from working on the problem; (3) illumination (today called insight), the sudden appearance of a solution. Wallas added that just before illumination, the person is likely to have the feeling that an answer is coming which he called "intimation"; (4) verification, the conscious effortful task of proving the insight. Wallas quotes Poincaré as saying that verification is not mechanical. The insight does not include how to prove it and once again, hard, effortful work is required. Poincaré's description provides clear evidence of Wallas's preparation stage, the 15 days of wrestling with a problem he set for himself. Wallas would also include his education in mathematics as part of the preparation. There was little or no incubation stage, a reason Wallas was less interested in this part of Poincaré's description than the ones that followed. And though Wallas placed the intimation stage as occurring during incubation, we have a suggestion that intimation came immediately after preparation on a particular day. For why did Poincaré abandon his usual schedule, drink black coffee, and stay awake through the night?

Another intriguing feature of Poincaré's description is the language he used to describe his experience on the fateful night. "Ideas rose in crowds and interlocked over time." He does not say, "I thought this" or "I tried that," which is the way he described the 15 previous days. Here he doesn't say he reflected on relationships among ideas. He felt the ideas collide. He was no longer trying. The description fits what psychologists have called *effortless attention* (Bruya, 2010) and *flow* (Csikszentmihalyi, 1999), a period when experience is focused yet spontaneous, with no self-consciousness or distraction interfering with what effortlessly comes to mind. Poincaré was living in the world of mathematical ideas, no longer centered on the everyday world around him.[2]

Note also, Poincaré did not solve the problem he set out to solve—that mathematical functions with certain properties could not exist. The flow resulted in an insight which was the opposite of what he set out to prove—the identification of a new set of functions which broadened the kinds of functions and the conditions Fuchs had considered. The solution brought with it a spontaneous reorganization of his understanding of what the problem was. This feature, insight emerging from spontaneous reorganization of the initial problem representation, was emphasized by the Gestalt psychologists, for example, Max Wertheimer (1936).

To continue with Poincaré's description, which is the next chapter of the episode:

> Then I wanted to represent these functions by the quotient of two series; this idea was perfectly conscious and deliberate, the analogy with elliptic functions guided me. I asked myself what properties these series must have if they existed, and I succeeded without difficulty in forming the series I have called theta-Fuchsian.
>
> *(Poincaré, 1908/1910, p. 326)*

The excerpt tells us that Poincaré knew what to do next: to ask himself questions about the properties of his new functions. And he had a strategy for finding the answer: use a related function as a guide. Once he posed the problem to himself in this way, there was a likely path to a solution. Psychologists call such strategies, which are likely but not guaranteed to bring progress toward a solution, *heuristics* (Duncker, 1945; Newell & Simon, 1972). The heuristics Poincaré used were "explore properties" and "use an analogy as a guide." The use of analogy is one of a number of heuristics psychologists have put forward as microprocesses that may be engaged by the creative process (Ward, 2001).

For this phase of his work, Poincaré called on generative, conscious problem solving using heuristics to come to a creative result. The creative process does not always proceed in the same way, not in different people, not in the same person on different occasions.

On May 28, 1880, Poincaré replaced his original entry with these new discoveries. The next day, Poincaré wrote a letter to Fuchs raising some questions which arose with respect to the new findings. That started a correspondence that continued through the year, Poincaré writing in French, Fuchs in German, both fully capable of understanding each other. Though Poincaré's discoveries went beyond Fuchs's work, the exchange kept him thinking about the conditions Fuchs put forward for his class of functions and Fuchs provided him with new equations to think about (Gray, 2013).

The Road to the First Supplement: Incubation in Life and in the Laboratory

His new entry submitted, it was time for Poincaré to take a vacation. Early in June, he put mathematics aside and went out of town on a geological expedition with a friend. Poincaré's description continued:

> Just at this time I left Caen, where I was then living, to go on a geologic excursion under the auspices of the school of mines. The changes of travel made me forget my mathematical work. Having reached Coutances, we entered an omnibus to go someplace or other. At the moment when I put my foot on the step the idea came to me, without anything in my former thoughts seeming to have paved the way for it, that the transformations I had used to define the Fuchsian functions were identical with those of non-Euclidean geometry. I did not verify the idea; I should not have had time, as, upon taking my seat in the omnibus, I went on with a conversation already commenced, but I felt a perfect certainty. On my return to Caen, for conscience sake I verified the result at my leisure.
>
> *(Poincaré, 1908/1910, pp. 326–327)*

That verification (at leisure?) involved 80 pages and constituted the first supplement that Poincaré submitted to his contest entry on June 28. It became the discovery that established Poincaré as a major mathematician. This description, along with two that followed also became major ones that Wallas drew on as evidence of the importance of an incubation stage, a period of turning away from the problem and doing something else.

The Research Study of Incubation

Wallas's framework, in turn, led research psychologists to ask: Can we find evidence that incubation facilitates the creative process more than continuous working on a task? And if so, why?

Teams of researchers selected laboratory tasks that seemed to capture an aspect of the creative process. One was presenting problems that demand insightful problem solving; another, the unusual uses test which contains questions such as "Think of uses for a brick," a test of divergent thinking (Guilford, 1950). (Divergent thinking contrasts with the traditional intelligence test because it calls for as many answers as possible rather than the one correct answer.) To demonstrate the effect of incubation, an experimenter typically had one group work continuously on divergent thinking questions and another either rest or do a distracting task. After a period, the experimenters again allowed the incubation groups to continue to work on the divergent thinking questions. Overall, experimenters found that the average scores of the incubation groups were higher than those who worked on the task continuously—laboratory evidence of the helpfulness of incubation.[3]

Psychologists have also put forward various theoretical suggestions for the mental processes underlying incubation: (1) a tired mind is rested during incubation; (2) there is opportunity to forget unsuccessful paths that had seemed productive; (3) something perceived in the environment gives a clue to the solution; or (4) unconscious associational and organizational processes below the level of consciousness take place during incubation with only the solution rising into consciousness. Each of these possibilities is supported by some research. Underlying all these explanations is the assumption that while the incubator's conscious mind was elsewhere occupied, the incomplete task was still active, creating a tension, and when an answer presented itself, it bursts into consciousness—suddenly, surprisingly, and with a sense of certainty (Topolinski & Reber, 2010).

Poincaré himself theorized about why incubation led to the insight. He, too, suggested that perhaps the mind was tired and needed rest. But he favored the idea that unconscious processes, perhaps resembling those he had consciously experienced on his sleepless night. Then he felt relevant ideas rising and making connections; after, the simultaneous reorganization of the problem and its solution came to him. He also wrote that his experiences of insight were not just cognitive. They came with an emotional element, an aesthetic emotion: "the feeling of mathematical beauty, of the harmony of numbers and forms, of geometric elegance...a true esthetic feeling that all real mathematicians know" (Poincaré, 1910, p. 331).

Poincaré's Experiences and Those of the Research Participants

Note some of the differences between Poincaré's experiences and those of the groups who worked in the laboratory. First, the research evidence that incubation facilitates creativity comes from demonstrating incubation groups produce more creative answers if they have an imposed, timed incubation period between the first and second presentation of a problem. Poincaré's insights came to him *during* the incubation period.

Second, though Wallas related Poincaré's bus insight to incubation, he had not consciously formulated a problem. So there was no initial problem his mind had been wrestling with and was now incubating on, no preparation period other than his education. Poincaré wrote: "the idea came to me, without anything in my former thoughts seeming to have paved the way for it." So this is evidence that there need not always be a clear initial problem. Poincaré's mind wandered to the world of mathematics[2] even when he was presumably on vacation and talking to a friend. Fuchsian functions were an active area of his thinking and he tended to think visually. So, his mind may have wandered to other visual subdomains in mathematics and suddenly he recognized the similarities between them. Or, perhaps he saw a form such as a saddle or a lettuce leaf, surfaces that mathematicians sometimes use to picture of non-Euclidian geometry and that was when the relation to Fuchsian functions came to him—again the problem and the solution coming simultaneously.

Third, generally, the laboratory researchers typically call on college students to participate in their experiments. The students tend to be cooperative but the tasks given are not tasks of major personal import. For Poincaré as a young mathematician, winning the contest promised prize money and prestige. Yet, the contest was not the beginning of Poincaré's work on differential equations. The subject was of deep intrinsic interest to him. He felt he had completed his entry when he went off and his correspondence with Fuchs was specifically on those functions. Perhaps wondering where he could take his new discovery next was on his mind without conscious awareness.

Fourth, the laboratory studies typically took place in a few hours or less. A period of working on the problem, an incubation period, and another period of working on the problem. Poincaré wrestled with the initial problem for 15 days, but he did not work on it all day. As Toulouse reported, he did mathematics in two-hour shifts with five hours in between—a much longer period than the typical incubation periods in the psychologists' experiments. So Poincaré had other occasions for incubation, but they didn't yield insights. Sometimes the Poincaré's turning away from the problem had no effect and sometimes it did. The difference was that the incubation leading to insight occurred when Poincaré stepped out of his usual routine, when he was prevented from his normal schedule. He left home for new places, and engaged in activities that did not allow his usual work.

Poincaré did not totally trust that sense of certainty. He knew the possibility of false insight. He had to prove the correctness of his solution to others, but he also needed to prove it to himself. He needed to find which logical steps could prove his insight valid by conscious, effortful work—Wallas's verification stage. The laboratory research on incubation usually does not require a verification stage.

The Road to the Second Supplement: Incubation and Streams Coming Together

Poincaré's descriptions continued with a second insight coming to him during an incubation period.

> Then I turned my attention to the study of some arithmetical questions apparently without much success and without a suspicion of any connection with my preceding researches. Disgusted with my failure, I went to spend a few days at the seaside, and thought of something else. One morning, walking on the bluff, the idea came to me, with just the same characteristics of brevity, suddenness and immediate certainty, that the arithmetic transformations of indeterminate ternary quadratic forms were identical with those of non-Euclidean geometry.
>
> Returned to Caen, I meditated on this result and deduced the consequences. The example of quadratic forms showed me that there were Fuchsian groups other than those corresponding to the hypergeometric series; I saw that I could apply to them the theory of theta-Fuchsian series and that consequently there existed Fuchsian functions other than those from the hypergeometric series, the ones I then knew. Naturally I set myself to form all these functions. I made a systematic attack upon them and carried all the outworks, one after another. There was one however that still held out, whose fall would involve that of the whole place. But all my efforts only served at first the better to show me the difficulty, which indeed was something. All this work was perfectly conscious.
>
> *(Poincaré, 1908/1910, pp. 327–328)*

So what does this description now tell us? His entry with his first supplement now completed, Poincaré took up questions in another subdomain of mathematics, number theory. His efforts seemed to go nowhere, so he took some time off and went off to a seashore. Walking on the beach, the relationships between non-Euclidian geometry and number theory came to him; he worked out the consequences but discovered a remaining problem.

Note the nature of the discoveries in the first two supplements. Mathematics, as many domains, had many subdomains. Just as fiction has many different genres, and most writers work in one of them, so there are many areas within mathematics and most mathematicians specialize in one of them. Now Poincaré's mind tore down the boundaries between subareas he had studied separately and allowed them to merge.

Merge

Several psychologists have put forward the idea that a property of the creative process involves remotely associated ideas coming together (Mednick, 1962; Ward, 2001). But in Poincaré's case, it was not simply associates coming together. He saw the relations among whole subareas of mathematics that traditionally have been seen as separate. Two psychologists have put forward concepts that capture what he achieved as a feature of the creative process. Gruber (1981) wrote of the interaction among a *network of enterprises* as possibly leading to creative work. Franklin (1989) wrote of the emergence of many new works as the result of the *convergence of streams*, each stream, an ongoing sphere of concern, activities, knowledge, skills, aims, wishes, and feelings that have unity for the experiencing person.[4] Note also that Poincaré had not first posed a problem to himself. Instead, two streams of mathematics were in the background of his thinking while his mind was occupied with a conversation with a friend. So there was no formal preparation. Instead, the solution and the problem that it solved happened simultaneously.

Poincaré's discovery emerging from the convergence of two mathematical streams made him set about writing a second supplement. Something else was on his mind as well. He began the supplement with these words:

> I fear that my first supplement was lacking in clarity, and believe that it is not pointless, before generalizing the results obtained, to go over these same results again in order to provide some additional explanations.
>
> *(Gray and Walter, 1997, p. 11)*

Poincaré had reflected on his own earlier work and evaluated it as wanting. Wallas had put verification at the end of a creative episode. Since then, psychologists have pointed out that evaluation of one's work is typically a feature of the creative process at one or, or perhaps more often, at several points in the process (Runco & Chand, 1994). Here Poincaré gave himself the same criticism as those on his doctoral committee had given him and this time sought to make corrections. Then he added the new insight which again brought two streams of math-making together. Here was another major discovery which now allowed mathematicians to draw from three subareas of mathematics: differential equations, non-Euclidian geometry, and number theory, each to illuminate the other. He sent in his second supplement with further elucidation of his first along with his new discovery on September 6.

Having sent in his second supplement, a problem still nagged at Poincaré—functions that eluded him and could overturn his whole idea. He was taken away from dwelling on this failure by the French government. He had to fulfill his military service. Again, the time away from thinking about his problem proved fruitful. He finished his account of the creation of his contest entry supplements this way:

> Thereupon I left for Mont-Valérien, where I was to go through my military service; so I was very differently occupied. One day, going along the street, the solution of the difficulty which had stopped me suddenly appeared to me. I did not try to go

deep into it immediately, and only after my service did I again take up the question. I had all the elements and had only to arrange them and put them together. So I wrote out my final memoir at a single stroke and without difficulty.

(Poincaré, 1908/1910, p. 328)

This third supplement arrived on December 20.

THE FIELD ANSWERS: CLOSE BUT NOT QUITE

Poincaré did not win the competition. As Gray and Walter (1997) put it "The jury, faced with this rush of activity from Poincaré and a more sober memoir from Halphen on differential invariants...opted for sobriety." The judges did award Poincaré one of two honorable mentions. The judges' report included these words:

> [The] author successively treated two entirely different questions, of which he made a profound study with a talent by which the commission was greatly struck... This is a fertile path that the author has not traversed in its entirety, but which manifests an inventive and profound spirit. The commission can only urge him to follow up his research, in drawing to the attention of the Academy the excellent talent of which they give proof.
>
> *(Darboux et al., 1916, p. 73 quoted in Gray, p. 220)*

The ideas that formed the entry with its three supplements incorporated four different, original, groundbreaking discoveries, as Gray (2013) pointed out. Though Poincaré only won an honorable mention, the discoveries themselves made Poincaré's name famous among mathematicians.

POINCARÉ AFTER HIS ENTRY

Poincaré continued to develop the ideas that arose from his entry and his mind continued to roam among related fields. He made contributions to mathematics, mechanics, geography, navigation, and physics. He won a competition in astrophysics solving the problem of how to deal with three bodies in orbits around each other. When someone found an error in his proof, Poincaré's correction led him to anticipate chaos theory. He anticipated the special theory of relativity as well. And he made a contribution to the study of the creative process, with his description inspiring Wallas and later investigators.

POINCARÉ'S CREATIVE PROCESS: SUMMARY AND REFLECTIONS

By examining Poincaré's account closely in the context of his life, we found instances of properties later psychologists identified from psychological research as well as new insights into how the creative process is lived. His creative episode took place in the context of domain and field, embedded in culture and a particular time in history. Faced with a tiresome task, his mind wandered to an intrinsically motivating incomplete project. The mathematics competition added extrinsic motivation to his internal attraction to creating in mathematics. His creative process featured both effortful preparation and effortless cognition. Parts of his episode roughly exemplified Wallas's four stages, dramatically showing how turning away from his task (incubation) and going to new environments resulted in sudden, surprising insights. Some of his insights brought together two different streams of mathematics. Insights sometimes came to him during incubation; sometimes, they emerged from a conscious, but intuitively guided flow. The insight sometimes consisted of spontaneous reorganization of the original problem representation, sometimes brought separate streams together. Verification and reflection were part of evaluating his conclusions.

The different chapters of Poincaré's creative episode show that the creative process does not always proceed in the same way, even with the same person. Poincaré's episode included several chapters that roughly followed Wallas's stages, giving dramatic examples of incubation leading to insight, but Poincaré did not describe intimation of a coming insight during incubation (Wallas surmised Poincaré just didn't notice). Poincaré did have an intimation in the wake of a preparation period, one that led him uncharacteristically to work in the evening. Another example, one of his creative results came as he moved directly from a problem to conscious use of heuristics to a solution.

Finally, Poincaré's account also makes clear that there are necessary differences between the laboratory studies of the creative process and the way it unfolds in life. The time involved is vastly different—an hour or two versus three-quarters of a year with routine and special interruptions. The laboratory task is chiefly extrinsically motivated—cooperating with an experimenter, a small cash reward, or course credit in a psychology class. Poincaré's creative process was intrinsically motivated and followed a history of learning and thinking in the world of mathematics. The task in incubation research is presented a second time after an imposed incubation. Poincaré's insights came to him during an incubation period he sometimes chose. One insight came to him without even having posed a problem to himself consciously, something that could not emerge from laboratory research. And there was an emotional difference as well. The students who were given a problem to solve that required insight surely felt pleased when they solved it but probably were not flooded with emotion. Poincaré's insights were accompanied by aesthetic feelings, as he felt the beauty and harmony of numbers and forms.

NOTES

1 Psychologist Kurt Lewin (1926/1951) had suggested that incomplete tasks create a tension in the mind until they are completed—a phenomenon that has come to be known as the *Zygarnik effect* after one of his students who found memory for interrupted tasks superior to completed tasks. Later research, e.g. by Atkinson (1953), and the mind wandering studies showed that Lewin's principle applied especially to cases where the task was important to the person.

2 The concept of inhabiting different psychological worlds is developed more fully in Chapters 4 and 5.

3 See Sio & Ormerod (2009) for a summary of the laboratory studies on incubation.

4 Note that the idea of streams includes more than concepts. Not only does it include the area's knowledge and previously developed skills, but also emotional aspects: concerns, aims, wishes, and feelings that are part of the ongoing experiences with the area. Poincaré's tension from incomplete tasks, wish to explore further, and pleasure in coming to insight were part of his experiential stream of each mathematical subarea.

REFERENCES

Amabile, T. M. (1996). *Creativity in context: Update to "the social psychology of creativity."* Boulder, CO: Westview Press.

Atkinson, J. W. (1953). The achievement motive and recall of interrupted and completed tasks. *Journal of Experimental Psychology, 46*(6), 381–390. doi:10.1037/h0057286

Bruya, B. (Ed.) (2010). *Effortless attention: A new perspective in the cognitive science of attention and action.* Cambridge, MA: MIT Press.

Csikszentmihalyi, M. (1996). *Creativity: Flow and the psychology of discovery and invention.* New York: HarperCollins.

Csikszentmihalyi, M. (1999). If we are so rich, why aren't we happy? *American Psychologist, 54*(10), 821–827. doi:10.1037/0003-066X.54.10.8215.

Doyle, C. L. (2016). The creative process: Effort and effortless cognition. *Journal of Cognitive Education and Psychology, 15*(1), 37–54. doi:10.1891/1945-8959.15.1.37

Duncker, K. (1945). On problem solving. *Psychological Monographs, 58*(5), i–113. doi:10.1037/h0093599

Franklin, M. (1989). A convergence of streams: Dramatic change in the artistic work of Melissa Zink. In D. Wallace & H. Gruber (Eds.), *Creative people at work.* Oxford: Oxford University Press.

Gray, J. J. (2013). *Henri Poincaré: A scientific biography.* Princeton, NJ: Princeton University Press.

Gray, J. J., & Walter, S. A. (1997). Introduction to Poincaré's three supplements. In J. J. Gray and S. A. Walter (Eds.), *Three supplements on Fuchsian functions by Henri Poincaré* (pp. 1–25). Berlin: Akademie-Verlag.

Gruber, H. E. (1981). *Darwin on man: A psychological study of scientific creativity* (2nd ed.). Chicago: University of Chicago Press.

Guilford, J. P. (1950). Creativity. *American Psychologist, 5*(9), 444–454. doi:10.1037/h0063487

Lewin, K. (1951/1926). Intention, will, and need. (D. Rapaport, Tr.). In Rapaport, D. (Ed.), *The organization and pathology of thought* (pp. 95–153). New York: Columbia University Press. (Originally published in German in 1926.)

Mednick, S. (1962). The associative basis of the creative process. *Psychological review, 69,* 220–232. doi:10.1037/h0048850

Newell, A., & Simon, H. A. (1972). *Human problem solving.* Englewood Cliffs, NJ: Prentice-Hall.

Poincaré, H. (1908/1910). Mathematical creation. (G. B. Halsted, Tr.) *The Monist, 20*(3), 321–335. doi:10.5840/monist19102037. (Originally published in French in 1908.)

Runco, M. A., & Chand, I. (1994). Problem finding, evaluative thinking, and creativity. In M. A. Runco (Ed.), *Problem finding, problem solving, and creativity* (pp. 40–76). Westport, CT: Ablex Publishing.

Sadler-Smith, E. (2015). Wallas' four stage model of the creative process. *Creativity Research Journal, 27,* 342–352.

Sio, U. N., & Ormerod, T. C. (2009). Does incubation enhance problem solving? A meta-analytic review. *Psychological Bulletin, 135,* 94–120. doi:10.1037/a0014212

Smallwood, J., & Schooler, J. W. (2015). The science of mind wandering: Empirically navigating the stream of consciousness. *Annual Review of Psychology, 66,* 487–518. doi:10.1146/annurev-psych-010814-015331

Topolinski, S., & Reber, R. (2010). Gaining insight into the "aha" experience. *Current Directions in Psychological Science, 19,* 402–405. doi:10.1177/0963721410388803

Toulouse, E. (1910). *Henri Poincaré.* Paris: Flammarion.

Verhulst, F. (2012). *Henri Poincaré: Impatient genius.* Springer.

Wallace, D. B. (1985). Giftedness and the construction of a creative life. In F. Degan & M. O'Brien (Eds.), *The gifted and talented: Developmental perspectives* (361–385). Hyattville, MD: American Psychological Association.

Wallas, G. (1926). *The art of thought.* London: G. J. Cape.

Ward, T. B. (2001). Creative cognition, conceptual combination, and the creative writing of Stephen R. Donaldson. *American Psychologist, 56,* 350–354.

Wertheimer, M. (1938). Laws of organization in perceptual forms. In W. D. Ellis (Ed.), *A source book of Gestalt psychology* (pp. 71–94). London, England: Routledge & Kegan Paul. (Originally published in 1923.)

CHAPTER 2

Darwin's Path to Evolution Theory

Changing Frameworks and Feelings

Charles Darwin's work on evolution altered the biologist's understanding of the development of life on earth. Coming at a time when literal interpretation of the Biblical account of creation was taken for granted by the majority in his native England, Darwin told a different story. The experience that set him on a path of revolutionary theorizing was a five-year round-the-world trip on the HMS Beagle. When he boarded the ship, Darwin, too, was a creationist on the way to becoming a clergyman who studied God's creation. Within three years of his return, he had developed an alternate framework. The process by which he came to his major insight and his emotional life as his theory evolved are this chapter's story.

Cognitive psychologist Howard Gruber (1981), in a landmark case study of the creative process in science, pored over Darwin's notebooks. Gruber identified the changing frameworks in Darwin's thinking, the conditions that gave rise to them, and concepts that captured the process. This chapter reviews many of Gruber's insights. Additional material came from Darwin's diaries, letters, and notebooks now available online (Darwin, 2002). Two excellent biographies (Desmond & Moore, 1994; Browne, 1996) served to put Darwin's work in the context of family, political events, and societal institutions as well.

DARWIN BEFORE HIS EVOLUTION THEORY

Charles Darwin (1809–1882) was born in Shrewsbury, England, the son of a prominent doctor and financier. As a little boy, he loved taking walks in nature and was an avid collector of shells, seals, coins, insects, and minerals. He and his older brother set up a chemistry lab in a shed on their property, young Charles's first experience of scientific experimentation. The family expectation was that he would become a physician like his father, but the sight of surgery made him sick to his stomach and the lectures at the University of Edinburgh bored him. Darwin, who was also an avid hunter, decided it

DOI: 10.4324/9781003013860-4

was more worthwhile to learn taxidermy, paying John Edmonstone, a freed Guinean slave, to teach him. That experience, as well as family tradition, made Darwin a fervent abolitionist.

The one subject that attracted him was natural history. The marine zoologist professor, Robert Grant, took students on field trips, taught research methods, and supervised Darwin's first original scientific experiments.

When it became clear that medicine was not likely to be his future, his father sent him to Cambridge to become a clergyman. There, Darwin met another important mentor, Professor John Henslow, a botanist who was also a parson, a possible role model. In addition to taking students on field trips and teaching research methods, now in botany, Henslow invited students to his home for chats on Friday nights. Darwin, with his deep interest and probing questions, became a Henslow favorite. It was Henslow who recommended Darwin for the Beagle voyage which was to be so crucial for Darwin's future and that of biology (Gruber, 1981; Desmond & Moore, 1994; Browne, 1996).

THE ERA IN THE DOMAINS OF GEOLOGY AND BIOLOGY

It was a time of ferment. Why did the surface of the earth look as it did? What accounted for the myriad forms of plant and animal life? The dominant position began with literal interpretation of the Bible—The Lord created the landscape; Noah's flood over the entire earth changed its topography (Scott, 2009). In the light of the fossil record, geologist Cuvier (1827) modified the creationist view by adding the idea that following Noah's flood, other catastrophes also changed the earth's forms (catastrophism). Species were stable, each exactly as God created it, each perfectly adapted to its environment.

There were doubters. In geology, Lyell (1970) asserted that the processes that formed the land were gradual and are still occurring today: volcanic activity, sediments piling up, and movements of the earth's crusts resulting in the rising or sinking of the land were examples. For living creatures, he produced a variation of creationism. As the earth changed, the Creator crafted new species of plants and animals, ones that fit perfectly into the new environments.

Biology had its skeptics of creationism as well, questioning that species are exactly as they were created. Instead they pictured gradual processes that resulted in the development of new species—evolution. French biologist Lamarck promoted that view and convinced Darwin's Edinburgh mentor Grant (Desmond & Moore, 1994). Even closer to home, Darwin's physician-scientist and poet grandfather, Erasmus Darwin (1796), had also put forward a theory of evolution (Gruber, 1981). These rebels were dismissed by most of the scientists Darwin knew. Furthermore, the suggested mechanisms for the workings of evolution were without proof.

Evolutionists were considered dangerous radicals in the larger society; they were seen as threatening the social order, the authority of the church, the basis for morality, and hope in the face of death. Darwin, as a student was exposed to the radical views, but, like his mentor Henslow, remained a catastrophist and creationist. Henslow's life as a clergyman-naturalist seemed ideal. Ironically, Henslow unwittingly helped to sow the seeds of doubt when he recommended Darwin for the scientific expedition to explore the geology and biology of the Southern Hemisphere (Desmond & Moore, 1994; Browne, 1996).

That voyage of the Beagle became the next chapter of Darwin's education, a phase that, in one sense, was the first chapter of the episode that led him to his decisive evolutionary framework.

THE VOYAGE OF THE BEAGLE

The Beagle voyage meant five years of travel on sea and land circumnavigating the coast of South America, visiting Pacific islands, Australia, and New Zealand before returning to England. What an adventure for a young man! As a budding naturalist, Darwin, aged 22 when the voyage began, found new worlds as he studied the geology, flora, and fauna at every stop. He also recorded what he was seeing in a diary—a general record of shipboard life, his thoughts and feelings, and his observations (Darwin, 2001). He called what he was seeing "a chaos of delight" (Darwin, 2001, p. 42): plants he had never seen before, varieties of coral, all sorts of new sea creatures, mountains with strata of fossil seashells, species of living birds and animals that were new to him, huge mammal fossils. He was also reading Lyell's book on geology, a present from the ship's captain, learning the argument for uniformism. Darwin's primary interest was geology, but he had what Gruber (1981) called an interrelated *network of enterprises*: geology, fossils, sea creatures, coral reefs, land animals, and plants.

Darwin's Multiple Frameworks

Piaget (1936) described the development of children's frameworks for thinking in terms of assimilation, accommodation, and reorganization of frameworks: experiencing the world in terms of given structures (assimilation), modifying the structure in small ways when observations don't quite fit (accommodation), and when experiences become confusing or and as contradictions pile up, there may be a total reorganization of the framework. Pioneering scientists may go through that process as well (Gruber, 1981; Kuhn, 1996). Darwin had two geology frameworks by which to understand the physical features of the land: catastrophism and Lyell's uniformism principles. During the first two years, as he recorded his observations of the landscapes, he sometimes interpreted what he was seeing in terms of catastrophes such as floods; sometimes according to the gradual processes Lyell's principles suggested. After two years, he stopped vacillating. Lyell provided the more powerful framework. Gradual change with land progressively rising, sea beds gradually falling and other principles accounted for more of the facts (Gruber, 1981). That band of fossil seashells in the mountain was intact with no signs of a flood: that provided evidence of elevation of the land. He witnessed an earthquake and the land seemed to rise before his very eyes.

The animal life, too, was intriguing. And it left him with questions creationism did not answer. He found a huge skull of an extinct creature he called a mastodon. Why did it die out? Some of the creatures of Australia were exceedingly strange to a European eye: kangaroo, platypus, koala, yet they shared the country with other animals similar to those of distant lands.

Darwin's primary task as a naturalist was to collect and describe. In his diaries, it is clear that asking questions about what he was seeing and trying out existing frameworks to explain his observations were features of his cognitive style. Lyell's principles explained the landscapes; for example, how the different layers of mountains came to be. But what about plants and animals? Was Lyell right that as the land changed, the Creator went back to work with new creations? Did He also create similar species in two distant places or was migration part of the answer? Lyell's theory provided a framework for understanding the geology of what he was seeing, but the plant and animal life raised questions for creationism.

On his visit to the Galápagos archipelago, he collected mockingbirds from four different islands. He ruminated about them in the notes he wrote on birds on the way back to England:

> The specimens from Chatham & Albemarle Isd appear to be the same; but the other two are different. In each Isld each kind is *exclusively* found... When I recollect the fact that [given] the form of the body, shape of scales & general size, the Spaniards can at once pronounce from which Island any Tortoise may have been brought. When I see these Islands in sight of each other, & possessed of but a scanty stock of animals, tenanted by these birds but slightly differing in structure & filling the same place in Nature, I must suspect they are only varieties. The only fact of a similar kind of which I am aware is the constant asserted difference between the wolf-like Fox of East & West Falkland Islds... *If there is the slightest foundation for these remarks the zoology of Archipelagoes will be well worth examining; for such facts would undermine the stability of Species.*[1]
>
> *(Barlow, 1963, p. 262)*

Looking back, we see the significance of his animal observations and ruminations as a first little crack in the idea that every species is in its place exactly as it was created. Yet most of his diary and his letters home to his mentors and science friends dealt with describing the geology and how it fit Lyell's principles (Gruber, 1981).

The many new findings brought enthusiastic attention. Lyell was delighted with the massive support to his framework. Darwin had embarked on the voyage an unknown young man; he came back a star among geologists, most of them creationists (Desmond & Moore, 1994).

A Network of Colleagues

The creative process in science often involves more than a single investigator working alone. Darwin knew he needed help in studying his plant and animal samples; the task was too big and he did not have enough expertise. Fortunately, he had what we can call a *network of colleagues* that included experts in these areas. Darwin convinced them to study his specimens and confirm his identifications. Each would be part of a multivolume series on the zoology of the Beagle voyage edited by Darwin.

Anatomist Robert Owen worked on the mammals of the dry pampas region of South America. The fossil findings were most spectacular. Among them was a giant rodent, a giant anteater, and what Darwin thought was a mastodon fossil turned out to be the skull of a giant llama. Once the mammals of the area were huge. Now similar, but much smaller animals roamed the plains. That intrigued Darwin because there was no evidence that the landscape or climate had changed.

Darwin handed ornithologist John Gould what he had assumed to be a motley collection: blackbirds, grosbeaks, wrens, and more, each species from a different island. Yes, Gould agreed, they were different species but…despite differences in their appearances, most notably in their beaks, they were all finch species. Also, to what had seemed to Darwin to be different varieties of mockingbirds, possible evidence suggesting a species could change a little, Gould said no. They were different enough to be called distinct species.

NEW FACTS LEAD TO CONSIDERING EVOLUTION

What could account for findings like that of the llama and the Galápagos birds? Darwin knew two possible explanations: Lyell's special creation theory and evolution. He pictured the Creator spending time creating all these different but related species. In the end, evolution made more sense. Creationism did not link up with other facts. The idea that the different finches evolved from a common ancestor did. It wasn't so much a sudden insight as a gradual realization as he pitted the evidence against the two frameworks. But the idea of evolution, that species gradually change did not satisfy Darwin. He needed a clearer picture of how the process of change took place (Gruber, 1981, Desmond & Moore, 1994).

Thinking in Words

Now, in addition to all his other enterprises—writing a book on his voyage, editing the others' zoology manuscripts, himself working on technical accounts of the geology—Darwin undertook a new one: Figure out how evolution works. What Lyell had done for geology, he would do for the living world. He began a notebook to put into words ideas about how evolution might come to pass.

Darwin's Problem Representation

In his notebooks, Darwin constructed what psychologists have called a problem representation; it includes an explicit statement or implicit understanding of the project goals, what is known at the beginning, a sense of what is missing, and strategies for reaching the goals (Duncker & Lees, 1945; Newell & Simon, 1972). The notebooks show that Darwin wrote out the questions that a complete theory should answer: How did life begin? Why do animals become extinct? What causes species to vary? How does heredity work? What role does the environment play? Whatever his ideas, he resolved to find decisive evidence to support or abandon them. He had a rich lode of observations to work with from the Beagle voyage. And when he needed more, he would go out and find them.

DARWIN'S FIRST EVOLUTION THEORY: DRAWING FROM BOTH RECEIVED FRAMEWORKS

That huge fossil llama skull buried in the land of smaller living llamas and those variations in Galápagos mockingbirds and tortoises made his questions more specific: Why do well-adapted species die out when the land doesn't change? What caused those island variations? His thought went to two ideas that were already present in the domain: Lyell had suggested that species have a fixed life span just as people do. And Lyell, though he didn't endorse it, wrote of the Lamarckian theory in which the building blocks of life were constantly emerging from non-living substances—the idea of spontaneous generation. Darwin played with that idea, calling the building blocks *monads.* The findings of biologist Ehrenberg fit. He had identified myriad, microscopic, constantly dividing single-cell organisms. Darwin wondered if they could be the monads. But if all these monads were the same, what accounted for the variety in species and how perfectly they fit their environments? Like Lamarck, Darwin theorized species were adapting by becoming more complex. But then, why did that huge llama species die out in an environment that didn't change? Darwin's first answer drew on Lyell's idea, that each species, like each individual, had a specific life span. Darwin modified the principle by applying it to monads; the monads have a life span and when their time comes, all the species that developed from them gradually die out and new monads evolve into a new species (de Beer, 1960a).

A Revolutionary Implication

If species evolve in adaptation to their environments, that meant how they evolve is an accident of the environment in which they find themselves. Darwin had been amazed at all the new species he had found—not a camel, but a llama, not a blackbird, but new species of finches. He was no expert on how plants and animals should be classified, but the systems he knew about did not fit the wild variety he had encountered. The systems were logical and symmetrical. For example, the Quinarian system divided the animal kingdom divided into five major groups; each had five major subgroups, and so on down. Lamarck pictured a ladder. Instead, Darwin was confronted with an unruly riot of variation (de Beer, 1960a; Gruber, 1981).

Thinking Visually

Then what were the relations among species as they evolved and adapted to different environments? Darwin pictured them, drawing a sketch of an irregularly branching tree. At first, he pictured whole branches dying when their monads' time had come (de Beer, 1960a). With his tree of life, he had what Gruber (1981) came to call "an image of wide scope," one of an "ensemble of metaphors" that guided thought (Gruber & Wallace, 2001).

The Fate of Monad Theory

Darwin's first evolution framework was clearly flawed, even bizarre. Still, in the course of constructing it, Darwin had two ideas that continued to be part of his thinking: the image of an irregularly branching tree, and the idea that the direction of evolution depended on the nature of the environment a species found itself in. Thus, monad theory was what Gruber (1981) called a helpful error.

Various enterprises in a network can advance thinking as the results of one become relevant to another (Gruber, 1981). All the while as he was puzzling about evolution, a major enterprise was writing up an account of his Beagle voyage for publication, reminding him of what he had seen at each stop of his journey. There was no fossil evidence of the simultaneous extinction of members of related species, something he would have expected if there was merit to the monad life cycle idea. Ideally, in science, theory is supposed to give way when it fails to be supported by observation, though it may be hard to do so. Darwin was able to give up a pet idea and stopped thinking in terms of monads. Instead, he theorized that species survived by changing, giving birth to new species (de Beer, 1960a; Gruber, 1981). But how?

GOING OUTSIDE THE DOMAIN FOR INFORMATION

His next guess was that a new species emerged when individuals of two different species or two variants reproduced giving birth to hybrids. Darwin sought information wherever it could be found. Zoologists might not know the answer but breeders and other animal fanciers might. He soon learned that crossbreeding was not the answer. Hybrids were often sterile and when they did appear, they were much weaker than the species they came from. Again this was a helpful error. He became fascinated by the art of breeding. This was not something biologists usually studied, but, for Darwin, it became a consuming enterprise in its own right. He talked to anyone he met who knew something about animals. In the course of informal conversation, he questioned zookeepers, dog breeders, pigeon fanciers, gardeners, farmers, even his barber. He found that breeders, for their own purposes, created "unnatural varieties": hairless dogs, pigeons with top-knots, cats without tails. Reproduction led to variation and the breeders, by selecting individuals with the traits they wanted for planned matings, "creating" animals to their own prescriptions via artificial selection. Darwin knew about natural selection, the fact that monsters were occasionally born, but they typically did not survive so they did not have a role in his thinking about species change. At this point for Darwin, natural selection was a process that kept the dominant species stable.

Still, the idea of natural selection as a force for evolution had appeared in his notebooks. Darwin wrote: "Whether every animal produces in course of ages varieties (influenced itself perhaps by circumstances) & those alone preserved which are well adapted"

(Darwin, 1837–1838, entry 90). In the same entry he noted the behavior of cocks, confronting each other, hens choosing the stronger males as mates. At this point, though, he was not yet ready to recognize natural selection as the major force in accounting for evolution. Nor was he ready when he read a pamphlet written by a breeder. The pamphlet mentioned that nature selects as well as the most skillful breeder; for example, cold weather can kill the weak whereas the strong survive (Desmond & Moore, 1994). Isolated ideas may lie dormant until they can be assimilated onto a framework. An important piece of what was to become Darwin's new framework was missing (Gruber, 1981).

Darwin's mind went elsewhere—to Lamarck's idea of the inheritance of acquired characteristics. Did the blacksmith's son inherit his father's big biceps? The idea of natural selection dropped out of his thinking.

The Most Controversial Hypothesis

From the beginning, Darwin's evolutionary thinking included human beings as evolved from a primate ancestor. Here too his Beagle observations were relevant. He was horrified by the brutality with which people treated another: a slave owner, for punishment, selling his slave foreman's wife and children away; gauchos wantonly killing young native women, the Beagle captain's harsh whipping of a miscreant. Darwin had marveled at the fierceness and nakedness of the mountain-dwelling Fuegians in their stark landscape at the tip of South America, was impressed by the mildness and intelligence of the comfortable Tahitians (Darwin, 1839). His experiences with his ex-slave taxidermy teacher taught him that culture and education could make the difference. For Darwin, humans were one family exhibiting variation depending on the particularities of their environment, capable of beastly cruelty and lofty ideals (Gruber, 1981; Desmond & Moore, 1994).

An orangutan named Jenny, who Darwin visited at the London Zoo, provided Darwin the kind of evidence he was looking for. Her keeper held out an apple, but did not enable her to get it. She acted exactly the way a three-year-old child might. Jenny threw herself to the floor, kicked, and cried—a temper tantrum Darwin had seen in young children (Darwin, 1945; Desmond & Moore, 1994).

DARWIN DISCOVERS THE SIGNIFICANCE OF NATURAL SELECTION

Darwin, as he was gathering evidence of the evolution of human beings, decided to read the major thinkers of the day. And late in September 1838, he picked up Malthus's essay on population. Now Darwin already was familiar with the outlines of Malthusian theory; it was well-known and talked about in intellectual circles; one of his friends was a fiery advocate (Desmond & Moore, 1994). Up to this point, Malthus was not yet a resource for Darwin's scientific theorizing, not yet part of the "how does evolution work" problem representation. His problem representation did include an unexamined assumption.

Darwin had taken for granted that in nature there was a natural balance between resources and populations; the reproduction rate would just meet the conditions to keep the number stable. When he read Malthus's book, its statistical reasoning startled him. The human population of the earth had the potential of doubling every 25 years and the food supply couldn't keep up. Yet, the population stayed in balance. The balance was maintained by the death toll from events like pandemics, wars, starvation from crop failures. The weak would succumb and the strong would survive to pass on their hereditary traits to their children (Gruber, 1981; Desmond & Moore, 1994).

Recent thoughts had primed[2] Darwin to see new significance in Malthus. He had just written a note remembering the wild reproductive rate of Ehrenberg's single-celled organisms; one creature, microscopic in size could, in four days, create so many others that its "children" together would be the size of a large stone. Finally, finally, it struck Darwin—more offspring are produced than resources to support them—superfecundity. Many different variations of a species emerge. Those best adapted to the environment will produce more of the next generation. The hereditary traits they carry will become gradually become more numerous in the population eventually giving birth to a new species. Nature will "thrust out the weak," and the strong continue to evolve (Barrett, 1974).

Darwin continued to read and make notes on Malthus throughout that fateful week. By October 3, he was confident that he had a theory to work with. He had to let go of some of the questions in his problem representation. He gave up trying to account for the origin of life, though he was convinced there was a single origin, the trunk of the tree of living species. He realized he knew neither the mechanisms of heredity nor the causes of variation, and that troubled by him. But the force of natural selection in the face of superfecundity was now so clear to him. Natural selection became the framework he tested again and again with further observations in the coming years. His long search for the mechanism of evolution had come to fruition (Gruber, 1981; Desmond & Moore, 1994).

EMOTIONS AND THE EVOLUTIONIST

The focus of our story of Darwin's creation of natural selection theory has been the thinking that resulted in his new framework. But what was Darwin feeling? And what about when he wasn't doing science? Let us consider Darwin's different modes of experience and the activities and emotions associated with each.

The World of Science[3]

Science calls for objectivity and it was Darwin's aim as well. In fact, he put it in stronger terms. Darwin wrote, "I believe there exists, and I feel within me, an instinct for the truth" (Darwin, 1985, p. 128). An instinct, an impulse, a strong motive—and as with all motives, every aspect of his scientific theory project was emotion-laden. Darwin was ever curious; he delighted in nature's every detail that caught his eye, calling being a naturalist his greatest pleasure. He compared his enjoyment of searching for fossils to that of the hunt. Guessing what a theory would lead him to observe next was akin to the excitement and elation of gambling. And for him, the pleasures of the fossil search and using theory to guess what he might see in nature far outweighed the earlier, more dissolute pleasures he had enjoyed as a young man (Desmond & Moore, 1994; Browne, 1996).

When he found his theoretical progress stymied, he may have experienced frustration, but remained determined and just dove into a related enterprise. And when he realized that combining superfecundity with natural selection brought him the answer he had been looking for, the insight, as insights typically do, brought with it a sense of certainty, the pleasure of completion, a feeling of competence (agency), and the experience of the beauty of a new synthesis (Skaar & Reber, 2020; Poincaré, 1908/1910).

The Professional Sphere

Being a scientist is more than doing the science itself. Scientific theorizing and observation are in the context of a social world, in particular a professional sphere peopled with mentors, colleagues, collaborators, and critics. The young man who became nauseated at the sight of surgery found himself attracted to a life like that of his idols. He identified first with the peaceful clergyman-naturalist life of John Henslow, then with the geology pioneer, Lyell. His new idol brought new ambition and a new purpose: what Lyell did for geology, he would do for natural history.

When Darwin gained professional status for his work in geology, he experienced pride and relished the new adulation he received from his family who had been concerned about his future. As he realized how much his natural selection idea would alienate old friends and mentors and might invite the attack of heresy from the church pulpit, he found the prospect devastating—one of several reasons he delayed making his ideas public to the science community and the larger society.

Gruber pointed out the conflict even penetrated Darwin's dreamworld. On September 21, seven days before his natural selection insight, with possible intimation of where his thought was going, he wrote:

> Was witty in a dream in a confused manner, thought that a person was hung & came to life, & then made many jokes, about not having run away &c having faced death like a hero.
>
> *(Darwin, 1837–1838, pp. 143–144)*

The Family Sphere

During the era he was working on evolution theory, his mind also went to the intimate family sphere. He considered marriage. Twice he hoped to make a logical decision, making lists of pros and cons. The first time the "logical" conclusion was no marriage. The second time he made a list, zookeepers had just told him about the sexual curiosity in monkeys. Darwin now added to the pros and came to the opposite conclusion—perhaps evidence of how one sphere can influence another. But again, there was conflict: Emma, his chosen mate, was religious. And given his commitment to truth, despite fatherly advice to the contrary, he confessed his religious doubts to her. He was elated when she accepted him nevertheless, lauding him for his openness and honesty. And she proved to be a loyal wife. In 1844, Darwin wrote a preliminary sketch of his natural selection theory. He was too anxious and conflicted to publish it without supporting evidence, but he asked Emma to arrange for publication in case of his death and she agreed (Gruber, 1981; Desmond & Moore, 1994).

The Body Sphere

Darwin also, intermittently, lived in a world of pain. He suffered seasickness and fever while on the Beagle. Recurrent bouts of stomach pains, vomiting, headaches, and boils plagued him throughout his life. There were many times when he was unable to engage in his scientific work. He sought various cures; some helped temporarily, none was permanent. Despite several suggested diagnoses, the cause of his misery remains unknown. Nevertheless, the stress of overwork and anxiety related to his conflict over making his theory public must have exacerbated his condition (Desmond & Moore, 1994; Browne, 1996).

Walking in Nature

Among Darwin's greatest pleasures was simply being in nature. When stress and conflict overwhelmed him, the so-called "water cures" doctors offered him typically involved beautiful natural environments that allowed him to walk under the trees. Just the pleasure of being in nature comforted him at his most difficult moments, and often was the gateway for further scientific observation.

Courage

Gruber (1981) pointed out that, as a plunge into the unknown, courage is part of doing science. Darwin had additional challenges, to continue his work in spite of pain and in spite of the hatred of the controversy he knew making his work public would cause. He found the courage and determination to continue. In 1854, he began work on a massive natural selection tome supported by all the evidence he had collected.

DARWIN AFTER HIS NATURAL SELECTION INSIGHT

Darwin was hard at work on his natural selection book in 1856 when he received a letter from Alfred Russel Wallace, a naturalist studying the flora and fauna of the Malay Archipelago. Earlier, Wallace had sent Darwin some specimens related to his work and they had become correspondents. Now Wallace wrote of his new theory—natural selection—and asked Darwin to arrange for publication. Darwin wanted to be fair and ethical, but his heart sank at the prospect of someone else being the theoretical pioneer when he had spent the last 20 years developing and finding evidence for his theory. He turned the problem over to his closest professional friends, friends to whom he had already "confessed" his natural selection framework. He also had documentary evidence for his priority: the 1844 sketch he had given to Emma and a letter he had written to a fellow biologist announcing his theory. What should he do? A few days later he hardly cared. His baby son Charles was dying of scarlet fever.

His friends found an equitable solution. They arranged for both the Wallace letter and excerpts from Darwin's sketch and letter to be read at a professional meeting and later to be published together as well. Darwin was not in the audience, but at home, felled by sickness and grief as he buried his son (Desmond & Moore, 1994).

That first public announcement strangely caused little excitement but propelled Darwin into a new project. He adapted portions of the natural selection book he had been writing into the book that made him famous and infamous, *On the Origin of Species* (Darwin, 1859). As he expected, the book was severely criticized by church officials and some of his former professional friends. Others defended him vigorously. Darwin, loving science and hating controversy, stayed out of the limelight and launched into less controversial projects such as studying climbing plants (Darwin, 1875).

Only later did he continue to build on his evolutionary ideas with *The Descent of Man* (Darwin, 1871) and *The Expression of Emotions in Animals and Man* (1872). His final activity involved a subject that others might have found trivial, but he found fascinating—earthworms. He did a series of experiments including the creation of an earthworm farm. That allowed him to document exactly how earthworms changed the soil—by aerating it with their movements and by eating it, and fertilizing it as it came out the other end—evidence that animals change the physical environment (Darwin, 1882).

DARWIN'S CREATIVE PROCESS: SUMMARY AND REFLECTIONS

To tell the story of the discovery of natural selection theory, it was helpful to review Gruber's account of the changing structure of Darwin's thinking, in and of itself. We have seen how his starting points were one of two competing frameworks in existing domains. He let go of one of those starting points when it was clear to him that the other explained more of his observations. He made useful errors. His flawed monad theory led to images and concepts which continued to influence his thinking—one of several helpful errors.

He had a network of enterprises; progress in one sometimes had fruitful implications for another. He had a network of colleagues he could call on to describe and identify his specimens. The search for a more complete theory included exploring breeding for one reason; it turned out to be useful for another. He knew Malthus's ideas, but did not consider them relevant to his project. He made natural selection notes prior to getting his major insight, but did not have a broad enough framework to consider their significance. His interest in human evolution led him to read thinkers outside his domain. That led him to Malthus and his realization that he needed to change a faulty assumption: that there is a natural balance between individuals and resources. Along the way, Darwin drew on thinking in words, playing with ideas, thinking logically, but also visual thinking.

Science is supposed to be free from the sway of emotion; the scientist is not. Each step of the journey drew on motives and feelings that spurred Darwin on or made going on more difficult. In the world of science, most of Darwin's activities brought pleasure:

delight in being in the natural world, zest for exploring phenomena that piqued his curiosity, enjoying theorizing and testing whether his predictions were confirmed, the excitement, satisfaction, certainty, and sense of efficacy when he came to insight—all moving him closer to the truth.

The honor bestowed on him by the professional world brought pride and spurred further ambition. The specter of being eclipsed by another naturalist led to disappointment and ethical conflict. Picturing the public attacks on his theory horrified him. He summoned the courage to persist, through his fears, through the misery of painful intermittent illness, through the deaths of children he loved. Courage was essential to his creative process.

THE FATE OF DARWIN'S THEORY

In his lifetime, Darwin saw his evolution theory recognized as groundbreaking the world over and he received many honors. At the same time, the religious opposition was fierce and has, to a lesser extent, continued to this day. Nevertheless, Darwin's theory has become a foundational framework for contemporary biology. He never found the hereditary causes of variation he was searching for, but Mendel's work on sweet peas provided one answer and the study of DNA, others. Together these constitute what has been called the modern synthesis,[4] a starting point for current research and theorizing.

NOTES

1 Italics in the last sentence of the quote added by the present author for emphasis.
2 Priming as a psychological concept is discussed more fully in Chapter 5.
3 The concept of distinct psychological worlds is discussed in Chapters 4 and 5. The professional sphere, the family sphere, and walking in nature are differentiated parts of the everyday world.
4 See, for example, Dobzhansky (1951).

REFERENCES

Barlow, N. (Ed.) (1963). Darwin's ornithological notes. *Bulletin of the British Museum (Natural History). Historical Series, 2*(7), 201–278.

Barrett, P. H. (1974). Early writings of Charles Darwin. In H. E. Gruber (Ed.), *Darwin on man. A psychological study of scientific creativity; together with Darwin's early and unpublished notebooks.* Transcribed and annotated by Paul H. Barrett, commentary by Howard E. Gruber. London: Wildwood House.

Browne, E. (1996). *Charles Darwin: Voyaging: A biography.* Princeton NJ: Princeton University.

Cuvier, G. (1827). *Essay on the theory of the earth* (5th ed.). London: T. Cadell.

Darwin, C. R. (1837–1838). *Notebook B: [Transmutation of species (1837–1838)].* Transcribed by Kees Rookmaaker. Retrieved April 23, 2020 from *Darwin Online,* http://darwin-online.org.uk/.

Darwin, C. R. (1838). *Notebook M: [Metaphysics on morals and speculations on expression (1838)]*. CUL – Transcribed by Kees Rookmaaker, edited by P. Barrett. Retrieved April 24, 2020 from *Darwin Online*, http://darwin-online.org.uk/.

Darwin, C. R. (1839). *Narrative of the surveying voyages of his Majesty's Ships Adventure and Beagle between the years 1826 and 1836, describing their examination of the southern shores of South America, and the Beagle's circumnavigation of the globe. Journal and remarks. 1832–1836*. London: Henry Colburn.

Darwin, C. R. (1859). *On the origin of species by means of natural selection, or the preservation of favoured races in the struggle for life*. London: Murray.

Darwin, C. R. (1871). *The descent of man, and selection in relation to sex*. New York: Appleton.

Darwin, C. R. (1872). *The expression of the emotions in man and animals*. London: Murray.

Darwin, C. R. (1875). *The movements and habits of climbing plants*. London: Murray.

Darwin, C. R. (1882). *The formation of vegetable mould, through the action of worms, with observations on their habits*. New York: Appleton.

Darwin, C. R. (1945). *Charles Darwin and the voyage of the beagle*. (N. Barlow, Ed.). London: Pilot Press.

Darwin, C. R. (1985). *The correspondence of Charles Darwin: 1847–1850*. Cambridge: Cambridge University Press.

Darwin, C. R. (2001). *Charles Darwin's Beagle diary*. (R. D. Keynes, Ed.). Cambridge: Cambridge University Press.

Darwin, C. R. (2002). *The complete work of Charles Darwin Online* (J. van Wyhe, Ed.) Retrieved April 10, 2020 from darwin-online.org.uk.

Darwin, E. (1796). *Zoonomia: Or, the laws of organic life*. Philadelphia: T& J Swords.

de Beer, G. (Ed.) (1960a). Darwin's notebooks on transmutation of species. Part I. First notebook [B] (July 1837–February 1838). *Bulletin of the British Museum (Natural History)*. Historical Series 2(2, January), 23–73.

de Beer, G. (Ed.) (1960b). Darwin's notebooks on transmutation of species. Part III. Third notebook [D] (July 15 to October 2nd 1838). *Bulletin of the British Museum (Natural History)*. Historical Series 2(4) (July), 119–150.

Desmond, A., & Moore, J. (1994). *Darwin*. New York, NY: W.W. Norton.

Dobzhansky, T. (1951). *Genetics and the origin of species* (3rd ed.). New York: Columbia University Press.

Duncker, K., & Lees, L. S. (1945). On problem-solving. *Psychological Monographs, 58*(5), 113. doi:10.1037/h0093599

Gruber, H. (1981). *Darwin on man: A psychological study of scientific creativity* (2nd ed.). Chicago, IL: University of Chicago Press.

Gruber, H. E., & Wallace, D. B. (2001). Creative work: The case of Charles Darwin. *American Psychologist, 56*(4), 346–349. doi:10.1037/0003-066X.56.4.346

Kuhn, T. (1996). *The structure of scientific revolutions* (3rd ed., Issr collection). Chicago, IL: University of Chicago Press.

Lyell, C. (1970). *Principles of geology* (Historiae naturalis classica, t. 83, pts. 1–3). New York: Lehre Verlag von J. Cramer.

Newell, A., & Simon, H. A. (1972). *Human problem solving*. Englewood Cliffs, NJ: Prentice-Hall.

Piaget, J. (1936). *Origins of intelligence in the child*. London: Routledge & Kegan Paul.

Poincaré, H. (1910). Mathematical creation. *The Monist, 20*(3), 321–335.

Scott, E. C. (2009). *Evolution vs. creationism: An introduction.* Berkeley, CA: University of California Press.

Skaar, Ø. O., & Reber, R. (2020). The phenomenology of Aha-experiences. *Motivation Science, 6*(1), 49–60. https://doi.org/10.1037/mot0000138

CHAPTER 3

Picasso's *Guernica*

The Creative Process in Art as Visual Thinking

Guernica is one of the most famous artworks of the 20th century (Figure 3.1). The mural is an artistic response to the first civilian bombing on European soil. By the time Picasso painted it, he had already been recognized as one of the era's most eminent and innovative artists. The mural itself, painted in 1937, has been the subject of at least two dozen books and myriad articles. Many are by art historians (e.g. Chipp, 1988, Van Hensbergen, 2004), who suggested possible precursors of the images both in Picasso's own work and in other important artworks from the past. Psychoanalyst Gedo (1980) found a source in a childhood trauma: Picasso's experience of being caught in an earthquake when he was three.

Picasso's Guernica: Genesis of a Painting by Rudolf Arnheim (1962), was a landmark in the psychology of creativity. Picasso himself had documented his process in creating *Guernica*; he dated and preserved his preliminary sketches. In addition, as Picasso painted on the canvas itself, stages of the mural were photographed, documenting the changes Picasso made. Arnheim examined the sketches and stages and used them to follow Picasso's visual thinking. For the first time, a psychologist studied the creative process in the making of a single complex work by analyzing the traces left behind. This chapter reviews Arnheim's perspective on how meaning is created in art as well as his insights into the sketches and states of the canvas. The perceptions of some art historians are incorporated as well.

Picasso himself occasionally spoke of his creative process, but he did so in enigmatic terms. He said, "basically a picture doesn't change…the first vision remains almost intact despite appearances" (Picasso quoted in Barr, 1939, p. 15). But he also said, "A picture is not thought out and settled beforehand. While it is being done, it changes as one's thoughts change" (Picasso quoted in Barr, 1939, p. 15) and "My work is like a diary" (Picasso quoted in Richardson, 1991, p. 3).

Years after Arnheim's book, some forgotten sketches were rediscovered, sketches that antedated the civilian bombing. Though some of the formal elements of the sketches resonated with the final mural, they appeared to be on an entirely different theme (Chipp, 1988). Or were they? This chapter suggests a way in which Picasso's enigmatic pronouncements might make sense if the forgotten sketches are seen as the first steps to the creation of *Guernica*.

DOI: 10.4324/9781003013860-5

FIGURE 3.1 Pablo Picasso. *Guernica*. Oil on canvas, 1937. Museo Nacional Centro de Arte Reina Sofía.

PICASSO BEFORE *GUERNICA*

Pablo Picasso (1881–1973) was born in Málaga, Spain, into a home surrounded by art. His father, an artist and teacher, was Picasso's first art teacher as well. The lessons began when Picasso was 7. By the time he was 18, he had perfected rendering a scene realistically. An early attraction to the domain of art combined with an environment rich with opportunity and support came together (Gardner, 1985; Franklin, 1994).

Picasso was fascinated by bullfights and they were the subject of his first oil painting. First bullfights and later, the characters from bullfights for various other purposes appeared in his art throughout his life.

The Era in Art and History

When Picasso first entered the art domain, it was in flux. Realistic portrayals of landscape and scenes from history and mythology, the styles favored by art schools, galleries, and museums, were being challenged by art movements such as impressionism. Paris was the center of the art world, and, in 1900, Picasso moved to Paris and experimented with various styles he was seeing around him. He was able to sell his first paintings and to make contacts with galleries; that allowed him a small income enabling him to eke out a living in Paris by making art alone.

Picasso as pioneer. Picasso himself became an innovator, experimenting with flat figures against the picture plane and making the first constructed sculptures. With Braque, he was the co-inventor of cubism; with Matisse, he co-invented collage. As Arnheim (1962) pointed out, by the time Picasso took on the task of painting *Guernica* in 1937, he had the whole history of artistic style possibilities to draw on.

Fascism and war. The 1930s—the age of Hitler, Mussolini, and Stalin—were turbulent times in Europe. A civil war began to rage in Spain as the legally elected government of Republicans—a coalition of socialists, communists, and liberals—was being overrun by the military, supported by the might of Fascist Italy and Nazi Germany. By 1937 they had driven the Republican government out of power. Many of Picasso's friends were members of the communist party, but Picasso never joined it.

THE PROCESS OF CREATING *GUERNICA*

The First Sketches

The story of the *Guernica* mural began with a commission in early January 1937. The elected Spanish Republican government, still legally recognized by France, was to have a pavilion at the 1937 Paris World's Fair. Many artists sympathetic to the Spanish Republican cause were to be represented. In early January, a delegation consisting of the pavilion's architect, Sert, and various embassy officials came to ask Picasso to create a mural for the pavilion. Picasso was wary; he insisted that serious art should not be used for propaganda. He was told that he could paint anything he wanted (Richardson & Picasso, 2005). As a world-famous artist, just his participation was message enough.

On January 8–9, Picasso spent two days quickly creating an etching—*The Dream and Lie of Franco*. It was like a comic strip; it consisted of a series of 18 panels, of which he completed 14. It pictured a monster but always with Franco's facial features, cavorting and destroying in various ways. In panel 14, the monster was finally demolished by a bull, representing Spain. The last four panels were left for later. Picasso was willing to create political cartoons mocking Franco and portraying a Republican victory. But he did not believe politics should enter serious painting. So how to paint the mural was a troubling problem. In addition, Picasso had never painted on commission with a deadline. So what to do?

He procrastinated. Instead he painted unrelated works. In March he painted a woman with a flower with the face of his mistress, Marie-Thérèse; in April, Marie-Thérèse at a window. He did visit the Spanish pavilion being built, and on April 18 made 12 preparatory sketches, the composition studies reflecting the relative dimensions of the mural. The subject? The one he returned to again and again throughout his life—the artist and his model. Chipp (1988) called a series of etchings on the subject created in 1933 a virtual diary of his life in the studio with his mistress as model. Picasso's first sketches for the mural had nothing to do with the war in Spain (Figures 3.2 and 3.3).[1]

On April 19, Picasso sketched again, this time a series of notations rather than a composition study: a female artist with an outstretched arm, an easel, two renditions of the pavilion wall with a blank mural, the face of a model. But then, drawn over other elements, were two upraised arms, the Republican salute. The fists were holding a tool with a hammer and a sickle (the communist symbol). His support of the Republican government had crept into his thinking about the mural. Picasso had drawn a similar image over a newspaper report in which the French minister suggested that all parties in the civil war should come to an understanding. At this point, with Picasso's outrage expressed, he again turned away from working on the mural. He painted still-lifes, and enormous nudes on a beach (Chipp, 1988).

FIGURE 3.2 Pablo Picasso. *Study for The Studio I: The painter and his model.* Pencil on blue paper, 1937. Musee Pablo Picasso Paris.

FIGURE 3.3 Pablo Picasso. *Study for The Studio XI: The painter and his model.* Pencil on blue paper, 1937. Musee Pablo Picasso Paris.

The Second Beginning: The Saturation Bombing of Guernica

On April 26, for three hours, teams of German planes kept flying over Guernica, dropping bombs of up to 1000 pounds and 3000 incendiary projectiles, the first saturation bombing of a civilian population on European soil. The city was on fire for three days, much of it destroyed. As people tried to flee, low-flying planes turned machine guns on them. The city and the surrounding fields were littered with corpses.

Picasso, in Paris, learned of the devastation from news reports and photos. Four days after the saturation bombing, he made a rough sketch with the characters that continued to be part of every subsequent composition sketch and the final mural: a bull, a wounded horse, and a woman leaning out of a high window holding a lamp with a horizontally outstretched arm (Figure 3.4). Picasso was not considering a realistic portrayal of events. There were no airplanes or bombs. He was portraying characters he had drawn again and again for a variety of purposes.

Picasso dated and numbered his sketches, and Dora Maar photographed states of the mural as Picasso worked on the canvas. Arnheim (1962) studied these as valuable clues to Picasso's visual thinking.

FIGURE 3.4 Pablo *Picasso Composition Study (1): Sketch for Guernica.* Pencil on blue paper, 1937. Museo Nacional Centro de Arte Reina Sofia.

Arnheim on Visual Thinking

Arnheim, a respected pioneer in the psychology of art, was also an accomplished amateur artist. He put forward the idea that the making of art involves thinking, but not in terms of abstract concepts or in words. The artist thinks in shapes, tries out shapes and their relation to one another, and then reflects on what his eyes are telling him—visual thinking. He wrote:

> Since the artist thinks by means of the shapes he creates, he is not likely to define his ideas neatly in the abstract and then search for the proper form that will make them visible. He will rather try to determine what he is thinking by experimenting with forms which will show his eyes the consequences of various thoughts.
>
> *(Arnheim, 1962, p. 62)*

And the shapes themselves are not necessarily consciously chosen. Both conscious and unconscious processes enter into much of what we do, Arnheim (1962) wrote. Some of the shapes that emerged for Picasso surprised him. He said to Gilot: "There are forms that impose themselves on the painter. He does not choose them… It's very mysterious and damned annoying" (Gilot & Lake, 1964, p. 126).

But how do shapes convey meaning? Arnheim (1962, 1969) pointed out that a shape can reflect several levels of meaning: In its representational meaning, identifiable aspects of the world are pictured, such as the horse and the bull. The image may be realistic or stylized. It may reflect learned cultural or mythological meaning as the bull standing for Spain in the etching. It also conveys emotional and abstract meaning, whether they are realistic or not. Shapes and lines, like music, convey rhythm, motion, and emotion. The spatial relations among the parts tell how the elements do or do not interrelate.[2] In this first sketch, the bull is turned away from the wounded, perhaps dying, horse. The horse is on his back, his legs in the air producing a central vertical line. Each character is isolated from the others.

Arnheim, as an artist, was very aware of the way the forms on a canvas were put together to become an integrated whole, the formal aspects of a painting. Yet he insisted, formal changes are more than formal; they also create changes in meaning. As we will see, at state 4 of the mural, Picasso made one formal change that invited others and yielded a major transformation in meaning.

Sketches for the Mural[3]

Style experiments. The day Picasso drew out his first vision of the *Guernica* mural, he completed five others. Three were sketches of the horse, some multiple on one page. They varied in style, from a cartoon-like horse with raised head falling, to a standing horse almost as a child would draw it, to a fully realistic horse, head raised to the right, feet collapsing. The style was in flux.

The other three May 1 sketches were composition studies. In the final one of the day, the style is simple, with classic lines, the identity of each character clear. The horse is wounded, a victim of violence, but a winged horse emerges from the wound, the psyche of mythology, a sign of continuing life. With neck raised and open-mouthed cry, the horse now relates to the light-bearing woman, who is thrusting her lamp out the window over the horse's head. As everything changed around her in the sketches through the final mural, the light-bearing woman remained in the same position. A new character lies on the bottom, another victim, a warrior from antiquity, dead, face up, still clutching his sword. The largest figure is that of the bull, standing behind the horse, taking up almost a quarter of the picture, looking away, uninvolved, serene (Figure 3.5).

As Picasso did on the first day, he would continue to do throughout: explore both the composition with sketches of the whole and in separate sketches, different versions of individual parts. May 2 found Picasso concentrating on the cry of a rising horse's head, culminating in a separate painting of it.

The horse collapses and the bull flies. The last sketch of the second day was a composition study now with the horse no longer erect. Now the horse's back was doubled over; the head bowed down. Whether the horse should be doubled over and collapsed or rearing up— two different meanings—remained unsettled even after Picasso was working on the actual canvas. A new addition, perhaps because the lower right-hand corner needed something, now had a face down dead woman, joining the warrior, now a decapitated statue and the

FIGURE 3.5 Pablo Picasso *Composition Study (1V): Sketch for Guernica*. Oil and pencil on plywood. Museo Nacional Centro de Arte Reina Sofia.

collapsed horse, according to Arnheim "a defeatist turn of thought." The bull is now flying over the scene, his face more human, still unperturbed, now staring straight ahead into space on the left. Arnheim asked, is the bull in flight from the scene or inspired by it? Picasso did no further sketching till May 8.

Mother with dead baby, bull now still and strong. The five-day rest brought a major addition and two omissions. The light-bearing woman and the small female profile are gone and a new character appears. Only one woman, holding a dead baby, is crawling in from the lower right. She is looking up in contrast to the head of the doubled-over horse. The composition sketch now shows the bull standing behind the horse, as Arnheim wrote, "proud and stable," perhaps the enduring symbol of Spain.

Mother and horse in relation. Later the same day, Picasso sketched just the doubled-over horse and the mother with both outlining a kind of triangular shape, in a way, as Arnheim points out, mirroring each other but with opposite emotions: the horse helpless, the woman appealing. And both, though not fully realistic, are more complexly presented and three-dimensional. On May 9, Picasso started the day with a more elaborate, more expressive full pen and ink sketch of the mother, her live breast contrasting with the bloodied dead child, the shape still triangular. The same day, Picasso also sketched the mother with the dead baby descending a ladder.

The May 9 composition: More women, fisted arms. The scene is full of shapes, almost exuberant. The low horizontal border has three prone women, one hugging the dead warrior, the mother with dead baby crawling in from the right. Houses, now three-dimensional, appear on either flank, one ablaze. And, for the first time, emerging haphazardly on the right and left, four upraised, fisted arms. Was Picasso considering a more political mural now? Yet, in the center, still the largest, most prominent shape, stands the bull, his head turned away from the chaos, emotionless, his human eyes staring straight out of the sketch. This was Picasso's last composition study before working on the canvas itself.

Color closeups: Mother, horse, and bull. May 10 found Picasso considering color. Of his five sketches, two were now in brightly colored crayons, one of a cubist horse, the other of the woman with the dead baby descending a ladder, outlined in colored crayon and surrounded by a background of red and orange.

The bull-man. For the first time, he also sketched a close-up of what Arnheim (1962) labeled the "bull's head." But it wasn't a bull's head. It was the head of a bearded man, similar to portrayals of the artist in earlier Picasso work, with horns and ears the only bull-like features. And the only sketch made the next day before tackling the canvas itself was of the full body of a bull with a man's head but crowned with bull's ears and horns. Was he considering a bull with the mind and soul of a human being?

The States of the Canvas[4]

Picasso chose huge dimensions for his mural: more than 25 feet long and 11.5 feet high. The step from sketches on sheets of paper to the canvas itself could not have been easy. Nor did he simply incorporate the shapes of his sketches onto the canvas. As he painted, he was also reimagining his characters, their relations to one another, and to the overall composition and these kept changing. As Picasso was working on the mural, he also paused to sketch, trying a new way one of the elements could look. The sketches were dated, so they help to get a sense of when the states of the mural were painted.

The first three states. Picasso began by laying out guidelines to the composition of the mural with a central triangle. This harked back to the Studio sketches from before the bombing. The content included a symbol of the Republican resistance with one arm of the warrior, upraised to near the top of the canvas, providing the central vertical and apex of the compositional triangle. In the first state, his arm ends in a bare fist; in the second state, it is plunged into a large sun, but holding flowers (Arnheim, 1962) or wheat (Chipp, 1988), an image suggesting a desire for peace. But did Picasso want his statement to be so obviously political? No, he did not. By the third state, the upraised arm is gone and in place of a round sun, the sun has the shape of a human eye (Figure 3.6).

The horse is doubled over in all three states, his teeth bared and his triangular, saber-like tongue extended as in the earlier states and horse sketches. The curve of his body covers the lower hindquarters of the bull. In state 2, his body is pierced by a javelin, indicating

FIGURE 3.6 Dora Maar. *Photo Report of the Evolution of Guernica*. Photograph of an early stage of Pablo Picasso's *Guernica*, 1937. Museo Nacional Centro de Arte Reina Sofia.

that his wounds were not caused by a charging bull, but as the result of human action (Chipp, 1988). The javelin remained in all the subsequent states of the mural.

The three women.   The mother, who was tried out in three different positions in the composition sketches, in the first state of the canvas now has a woman in all three positions, only one with the dead baby: a woman aflame falling from the high window of a burning building on the right; the triangular shape of a woman trekking in from the right and an upright woman with the dead baby on the left. Her head is right below the head of the bull, her nose and forehead touching the outline of his chin, her mouth agape, pleading. These are their positions in the final mural. In the first two states, a fourth woman lies prone on the bottom right in the tangle of shapes. She was eliminated.

The bull in the first three states.   He is the largest figure, taking up much of the area of the left side of the mural. He is unemotional, looking to a distant point to the left outside the mural. Though the day before, Picasso was sketching him with human features, here the only human features are his staring eyes. Amid the devastation, he seems uninvolved.

The fourth state brings radical change.

The horse rears up.   Where a human arm once stood as the center vertical in earlier stages, we find the horse's long neck rising up, his head facing the bull, his mouth crying out in agony. As Arnheim pointed out, the major change in form simultaneously brought a change in meaning. Though seriously wounded, the horse is alive, proud, dignified, directly confronting the bull. The center now belongs to a victim of the catastrophe.

The bull reimagined and positioned anew.   Up until now, the upper left-hand corner had been relatively empty. Picasso filled it by taking the bull out of the center of the mural, his body smaller and less prominent, now moved toward the action, his fiery tail, undulating into the corner. The vision of the bull has also changed. His features are somewhat more human, especially the eyes which stare directly out at the viewer. Rather than unmoved by the scene of suffering, his mouth is open with a saber-like tongue protruding, echoing the tongues of the mother and the horse. So important and sudden a change suggests that Picasso had taken a major step, with new insight into what the mural should be and say. With the fourth state, the horse and the bull found their positions in the final mural (Figure 3.1).

States 5 and 6: Simplifying, clarifying, and trying color.   The lower part of the mural was still too crowded and though the horse was clearly three-dimensional, the space was not. In state 5, the prostrate woman on the right is gone and a small but telling detail gave the first hint of a three-dimensional space in the mural's center. The warrior's lance is turned inward in perspective. The woman falling out of the window now has upraised arms. Chipp (1988) noted that this echoes a Goya image from *The Disasters of War* #14, an image Picasso was surely familiar with. In this echo of an earlier painter portraying the horror of an earlier war, the painting seems to be going beyond a specific event to the universality of war's victims.

Wallpaper rectangles covering possible clothes of the three woman reappear in stage 6. Was Picasso again considering collage or color? We don't know. We do know he rejected the idea.

Sketching the warrior and state 7. June 3 and 4 had Picasso returning to sketching the warrior. On June 3, he drew the warrior as human, lying face down. On June 4, a simplified head was turned up. That sketch of the face became the face of the warrior in state 7, the face turned up, joining all the others crying out. He is no longer the man in the June 3 sketch, but has become a statue as he had been in one earlier sketch. And Picasso also made the entire space three-dimensional, by tiling the floor and adding a table for a bird to sit on. Though there is an eye-shaped sun, it has acquired a lightbulb for a pupil at its center. Was Picasso portraying an outdoor space, an indoor space, or both?

The final mural. Picasso clarified the shapes. He made some of them gray rather than using exclusively using black and white, providing more contrast. The entire back and legs of the horse were stippled, making its shape more visible. And he made the indoor/outdoor enigma even more puzzling in two ways: the lines of an inside wall pass behind the eye-shaped sun. And a door on the right leads inside, as it did in two of the earlier Studio sketches.

SUMMARY: ON PICASSO'S CREATIVE PROCESS

The preceding description tells us just some of the highlights of Picasso's process as revealed by the sketches and states. A commission was the beginning of the idea of a mural. Before the bombing of Guernica, Picasso's first sketches for it pictured variations of a favorite subject, the artist and his model. The first sketches after the bombing had a familiar cast of characters, most in agony, but isolated from one another; Picasso experimented with possibilities and neither the composition nor the realizations of the characters were settled till late in the process. That experimentation involved both sketching composition studies and zooming in to concentrate on various elements separately. At times he multiplied characters (the women) and then omitted some (the women again). One element was replaced with another that had the same function or the same place in the composition (the fugitive for the first position of the mother with the dead baby, the horse's neck for the upraised arm of early states, and for the dying horse's legs in sketch 1). Only in the case of the warrior and in the open door in an early Studio sketch did Picasso use what he had sketched without altering it in the mural. Some characters were more complex in the sketches than in the final mural (the mother with the dead baby). And because an artist thinks visually, changes in formal characteristics were also changes in meaning (the horse collapsed versus the horse's raised neck, head facing the bull). With such a large mural to fill, Picasso had to find a composition that unified the canvas. By having matching vertical shapes anchoring the left and right flanks and because many of the characters are straining toward the bull, their desperate cries directed toward him, the mural achieved a unity despite its enormous size.

THE QUESTION OF MEANING

If the making of art is visual thinking, what was the meaning Picasso came to? Though there is disagreement, there is also some consensus. Clearly, this is a picture of the devastation and chaos brought by war, its victims crying out in agony and grief. The old heroism celebrated in the statues of warriors has been destroyed and women and children are war's innocent victims. The use of only black, white, and gray and the stippling of the horse suggest newsprint, reflecting the way that Picasso, sitting in Paris, learned about the bombing and are the colors of mourning as well (J. D. Dodds, personal communication, 2018).

The possible meanings of the bull have been more controversial. Picasso, who enjoyed speaking in riddles, simply said that the bull was a bull. Others have offered various interpretations, among them, bull as the enemy and bull as the spirit of the Spanish people. A third suggested interpretation is the bull is what we can call an *avatar* of Picasso—*avatar* meaning a representation of distinctive features of a living person without capturing all of them.

Arnheim, in the conclusion of his exhaustive analysis of the sketches and states in 1962, did not interpret the mural in any specific way. Forty-five years after Picasso painted it, the director of the Prado Museum invited Arnheim to lecture in front of it. In the meantime, he had assimilated the scholarship that had been written about Guernica. Now he hazarded an interpretation. First he noted again that a single image can have several levels of meaning. Arnheim found two principal meanings condensed in the single image of the bull. One was the bull as the enduring spirit of Spain. The other was the bull as an avatar of Picasso himself, as he had sometimes portrayed himself in earlier work—the bull as artist (Arnheim, 1982).

And what of the enigma of the inside/outside space? Arnheim embraced one of the major scholarly suggestions. Both inside and outside come together on a stage, the outside representations, a stage set. If the bull were an avatar for Picasso as artist, Picasso had put the horrors of war on a theater stage.

At this time, the original Studio sketches had not been recovered and so this had no part in Arnheim's understanding the mural. But suppose we consider those light, early pencil sketches of the artist and his model to be the glimmer of a beginning. Might there be another way of seeing the simultaneous presentation of inside and outside—the artist's studio?

Picasso was skeptical when he was urged to contribute to the Republican pavilion at the World's Fair. He did not want his art to be used for propaganda. He tried out compositions that were overtly political and rejected them.

Suppose the composition sketches and states were like a diary—Picasso, torn between not using painting for propaganda, yet enraged by the bombing's savagery and grieving for its victims. Perhaps Picasso came to see the mural as still another exploration of the artist and model in his studio. Now his models were no longer the passive voluptuous nudes of the Studio series, but phantoms of the innocent victims, now in agony, crying out, haunting the artist, pleading with him to do something? How should the artist respond? What do the sketches suggest about Picasso's visual thinking? With his avatar the bull looking away does he mean to say art should not be used for propaganda? Uninvolved as an artist sitting in Paris could be? Simply bearing witness? Serene as celebrating the survival of the indomitable spirit of Spain? Should the bull artist dominate the mural, filling much of half the canvas? No, he should be on the side, and the victims need be the center. The women, the horse, even the broken statue are all active, some moving toward him, all crying out, in agony and pleading. The bull himself, though stable, is no longer serene or disinterested, but affected, mouth open, swishing his fiery tail. He stares out of the canvas with human eyes, confronting the viewers, confronting us.

If the bulk of the mural is the artist-model painting, then who is the light-bearing woman with her arm outstretched? Some interpret her as the muse. Here is an additional possibility. An outstretched arm appeared in several of the Studio sketches, the arm of a painter, and, in some cases, the painter was a woman. In that sketch, the arm was the arm of a painter. If much of the mural could be considered the painting of the artist and his model, the light-bearing woman could be considered a second avatar, the painter whose work is shedding light on the relation of the artist and his models in the face of catastrophe.

These interpretations suggest that the Studio sketches were the beginnings of the mural, a decision to once again explore the relation between artists, their works, and life. Now the life he had been depicting in the past was upended. As he sat in his studio, the victims of civilian bombing were calling out to him. What can the artist do but highlight the tragedy, confront the viewers, asking the world to see, to feel, and to act?

Whatever the analyses of the meaning of various elements of the mural, one thing is clear from the sketches. Picasso wrestled with the question of what an artist should do in the face of national tragedy. Though he had political positions, he had previously kept two streams[5] of his life—serious art and his concern about events in his homeland—separate. An extended process of visual thinking led Picasso to discover how to bring those two streams together in a magnificent, moving, and challenging way; he came to understand how the artist can use all his skills to wake up the world to the terror and suffering wrought by war without stooping to cheap propaganda. We can see the change in his completion of the etching which still had the four missing panels. The last panel he had done in April was of the bull defeating Franco and the etching, a cartoon so far, had a jocular, satirical feeling. Now in June, after the process of creating *Guernica*, the last four panels were of women in grief, three with dead babies.

The mural itself demonstrates that the artist lives through historical events that can penetrate and enlarge private aesthetic concerns. Here human devastation called to the artist and demanded to be portrayed.

The mural was painted also knowing the context in which it would be viewed. Picasso's title is part of the meaning (Franklin, Becklen, & Doyle, 1993). By naming the mural *Guernica*, Picasso was calling attention to a specific event, suffering and death as the outcome of the saturation bombing. But in art, specificity points to more general concerns. The mural is now recognized as a passionate plea to recognize the appalling costs of war (Chipp, 1988).

NOTES

1　All the studio sketches described here are available online at the Picasso Museum Paris website: https://www.museepicassoparis.fr/en/collection-en-ligne#/artworks?filters=year%3A1937__1937&page=2&layout=grid&sort=by_author starting with works dated April 18, 1937.

2 In Chapter 2, we saw that Darwin drew on visual thinking to imagine the evolutionary relationships of species in a tree diagram.

3 In addition to the two sketches pictured here, all the sketches described in words are available online at the Museo Reina Sophia website: https://www.museoreinasofia.es/en/buscar?bundle=obra&f%5B100%5D=&fecha=&items_per_page=15&keyword=Picasso%20Guernica%20sketches&pasados=1. The sketches can be found on this site (and the following two pages for which you can find the links at the bottom of the first page). The sketches are not displayed in chronological order.

4 All the states of the mural described here are available online at the Museo Reina Sophia website: https://www.museoreinasofia.es/en/buscar?bundle=obra&f%5B100%5D=&fecha=&items_per_page=15&keyword=Dora%20Maar%20photographs%20Guernica&pasados=1. There is a link at the bottom to take you to the second page of the photographs.

5 Convergence of streams as a possible feature of the creative process is defined in Chapter 1.

REFERENCES

Arnheim, R. (1962). *Picasso's Guernica: The genesis of a painting*. Berkeley: University of California Press.

Arnheim, R. (1969). *Visual thinking*. Berkeley: University of California Press.

Arnheim, R. (1982). Forty-five years after Guernica. *Michigan Quarterly Review, 22*, 1–8.

Barr, A., Jr. (1939). *Picasso: Forty years of his art*. New York: Museum of Modern Art.

Chipp, H. (1988). *Picasso's Guernica: History, transformations, meanings* (California studies in the history of art, 26). Berkeley: University of California Press.

Franklin, M. B., Becklen, R. C., & Doyle, C. L. (1993). The influence of titles on how paintings are seen. *Leonardo, 26*(2), 103–108. doi:10.2307/1575894

Franklin, M. B. (1994). Narratives of change and continuity: Women artists reflect on their work. In M. B. Franklin & B. Kaplan (Eds.), *Development and the arts: Critical perspectives* (pp. 165–191). Lawrence Erlbaum Associates.

Gardner, H. (1985). *Frames of mind: The theory of multiple intelligences*. New York: Basic Books.

Gedo, M. M. (1980). *Picasso, art as autobiography*. Chicago: University of Chicago Press.

Gilot, F., & Lake, C. (1964). *Life with Picasso*. McGraw-Hill.

Richardson, J. (1991). *A life of Picasso: Volume 1, 1881–1906*. New York: Random House.

Richardson, J., & Picasso, P. (2005). *A life of Picasso: Volume 4*. London: Cape.

Van Hensbergen, G. (2004). *Guernica: The biography of a twentieth-century icon*. New York: Bloomsbury.

PART II

Creating as Navigating Among Different Psychological Worlds

Creating Novels and Short Stories

The Writing Realm and the Fiction World

Kathleen Hill, Mary LaChapelle, the late Jerome Badanes, and the late Grace Paley are four writers who have been honored for their fiction. Though their works are very different, they described their creative process in similar ways. For example, one common theme was a sense of uncertainty about how their stories would unfold. Paley put it this way:

> I have this paragraph or this sentence and I haven't the vaguest idea what the story is. There isn't one story in that book where I had the vaguest notion what page 3 was going to be like, let alone later on…maybe after a couple of months I might write the next two pages, the next three pages, and then I'm really stuck.
>
> *(Grace Paley, 1992, unpublished interview)*

This chapter is based on qualitative interviews with the writers, the interviews centering on how particular works of fiction came to be.[1] There was variation in the role that writing played in their lives and in some aspects of their experiences as they were creating. Nevertheless, there were many common themes and those themes are the subject of this chapter's story.[2]

The writers' descriptions suggested the work of several psychologists and philosophers, most prominently the work of Alfred Schütz, a phenomenological philosopher. Schütz's concept of multiple, psychological worlds illuminates the experience of the creative process in other domains as well[3] and so is presented here in some detail.

The writers' accounts (plus a few excerpts from other published interviews) and their resonance with concepts put forward by theorists is this chapter's story.

BEGINNINGS

Jerome Badanes

Badanes (1937–1995) was a poet, a creator of street theater, and a filmmaker before he published his first novel, *The Final Opus of Leon Solomon* (Badanes, 1989). As he was

DOI: 10.4324/9781003013860-7

doing street theater, he noted in his journal that he was writing more and more about the fiction he was reading—studying it, devouring it. He decided to try it himself, and started an autobiographical novel about street theater.

Amid working on this, he was asked to make a film. It was to deal with life in Poland prior to the Holocaust. His interviewing brought a problem:

> Most of the people were survivors and they couldn't really talk about the world except in this official way they had invented for themselves, which was...all gray and condemning. But if they talked about their Holocaust experiences first, and told me what they needed to tell me, then they could work their way back to a time before the Holocaust.

The film did not include those Holocaust experiences. But the stories told by the survivors haunted him. He said, "There were all these crazy voices in my head. And they had become crazy because I hadn't given life to them. I felt like they were the Furies. I was writing this other book and the Furies were saying, write about us."

Still he worked on the novel he had started for about a year. Then he read about someone stealing Holocaust documents from an institute library; that incident got all mixed up with the survivors' voices and he abandoned writing the earlier novel. Instead, he started out to write about a filmmaker, somewhat like himself, who interviewed survivors. His interview told what happened next.

Kathleen Hill

A New Yorker, she always loved literature, but did not begin to write until her 40s. She said, "I started writing when my daughters were in their teens. I started with stories— I guess there were about five or six of them—and they were published, so I thought I would work toward a collection."

One short story, *Willie* (Hill, 1983), was based on a family anecdote that always intrigued her. She had a grandfather, a martinet, who had made the lives of the grandchildren difficult. After his wife's death, the grandfather took his daughter, Hill's mother to Paris. On one of their walks, she stopped in front of a shop window and said, "Oh what a beautiful dress." Characteristically Hill's grandfather criticized his daughter for thinking about herself instead of her sisters back home. Later that day, the grandfather presented that very dress to his daughter. Hill started off to write, as she said, "a biting little picture of Willie, almost angrily."

She finished *Willie*, but never completed the story collection. What interrupted was a visit to her daughter, working in a clinic in Africa. It was Hill's third visit. She had lived in Nigeria with her husband when she was in her twenties and gave birth to two children there. A few years later, now with a third child, the family lived in Niger, on the rim of a desert.

The third visit 17 years later was also to Niger, a visit to her adult daughter who was working in a clinic there. Hill was overwhelmed by what she saw. The clinic was in a drought area and children were dying of starvation. Hill said, encountering mothers and starving children "was so profound, I just didn't know what to do with it." Hill started to write about the village in journal form.

In her interview, she spoke both of writing *Willie* and her novel, *Still Waters in Niger* (Hill, 1999).

Mary LaChapelle

Born and raised in the US Midwest, LaChapelle is known for writing about its rural and small-town characters. Once she determined she wanted to write, she took a job as a night counselor at a halfway house for juveniles with emotional and/or cognitive problems. There, she was able to sleep some of the night and write during the day.

Speaking of writing, LaChapelle said, "There is something in the original impulse or image…I trust to guide me when, by and by, I feel lost writing it. And even when it's a mess in progress, I love that I can hold the whole of a short story's form in my head" (LaChapelle, 2017, para. 3).

Most of her stories began with an experience. *The Meadow Bell* began when on the way to somewhere else, she stopped in a farm cheese store, the kind where the farmer himself makes the cheese. There, on a crate, stood a little boy, with shoes on the wrong feet, shirtless, shuddering. "Are you cold?" she asked. The boy shook his head. "No," but then crossed his arms over his chest. As she drove off, LaChapelle wished she could talk to someone about what she had seen, but in the absence, her mind began to form a story.

The Understanding was written at a time when she was living in the home of a woman 101 years old, an exceptional woman in some ways. One day, while sitting across from the woman, LaChapelle got the impulse to write a story about the woman and wondered how best to go about it.

LaChapelle's interview dealt with these and other stories collected in her book *House of Heroes* (LaChapelle, 1988).

Grace Paley

Paley grew up in the Bronx in New York as part of a large extended family. She always thought of herself as a writer, but, at first, she wrote only poetry. She was a mother of two children and active politically. Being a good mother and working for peace and justice were as important to her as her writing.

She said that her shift to writing stories came when she and her husband were supers in a building in Greenwich Village. When her children were young, she spent hours in a local park getting to know other mothers and meeting other people from the neighborhood. Paley said, "I just took a look around and I simply couldn't understand mostly the young women. Something appalled me about the way they were living, the relations between men and women. It was as if I hadn't noticed."

Her Greenwich Village experiences started her stories. In one, her husband handed her a broom and laughed uproariously. That incident was transformed into beginning a story of a different marriage.

Another story was sparked by meeting a man in the park, one she knew to be a racist. He had an African-American boy in tow. She asked him, "Who's this little black kid?" He said, "It's my grandchild… Tell her how smart you are." Intrigued, Paley began a story about a woman somewhat like herself telling her husband about being in the park and meeting a racist with an African-American boy in tow. She wrote two pages and then, as she told it, "I was absolutely stuck and I didn't know what to do. I'd say for two years."

In her interview, she told what happened two years later as well as the story of several other stories.

THE WRITERS' CREATIVE PROCESS

The Seed Incident

Badanes was haunted by the Holocaust stories he heard, but he continued to work on another project until he read about the thief who stole Holocaust documents. Hill had finished the story based on the family tale that mystified her; she abandoned another story start she was having trouble with after being overwhelmed by her third trip to Niger. LaChapelle was puzzled by a shirtless little boy standing on a crate and shuddering; the start of another story came from being intrigued by her ancient landlady. Paley was bewildered when a man she knew to be a racist introduced her to his African-American grandchild and had puzzling feelings when her husband handed her a broom. These incidents, which we can call *seed incidents*, have something in common. The writers spoke of them as overwhelming, intriguing, mystifying—the incidents did not fit the narrative logic through which we make sense of everyday experience (Bruner, 1986). Hill said of her story of the dress, "it seemed full of meanings I couldn't even begin to grasp." Paley said, "You have to be sort of buffaloed by something." As an example, Paley explained that if she wanted to understand a commune, she would have to write a story about it. Grasping the meanings of a seed incident meant making it into an imagined story that somehow illuminated a mystery.

Psychologists often use problem-solving as a model for the creative process, but the problem in fiction writing seemed elusive. Gadamer (1989) pointed out, asking a question already points in the direction of an answer. Here we see that the seed incidents provided a mystery to be solved, and the narrative logic of how human events happen became the writers' means, but now in an imagined world of their own creation. The goal is also very vague. The seed incident seems pregnant with meaning, but often the writers had no idea where the imagined story should go and, at times as we shall see, it veers away from the original direction.

Commitment to Creative Work

The seeds grew into stories only after something else had already happened. The writers had committed themselves to writing fiction. As Franklin (1994) pointed out, creative development has more than one beginning. It starts by being attracted to a domain such as literature in childhood. Then, at some point, there is a commitment to creating in the domain. The four writers made a clear commitment to themselves before they wrote their first fiction.

That commitment was more than saying to themselves, "I am a fiction writer." As Wallace wrote, "a creative person, with greater or lesser difficulty, fashions a personal context…that provides the fullest opportunities for the realization of creative work" (Wallace, 1985, p. 371). That typically included finding time and a place to write.

Hill was explicit about this. She said,

> I was beginning to set my life up. I had a friend who went out every day and I rented her place. Three days a week I would go and—I would leave our apartment—and I would go to her apartment and that gave me a sense of sanctuary. I wasn't going to read her books. I wasn't going to answer her phone… It was like going to work.

LaChapelle, as we saw, took a job partly because it would allow her to sleep part of the night so that she could write the next day. Badanes had an office and time in his schedule for writing poetry which now became time and place for writing fiction. Only Paley did not at first do so, but a time when illness required complete rest gave her opportunity. She could no longer take care of her lively children; they went to daycare (Arcana, 1993). That solitude gave her time and place to write. Later on she said she wrote whenever she had a spare minute in her busy life, sometimes on subways and buses, but even she realized she needed what we can call a "writing place" when the writing told her she needed a special context to pull things together. At those times, she rented a hotel room.

Multiple Realities: The Writing Realm

The places where the writers came to write were more than geographic locations. They were invitations to an experience outside the hurly-burly of everyday life. The works of William James and Alfred Schütz are relevant here. In describing the varieties of conscious experience, James (1915) wrote of different worlds, among them the world of sense and physical things (as the paramount reality), of science, of religion and myth, and of madness. "Each world," James wrote, "whilst it is attended to, is real after its own fashion; only the reality lapses with the attention" (p. 293). Schütz (1945) continued the theme in his paper, "On Multiple Realities" and gave these examples:

> the paramount world of real objects and events into which we gear our actions [the everyday world], the world of imaginings and fantasms such as the play world of the child…the world of the insane, but also the world of art, the world of dreams, the world of scientific contemplation.
>
> *(p. 341)*

Schütz then described how the worlds differ; they are distinguished by a particular sense of self, specific kind of sociality, a typical form of action, a change in time perception, and an epoché by which he meant, what is taken for granted. In the everyday world people are wide-awake to the surrounding concrete world and its possibilities. Its existence is taken for granted—it's the "real world." The prevalent form of action is doing for a purpose by acting bodily in and on the world to fulfill goals. The everyday world is furnished with things and peopled with family, friends, colleagues, and strangers. The everyday self includes our place in the world, the stories we tell ourselves about ourselves, our sense of our capacities and weaknesses, our hopes and fears for the future.

Wherever their writing places, the authors entered a sphere of experience that has been called the *writing realm*. For the most part their sociality was aloneness. (Even Paley, riding trains and buses, when she was writing, tuned out the outside world.) The sense of self was as a writer, self-consciously aware that their task was to write. The typical forms of action were reflections on what to write, thinking about how to go about it, and jotting down notes.

One day, LaChapelle was substantially alone sitting across from her 100-year-old landlady who was dozing. She thought to herself,

> Oh I wish I could write a story about Carrie (her landlady)...then I thought, you can't...because you'd be right in the middle of it...as Mary who's living with Carrie... I just wanted it...more about...Carrie's life. It was just too narrow of a scope... My experience of her was limited.

Beside Carrie's rocking chair, also dozing, was Carrie's poodle, a dog that would have to go because he was beginning to bite her. LaChapelle asked herself, "Could I ever take a poodle's point of view? How would that work?" LaChapelle went downstairs to her room, her writing place, to try that out.

The Fiction World

But how do the seeds and the reflections that follow become stories? The interviewed writers answered, "I wrote a sentence" or "I got an image" or "I wrote a paragraph or "I heard a voice." Beginning the Carrie story, LaChapelle wrote the line, "I am a poodle. The mailman comes." She explained, "You don't figure it out. You become the poodle and see how it feels."

LaChapelle was no longer her reflective, self-conscious writer self, but had entered a world in which she was a poodle. She saw his sights, smelled his smells. She was in the dog's social world, aware of the mailman. She was now experiencing an imagined world from the poodle's point of view. She had entered a mode of being which has been called, the *fiction world*, experiencing the unfolding of imagined events as a self different from her everyday self.

But as often happens, sometimes this early, sometimes later, she was thrown back into the writing realm, evaluating what she had written. LaChapelle said of her beginning, "it just wasn't true... It was too farcical. So then I tried a third person poodle. And it seemed more real. Also I realized it was now a melancholy poodle."

Thus after the evaluation, she returned to the fiction world with a different narrative voice, discovered something new in the writing, and was able to find a narrative flow.

Impasses and the Search for a Narrative Voice

Each of the writers spoke of the search for the right narrative voice, and the wrong voice sometimes led to an *impasse*, also called *the point of creative frustration* (Sapp, 1992). Paley told, that after she wrote two pages about the woman telling her husband about meeting the racist in the park, she was stuck. She just couldn't go on. What Paley did when that happened was to put the story aside, turned to other parts of her life, or worked on other stories.

Hill had difficulty with her Niger story, too. Perhaps she didn't enter the fiction world at all as she started with writing about the village in journal form. She said, "The voice wasn't there. Nothing was happening." At that point she had health problems requiring surgery and after, as she tried to get into the story, she told, "I felt, 'this is a catastrophe. I don't know what to do anymore… It was an anguished year.'" Then she arranged to spend a summer at Yaddo, a writer's colony, but promised herself she would spend the time simply to get her strength back without putting pressure on herself to write.

Badanes wrote 50 pages about the filmmaker who interviewed Holocaust survivors but realized it was getting him nowhere. Back in the writing realm, he reflected on why and realized what was wrong. He didn't know the story. He didn't know what he could do about it.

Impasses such as these are commonly reported by fiction writers. Sometimes they get discouraged and question their abilities. John Steinbeck wrote in his journal mid-writing *The Grapes of Wrath*, "I am not a writer" (Steinbeck and DeMott, 1989, p. 36); this kind of questioning of self has been called the *inner critic* (Goodman, 2001).

Yet turning away from writing for whatever reason sometimes proves very productive, more examples of *incubation leading to insight*. And, as with LaChapelle, the impasses are sometimes resolved by discovering the narrative voice that allows the fiction world to unfold.

Paley, two years after leaving her racist story, was struck by the thought, an insight: "It's his story. Why don't you let him tell it for Chrissake?" Similarly, Badanes realized something was wrong with writing from the filmmaker's point of view and needed to make a survivor speak for himself. The paradox was that neither Paley nor Badanes knew much about their narrators' lives. As Badanes said, the survivor was "not like me and a person whose life is…a mystery to me, but I had…to see what I could do with it, living with that uncertainty, leaping into that void and writing in his voice."

Hill did not change the narrator of her Niger novel, but after a long forced incubation, she remembered seeing Niger children with their backs to the desert. That was when the first words of her novel came to her, and a writing flow followed.

The narrative voice is more than a way of talking. As philosopher Bakhtin (1981) taught, the narrator's voice reveals a stance in the fiction world, a situated consciousness with attitudes and values. The right narrative voice leads writers into their characters' fiction worlds through the process of narrative improvisation. The writers become their characters, let them speak, and tell of their lives. As Badanes said, "It happens in the voice. I really got to the point where he (the survivor narrator) was doing my thinking."

Features of the Fiction World

The typical form of action. In the interviews, the writers' own way of speaking changed as their descriptions moved from the writing realm to the fiction world. When describing the writing realm, they spoke of reflecting about their writing, what they as active agents intended in their stories: "I wanted to," "I asked myself," "I decided to." Once into the fiction world, they described themselves as letting experiences happening to them. "I had to let Zagrowski see it with his own eyes," Paley said of her racist. Badanes described finding his Holocaust survivor's voice by saying, "that opening sentence…somehow came to me one day." The typical form of action is allowing scenes and words to come to them.

The fiction world as creative flow. The descriptions of living in the fiction world fit many of the features of Csikszentmihalyi's (1990, 1999) concept of flow, an experience of total engagement in activities such as sports (the zone), video games, and religious rituals. Its features include the sense of having stepped into a different reality, effortless attention, spontaneity, time distortion, and no distractions or fears of failure (Clark, Teevan, & Ricciuti, 1956), none of the usual self-consciousness of everyday life. But Csikszentmihalyi's description of flow also includes clear goals, unambiguous feedback, and sense of control, features typical of domains such as playing tennis. Mace (1997) and Cseh (2016, 2017) reported that their interviews with visual artists found no evidence of these. Similarly the four interviewed writers did not have clear goals (Paley's having written a paragraph and not having "the vaguest idea what the story is"). They allowed scenes to come to them (giving up conscious control), and they did not get unambiguous feedback. That is, they didn't reflect on what emerged in the fiction world as "working" until they left it for the writing realm. Badanes had written 50 pages of his Holocaust novel before he realized he was moving in the wrong direction. Creative flow in artistic worlds, such as the fiction world, have some unique features. Csikszentmihalyi (1999) wrote of the paradox of control, thinking that the organized creations that emerge in flow must mean that there is control. One of the mysteries of the fiction world is that intentions from the writing realm often infused the narrative flow without the sense of controlling it.[4]

Characters in the fiction world. The fiction world is a social world, peopled with characters that emerge with narrative improvisation. As their stories unfolded, writers spoke of "getting to know" their characters, hearing their conversations, smelling their smells, feeling their emotions. When writers are in the fiction world, the characters are "real." As Zagrowski's voice became her own, Paley felt his annoyance at the intrusive question, "Who's that black kid?"

Sometimes the characters of the fiction world continue to appear in the experience of the writers, even after the completed story. Paley's broom story is told from the viewpoint of Virginia, the recipient of the broom. She had a very negative view of her neighbor, Mrs. Rafferty. Paley said,

> I always felt that girl Virginia didn't see her straight, that she hasn't given that woman her due somehow, that there's more to her than met Virginia's eye. That bothered me. I didn't like leaving her in that rotten condition…(in another story) she turned out a lot different than Virginia gave her credit for… It's sort of eerie when I think about it sometimes.

Though the writers' characters sometimes began by being based on someone from their everyday world, they typically changed spontaneously, often combining the features and experiences of people from the everyday world. In Hill's story, *Willie*, she began by writing about her martinet grandfather with the bitterness she felt as a child. But, when the second paragraph came to her, Willie teaches his daughter to swim, just as Hill's father had taught her to swim—a happy, tender memory. Then a scene in which Willie feels the kind of shame Hill herself had once felt in the everyday world appeared. Willie became a much more complex, sympathetic character.

Even characters who start out to be autobiographical change to a greater or lesser degree. Grace Paley often has a character named Faith in her stories and Faith has many experiences and values resembling Paley's. (In the *Zagrowski* story, he tells of meeting Faith asking her intrusive question in the park.) But Faith had a different history; she was a single mother with two sons whereas Paley was married and had a son and a daughter. In public presentations when she was asked about Faith, Paley refused to say Faith was autobiographical instead insisting, "Faith works for me." Badanes said this about his semi-autobiographical street theater character, "he wasn't exactly like me. He didn't exactly have my experiences and the way he thought about the world was a little different."

Hill drew heavily on the journal she kept during her visit to Niger. But asked about whether the woman who visits her daughter in the novel was Hill herself, she said, "Once you begin to write something down, it becomes different, it's not your life anymore." She added that the character was "very different from her social self, more ungoverned, much more freed." And the scenes and the conversations were fictional. We can think of the semi-autobiographical characters as *fictional avatars*, representations of some experiences and aspects of the writer's self, but not others.

Intermittency and Surprises

The writers tended to go in and out of the fiction world, writing, reflecting on what they had written, and then living in the fiction world once again as they wrote. Badanes had written half a manuscript when, in the writing realm, he thought something was missing in his novel, but did not know what. Then,

> she came to me...as I was writing. And I wrote her name—Malkala...and I could see her face, something about her large lips and a certain sort of like a clown smile... When the sister came to me, the whole book fell into place.

Again and again, writers spoke of surprises that came to them as the fiction world unfolded for them. In her story of the little boy on the crate, LaChapelle was writing from the cheesemaker's point of view. The story opened with him seeing and talking to the boy. Later as the fiction world developed, this scene came to her:

> He's lying in bed with his wife. And there was a feeling...people lying together but not being together. I was in his point of view...and there was this sense of her looking down on him as he's lying there...and she says to him, "Lakund, is it happening again? Are you trying to talk about Jimmy again? Jimmy's not real." It was just so awful. Oh, he's not real.

Here again, writers were feeling their characters' emotions. LaChapelle felt Lakund's shame and horror when he was jarred into realizing that hallucinations once again had led him astray. Badanes reported getting chills when, as his narrator, he suddenly saw the face of his dead sister.

Such surprises in the fiction world can change stories drastically from original writing realm intentions. No longer did the cheesemaker have a living son in LaChapelle's story. In Badanes's Holocaust novel, the survivor's guilt over what he failed to do for his dead sister became crucial. And Hill's Willy turned out to be a character we sympathize with.

These drastic changes usually require reflecting on what had already been written, a return to the writing realm, looking for places where the story has to prepare for the new development. Now that LaChapelle knew Lakund better, where did there have to be other clues to his condition? Now that the image of the dead sister came to the survivor, where does he remember her earlier in the story?

At times, the surprise comes when reflecting after a period of creative flow. Hill did not know the major theme of her Niger novel as she was being carried along in the fiction world by the rhythm of what she was writing:

> When I wrote this—Orpheus searching for his beloved, Demeter crying for her daughter—I had no idea that that was exactly the whole thing. I had no idea. Afterwards, not even too long afterwards, I said, of course. This is what this story is, but I never thought of that when I wrote it.

So the theme, a mother grieving for her lost daughter was recognized in the writing realm after words suggesting it emerged without conscious thought in the narrative flow.

All the writers spoke of going in and out of the fiction world, living its reality in words and images and then, inhabiting the writing realm—studying the structure, evaluating, reflecting, asking new questions—then returning to the fiction world once again.

There was forced intermittency from the everyday world as well. The writers had responsibilities as parents, partners, wage earners, sons and daughters, close friends who needed help. Each writer told about long periods during which their writing could not claim their attention. Two told of serious medical problems that took away months from their creative projects.

The writers were college teachers and, at times, teaching responsibilities made great demands on their time. After long interruptions it was sometimes difficult to re-enter the fiction world. Badanes spoke of a very heavy teaching semester. He said, "I couldn't work. When I came back to it, I thought I'd lost the voice. Lost the voice. I could not write the way he wrote." It was easy to get discouraged, but Badanes continued to struggle. Then one day, in the writing realm, he realized what was wrong. In explaining his life, the survivor had made asking questions part of how he told the story; now he was not. So back in the fiction world, he again moved the story along by asking questions and the writing once again began to flow—an example of conscious writing realm intentions somehow infusing the fiction world that follows without consciously trying to do so.

Thus, fiction writing rarely comes out whole all at once. Something internal to the work or demands from the everyday world take away attention. Intermittency among the different experiential worlds is typical of the creative process in fiction writing.

Revisions

All the writers spoke of revising. Hill said she "endlessly, endlessly" revised each major section. Paley did it by "writing out loud." She said, "I talk these people all the time... I must talk them sixty times before I'm sure they sound right." LaChapelle, reflecting in the writing realm, noticed patterns as she went over and over a draft. "You see a pattern that has meaning...and it's like music, you just keep repeating the pattern so it becomes more and more clear."

After completing a draft that felt satisfactory, they showed it to trusted writer-friends or respected editors. The comments that came back led to more reflection. Was that suggestion in the spirit of the story? If not, what in the story elicited the comment? One of LaChapelle's readers noticed an incest theme in a story. That distracted from the core meaning and so she located and took out the elements that might have suggested incest. Badanes's editor found the survivor's wife to be too weak in a family argument and he realized she was right. He now asked his wife what she would have said. "She started screaming all these things," he said, "She really let me have it." He just took notes. Then he went back to his writing place, re-entered the fiction world. As the survivor, he had to fight back.

Sharing the Work

The fiction writing project did not feel complete without sharing the work. LaChapelle put it this way: "The other big part is the sharing of the experience with somebody else. You make something overwhelming sort of understandable in an experiential way. You try to render it so that somebody else can also kind of get it." Badanes spoke of having privileged information from Holocaust survivors, information he felt compelled to share. Others spoke more generally of what they had discovered in the writing and wanted to share: "how we are" (LaChapelle) and "how life is" (Paley), "underlying truth" (Hill).

Getting published. In order to share the work, writers sent their work to agents or publishers. Though three of them had been stung by rejections in the past, these four writers had the happy experience of finding editors who respected their work—in literary journals and later, in books. Their identity as writers thus became part of the experience of self in the everyday social world as well.

THE CREATIVE EPISODES IN FICTION WRITING: SUMMARY AND REFLECTIONS

Schütz's framework describing the features of different psychological worlds illuminated the experiences of these four writers as they went from a reflective writing realm, to the fiction world, to the everyday world—often a long and, at times, frustrating process. Yet the process was also marked by surprises, insights into how the work has to go. There were periods of flow in the fiction world, the sense of self was their characters, the work unfolding without conscious control. Yet that experience was remembered as wondrous, even ecstatic once recalled by the everyday self in the everyday world. Such experiences were at times followed by impasses. The pull to completion had to be sustained for long periods of time, from seed, through awkward first steps, impasses, inner critic's voices, interruptions, and the feeling that the work needed revision after revision. The writers did not speak of completion as choice. Badanes was "haunted by the Furies"; Hill was obsessed with getting to the end of her story; Paley felt compelled "to tell the truth" about an invented reality.

THE FATE OF THEIR WORK

Each of the writers had the pleasure of having their work recognized as excellent by the field. Badanes's book won the Edward Lewis Wallant Prize; LaChapelle's *House of Heroes* won the Pen/Nelson Algren Award and she has continued to write stories. One of her recent stories was selected as one of the best short stories of the year. Grace Paley's collected short stories were nominated for a National Book Award and thereafter she continued to write stories, poems, and essays until her death in 2007. Kathleen Hill's Niger novel was selected as a notable book of the year by *The New York Times* and other newspapers; she has since written both fiction and non-fiction. The writers' commitment to discovering "how we are" through writing continued.

NOTES

1 Unless otherwise indicated, the excerpts in this chapter come from unpublished interviews conducted by the author in 1992. An earlier version of the material appears in Doyle (1998).
2 See Chapters 8 and 9 for fiction writers whose work unfolded differently.
3 See, for example, the description of Poincaré's sleepless night in Chapter 1.
4 This problem is taken up again in Chapter 5.

REFERENCES

Arcana, J. (1993). *Grace Paley's life stories: A literary biography*. Champaign, IL: University of Illinois Press.

Badanes, J. (1989). *The final opus of Leon Solomon*. New York: Knopf.

Bakhtin, M. M. (1981). *The dialogic imagination: Four essays*. M. Holquist (Ed.), C. Emerson & M. Holquist (Trans.). Austin: University of Texas Press.

Bruner, J. (1986). *Actual mind, possible worlds*. Cambridge, MA: Harvard University Press.

Clark, R. A., Teevan, R., & Ricciuti, H. N. (1956). Hope of success and fear of failure as aspects of need for achievement. *Journal of Abnormal Psychology, 53*, 182–186. doi:10.1037/h0046496

Cseh, G. M. (2016). Flow in creativity: A review of potential theoretical conflict. In L. Harmat, F. O. Andersen, F. Ullén, J. Wright, & G. Sadlo (Eds.), *Flow experience: Empirical research and applications* (pp. 79–94). Cham, Switzerland: Springer International Publishing.

Cseh, G. M. (2017). Ambiguous feedback, control & creative flow: A qualitative investigation of flow with fine artists and graphic designers. Retrieved on June 28, 2017 from https://researchgate.net/publi cation/317081880_Ambiguous_Feedback_Control_Creative_Flow:A_Qualitative_Investigation_of_ Flow:with_Fine_Artists_and_Graphic_Designers. doi:10.13140/RG.2.2.13448.62729

Csikszentmihalyi, M. (1990). *Flow: The psychology of optimal experience* (1st ed.). New York: Harper & Row.

Csikszentmihalyi, M. (1999). If we are so rich, why aren't we happy? *American Psychologist, 54*, 821–827. doi:10.1037/0003-066X.54.10.821

Doyle, C. L. (1998). The writer tells: The creative process in the writing of literary fiction. *Creativity Research Journal, 11*(1), 29–37.

Franklin, M. (1994). Narratives of change and continuity: Women artists reflect on their work. In M. Franklin & B. Kaplan (Eds.), *Development and the arts: Critical perspectives* (pp. 165–191). Hillsdale, NJ: Erlbaum.

Gadamer, H. G. (1989). *Truth and method.* (2nd revised ed.). J. Weinsheim & D. G. Marshall (Trans.). New York: Crossroads. (Original work published 1975).

Goodman, A. (2001). Writers on writing: O.K. You're not Shakespeare. Now get back to work. *New York Times.* Retrieved May 1, 2020 from https://www.nytimes.com/2001/03/12/arts/writers-on-writing -ok-you-re-not-shakespeare-now-get-back-to-work.html.

Hill, K. (1983). Willie. *Arizona Quarterly, 38*(1), 38–46.

Hill, K. (1999). *Still waters in Niger.* Evanston, IL: TriQuarterly Books.

James, W. (1915). *The principles of psychology.* New York: Henry Holt.

LaChapelle, M. (1988). *House of heroes.* New York: Crown.

LaChapelle, M. (2017) Author Spotlight Archive: Mary LaChapelle. In The O. Henry Prize Stories. Retrieved May 2, 2020 from http://www.randomhouse.com/anchor/ohenry/spotlight/lachapelle .html.

Mace, M. (1997). Toward an understanding of creativity through a qualitative appraisal of contemporary art making. *Creativity Research Journal, 10*, 265–278. doi:10.1207/s15326934crj1002&3_15

Sapp, D. D. (1992). The point of creative frustration and the creative process: A new look at an old model. *The Journal of Creative Behavior, 26*(1), 21–28. doi:10.1002/j.2162-6057.1992.tb01153.x

Schütz, A. (1945). On multiple realities. *Philosophy and Phenomenological Research, 5*, 533–576. doi:10.2307/2102818

Steinbeck, J., & DeMott, R. J. (1989). *Working days: The journals of the grapes of wrath, 1938–1941.* New York: Viking.

Wallace, D. B. (1985). Giftedness and the construction of a creative life. In F. Degan & M. O'Brien (Eds.), *The gifted and talented: Developmental perspectives* (pp. 361–385). Hyattville, MD: American Psychological Association.

CHAPTER 5

Acting for the Stage

How Three Actors Created Their Roles

Leon Addison Brown, James DeMarse, and Lois Smith are professional actors who have appeared on Broadway, off-Broadway, film, and television. Though actors are often lauded for individual performances, these three emphasized that the world they create, the drama world, typically emerges out of interactions with their fellow cast members. In performance, they were speaking scripted words, yet the three told of creating the world of the play anew each night. It may seem paradoxical, but memorized words and repeated rehearsals of the same scenes came to allow spontaneity.

The clues to the actors' creation of their roles come from unpublished interviews with Brown, DeMarse, and Smith each focusing on work on one particular play. They were asked to describe their experiences from the time they were cast in a play through to the end of their performance run.[1] The interviews resonated with Schütz's psychological worlds framework.[2] For example, Smith described her transformation from her everyday self into her character this way:

> The facts are going to be: the (stage) lights are going to go out, it's going to be darker than I wish it were…I'm going to have to get in the dark—here's a piece of glow tape, here's a piece of glow tape—I'm going to sit. I'm going to make it… Still now, here I am in this chair, my chair. This night. Awake. Moonlight…I'm looking out the window. I know what's there. I know what I'm hearing (Carrie's son and his wife talking in the next room). I know what it means to me…it's not quite what it meant last night.[3]

A change in her sense of self took place. In the theater wing, she was Lois, concerned about getting to a predetermined place on the stage. When the lights went up, she became Carrie, lived in Carrie's world, listening to Ludie and Jessie Mae talking about her.

The experiences that allowed the transformations such as this to take place, the ways in which the psychological worlds framework illuminated the process, and the extensions of the framework suggested by the interviews—these are this chapter's story.

DOI: 10.4324/9781003013860-8

THE ERA IN ACTING

In contemporary, English-speaking theater, actors tend to be trained in one of two ways. The first is the British "outside-in" tradition taught by the Royal Academy of the Dramatic Arts; it begins with learning skills: singing, speaking, movement, and mime. The actor is also asked to observe the appearance, gestures, movements, accents, and phrasings of others, assembling a catalogue from which they can draw in building a part. (See, for example, Olivier, 1986.) The second approach is the Russian-American "inside-out" tradition, "The Method" taught by The Actors Studio; it asks actors to think of their characters as aspects of themselves. To capture characters' emotions, intentions, and goals, they may relive memories in which they felt similarly or place themselves in the characters' circumstances (Stanislovski, 1986; Strasberg & Morphos, 1987). One of the interviewed actors was trained in the British style; the other two were members of The Actors Studio and attended Method workshops, but they draw on them in different ways as part of their work.

BECOMING ACTORS

Leon Addison Brown grew up in a small town in South Carolina and had never seen live theater before he entered college. He expected to major in biology, but an unforeseen development put him on a new path. The course whose hours fit his schedule was a theater class. He loved it and resolved to become an actor. He attended the North Carolina School of the Arts, an academy modeled on British-style training at the Royal Academy of Dramatic Arts. What he learned there continues to be the major influence on his acting.

James DeMarse acted in his first play in his Rochester, NY high school. After one year of college theater, he came to New York City to become an actor. He studied with Joseph Chaikin and worked with the Open Theater, an experimental group that developed plays through improvisation with an emphasis on movement. He appeared in off-Broadway and regional theater plays, picking up other skills from those experiences. He also attended workshops in voice and script analysis. Later, he became a member of The Actors Studio— what he learned there transformed his approach to acting.

Lois Smith was born in Topeka, Kansas. When she was 11, the family moved to Seattle, Washington. Her father put on plays in the church they attended; young Lois loved performing in them. She studied acting at the University of Washington, but much of her learning came from acting and interacting with seasoned professionals. When she won a small part in the film *East of Eden* (Kazan & Osborn, 1955), the director, Elia Kazan, suggested she study with Lee Strasberg at The Actors Studio. She auditioned, was admitted to the Studio, and became a lifetime member.

THE CREATIVE PROCESS IN ACTING

The creation of a character in contemporary scripted theater has distinct, but overlapping phases. The three actors began to work on their scripts independently as soon as they were cast. Their only collaborator then, living or dead, was the playwright. Independent work continued throughout the other two phases, rehearsal, and the performance run. The independent work began with reading and rereading the script. That was barely the beginning. As DeMarse said, "when you read the script, you know the story and have an emotional reaction to it, but it's not in your bones."

Actors' Independent Work

James DeMarse in The Orphans' Home Cycle. DeMarse played two roles on successive nights in *The Orphans' Home Cycle*. Foote (1989) had written nine rather short plays in which a continuing character, Horace, parallels the life of Foote's father. Foote cut the plays so that at each of the three performances, performed in repertory, three earlier plays became three acts. On the first night, DeMarse starred in the second act, *Convicts*. Fourteen-year-old Horace, now orphaned, has been sent to work on a sugar plantation. The owner, old Sol (DeMarse), used convict labor, men he feared, exploited, and treated with disdain and cruelty. Now old, sick, alcoholic, and demented, Sol goes wild, shooting into a closet at an imagined convict, going hunting and shooting at a hallucinated bear. But he forms a bond with young Horace, a bond he cherishes as he is dying. On the other two nights, DeMarse played Mr. Vaughn, Horace's father-in-law. Himself an orphan, Mr. Vaughn has become a successful businessman and an influential citizen in the community by fierce self-discipline. He loves his daughter dearly and finds the idea of her marrying the penniless Horace unacceptable. Mr. Vaughn expects to be listened to. When she marries Horace anyway, he cuts off all relations with her, but later relents.

DeMarse's independent work. The Method learned at The Actors Studio guided DeMarse's preparation of his two characters. After reading the scripts multiple times, he analyzed them systematically. He divided the scenes into beats, drawing a line in the scripts each time his characters' goals, intentions, or feelings changed. In the margins, he jotted down a few words to capture the feeling in the scene. Then he reflected on his life, identifying an event in which his feelings and wishes were something like his characters.

The words "parental love and protection" captured the feeling DeMarse wanted to enact when meeting his daughter to forbid her to marry. DeMarse entered a memory world, going back to the time he held his newborn son for the first time. He didn't just recall it; he re-enacted the scene in all its sensory and body fullness. He smelled the smell of the hospital. He "heard" the baby crying. DeMarse bent his arm, cradling the baby, and said aloud as he did then, "I am going to take care of you." He "heard" the crying cease, and once again was overwhelmed.

Old Sol, the plantation owner, was dying and feared death. DeMarse went back to the time he felt as though he was having a heart attack and reinstated the scene, the look of the room, the feel of his body, the terror.

DeMarse imagined the earlier lives of his two characters as a writer might. They were both orphans, but unhappy circumstances led Sol into alcoholism and cruelty; opportunities in Mr. Vaughn's life he took advantage of made him respected and powerful.

DeMarse saw a photograph of the playwright's uncle wearing glasses. He recognized a possible Mr. Vaughn in the picture. Locating an optician who stocked antique glasses, DeMarse borrowed them for the run of the show.

Lois Smith in *The Trip to Bountiful*

Smith played Carrie Watts, an old woman who lives in Houston, Texas with her over-protective son, Ludie, and her disapproving, manipulative daughter-in-law, Jessie Mae. Carrie longs to return to Bountiful, her childhood home. Jessie Mae usually seizes Carrie's pension check, both to supplement Ludie's income and to prevent Carrie from running away again. When the play opens, Carrie is listening to Ludie and Jessie Mae's conversation about her. She has already hidden the check with plans to escape to Bountiful. She succeeds in getting away, but finds that neither train nor bus still stops there. She finally takes a bus to a nearby town and a friendly sheriff drives her to Bountiful. She learns her childhood friend, with whom she had hoped to live, is dead and that the town and the house are deserted. Ludie and Jessie Mae arrive to retrieve her. The conversation between Ludie and Carrie brings them closer together as they remember their time in the old house. He admits he should have taken her there earlier. Completing the trip she has so long yearned to take, seeing that the land where she grew up is still there, and sharing precious memories with Ludie provide fulfillment and she is ready to return to Houston.

Smith's independent work. She started with questions: "Who am I?" "What is the personality?" "What the way of dealing with things is…" The answers came from reading the play again and again. In the process, she realized what is going on in scenes, but she did not explicitly break them down or paraphrase Carrie's feelings and intentions. "Because it's better expressed here," she said, pointing to the script.

Memorizing was her way of becoming more deeply acquainted with her character. She was meticulous about accuracy. "It all matters," she said, "Every comma, every ellipse, every oddity." The lines told her how Carrie talks, what her relationships are, how she responds. Reading and memorizing the first scene, she realized that her son would help his wife prevent her from leaving.

The first passage she memorized was a long speech telling a fellow bus passenger the story of her love life, how she loved one man, but married another. Learning the words was her way of finding meaning in the speech and what it revealed about the nature of Carrie's character.

Smith's everyday posture tended to sag. That felt wrong for Carrie. One day she gave herself the more upright posture of her mother.

As Smith read and memorized, associations came to her. Carrie had been raised on a farm in Texas. Smith was not, but had close relatives who were farmers, so the context was already part of her experience. As she realized what was going on in scenes, memories of her experiences in similar circumstances came to mind spontaneously. They "became part of the flowing river," later drawn into scenes implicitly. What was still puzzling before rehearsals began, she trusted to become clear in rehearsal, in interaction with her fellow actors.

Leon Addison Brown in *The Train Driver*

The play is set in South Africa in a graveyard outside a squatter camp. Brown played Simon, the old caretaker of the cemetery for the Black nameless ones, dead bodies no one had claimed. His hard but quiet life is overturned when a white man, Roelf, barges in demanding to find a particular grave. Roelf, a train driver, had hit a young mother with a baby on her back when she jumped onto the tracks—so suddenly, there was no way he could stop. He is traumatized and came to the graveyard to yell out his rage against the young woman who had torn apart his life. Simon knew the white man spelled trouble for him, that there was no way to identify which grave the victim was buried in; he says little as Roelf rants almost continuously. As the play proceeds, Roelf falls apart as he faces the victim's desperation. Rage turns to grief and the desire to make amends for the horrible conditions she lived under. Simon realizes Roelf is a good man and becomes protective, inviting Roelf to spend the night in the shack. Simon suggests burying the next nameless body in the name of the victim. Roelf does so, but carries it out in a way that ends in tragedy for both men.

Brown's independent work. Before rehearsals began, Brown had a previous commitment to help build sustainable housing. His task was to dig a trench. The feel of the shovel, the frustration as sides collapsed inward, his tiredness and muscle aches at the end of the day—all became part of Simon's mind and body. As an outside-in trained actor, he was sensitive to the appearance and demeanor of others. Relaxing after the day's work in a tavern, he took note of an old man whose look and demeanor suggested Simon.

Returning home, he reread the play every day. He raised questions, looked to the script, and did research about the setting to answer them. What constraints does Simon live under? What are his needs and wishes? What is Simon's emotional journey through the play?

Brown surfed the internet for a Simon-like image, and downloaded one. He sought to enter the world of the pictured man. Where was his body tense, where relaxed? What was he thinking? How would he walk out of the picture? The answers were not just words but doing—making the pictured body his own. "It has to come inside," Brown said.

Simon had a line about fishing as a boy. Fugard, the director and playwright, asked Brown if he liked to fish. Brown loved fishing. Fugard gave Brown a picture of a little Black boy at a fishing site, and asked Brown to make up a speech about the boy's fishing. Brown researched South African fish species, entered into the picture, and allowed Simon's speech to come to him. Now having a keener sense of Simon's prior circumstances, Brown realized Simon's life, once full of possibility, had been crushed by the apartheid culture and led to the poverty-stricken constrained life of the present.

A Comment on the Independent Work

The three actors worked on their plays in different ways. DeMarse drew on his Method training. Brown took note of people he encountered and studied photographs for clues to his character—outside-in techniques. Smith allowed spontaneous realizations to come to her. Nevertheless, the actors were not dogmatic and pulled in techniques from other traditions as well. Brown's digging experience fed his creation of Simon. He put himself in Simon's circumstances as he imagined a scene in his boyhood, both inside-out tech-niques. DeMarse was influenced by a photograph for the stance and look of Mr. Vaughn; Smith modeled Carrie's posture on her mother's—outside-in approaches.

And there was commonality in how they worked. They all theorized about the play, analyzing it explicitly or implicitly, putting together the characters' emotional jour-neys. They all found their character's bodies—literally embodying the characters. They embodied their characters in another way as they came to feel their characters' emotions by drawing on prior experiences—their own or others. The different techniques had common outcomes, possible building blocks for the characters they were to play.

The Rehearsal Period

These three actors loved rehearsals. They were a time of bringing the drama world to life, a time of problem finding, a time for discovery.

From independent work to listening. Rehearsals began with several read-throughs of the plays, discussion about the plays, and information conveyed to them by the dramaturge, the set, lighting and costume designers. On following days, scenes were rehearsed one at a time. The actors brought the fruits of the independent work to rehearsal—their senses of the characters' emotions, goals, and expectations and how to embody them. The "interactions" didn't always mesh. Once the words were memorized—taken for granted, the actors could listen and respond more spontaneously. "90% of acting," Brown said, "is reacting."

Discoveries from scene interaction. With repeated rehearsals, scenes gradually came to life with actors inhabiting the drama world to a lesser or greater extent. The spontaneous interactions sometimes led to actors feeling and doing what they did not expect. Brown as Simon in his hut, had been offering Roelf water, which he refused. One day Roelf accepted the water, and that, Brown said, affected his performance for the rest of the play. DeMarse's Mr. Vaughn, stiff and reserved when finally visiting his daughter and Horace, was moved by something Horace said and did. DeMarse/Vaughn found himself softening and appreciating Horace's good character. Vaughn's demeanor, phrasing, and tone of voice made the change which was only implied in the script into a dramatic moment though not a single word had been altered.

Discoveries from mistakes. Sometimes what is discovered is an unexpected problem. Smith found that well-memorized lines suddenly weren't there for her in the middle of a scene. Something about the meaning created by the interaction did not allow her next line to come out. "Then," she said, "You have to figure out what you don't know… I'm involved in what I am listening and seeing…maybe you have to stop and cry or stop and walk across the room or hit somebody first before you go on…to the next word."

Discoveries from the director's comments. The director is in charge of rehearsals and this can sometimes lead to friction between the ideas of an actor and the instructions of the director. With these three actors under the guidance of these three directors, that did not happen. There was mutual respect and trust between them.

The actors took the instructions and suggestions of the directors seriously and worked to carry them out. DeMarse said, "You give him…broad strokes on the palette and he gives it shape and colors and texture. Then it's up to me to translate it." DeMarse was playing Sol, close to death, as weak and afraid. The director said Sol was still strong. DeMarse realized that the still powerful hate for the convicts could give racist Sol strength. DeMarse re-experienced a time when he hated, not racism like Sol's, but still experiencing the arousal that hate brings, adding strength to the dying Sol.

When director and actor disagreed, it became a time for trying things out and finding integrations. Smith's Carrie, after reviewing the devastation of her childhood home with her son, had a speech in which she realizes what will remain—the fields, the trees, the smell of the Gulf. She was directing the lines to her son. The director thought Carrie was saying it for herself. Smith said, "We just kept working on it. It is obviously both things."

Actors sometimes see the moment when fellow actors "disappear" into their characters, embodying a mode of being in the drama world that brings together all the bits and pieces worked on separately. Director Fugard triggered something like that for Brown. Fugard told Brown in one scene he was playing Simon "too young." Brown's Simon now slowed down and that was the missing ingredient. Brown said, "that's when I start to feel, 'Yeah, that's it.'" Ritchie Coster, who played Roelf, told Brown he had disappeared.

After a scene was rehearsed the directors discussed what they saw and made comments. With these directors, actors felt free to make suggestions. Directors typically decide on the play's blocking: the entrances, placement, and movements of the actors on the stage. DeMarse felt one of his entrances was awkward. Wilson suggested another entrance which felt much better. The directors also established an atmosphere where mistakes could be made without feeling humiliated. Stumbles by the actors became opportunities to laugh together. All this contributed to the actor's ease in immersing themselves in the drama world, making the scenes when next rehearsed more vivid.

The everyday social context. There were breaks, times when actors interacted informally as their everyday selves. With these actors in these productions, the informal conversations among actors often took the form of supporting one another: bonding through joking, sharing anxieties, commiserating about the difficulties of their acting challenges, praising each other's work. So the breaks often resulted in greater confidence in their fellow actors and in themselves. With everyday concern about themselves lessened, they were able to enter the drama world more fully.

The complex role of intentions. Actors often came to rehearsals with new intentions—from their past discoveries, from directors' suggestions, from new insights as they reread the script. Nevertheless, the aim in rehearsing scenes was to listen and be spontaneous, not to control what they were doing. Yet the intentions often, but not always, influenced what the actors did in the scene spontaneously. The new intentions, which the actors tended to review just before rehearsing a scene, made embodying the intended action available, more likely, without determining it. The spontaneous action in the drama world was an integration of many possible influences. The actors were listening and watching what else was going on currently and what they did was a response to that.

The intention, perhaps lingering in the background of consciousness, became a possible stream to draw on, but only if it fit. DeMarse told of coming to rehearsal with the intention that Sol look at the stars. Performing the scene, he was no longer thinking about his intention. "It either happens or not," DeMarse said.

What is taken for granted. As rehearsals proceeded, the words, the events, and the blockings became increasingly automatic, a strong taken-for-granted structure within which the actors reacted spontaneously to what they were hearing and seeing in the present. Smith called it "building the nest to live in."

Discoveries continued. When Smith as Carrie first saw her deserted childhood house, she had been saying with satisfaction, "I'm home." And a few lines later, she speaks of half-expecting that her mother and father would come out. One day, when rehearsing the scene, she found herself calling out, "I'm ho-ome," as if she were letting her parents know she had come back, a new way of understanding the line that delighted both the director and the playwright who was also present.

Tech and dress rehearsals. The approach of performances for audiences brought a grueling period. Tech rehearsals were about lighting, prop, and sound cues, with actors going through the motions while problems were ironed out, sometimes 12-hour days. Dress rehearsals brought clothes, hairstyles, and props that sometimes were not comfortable, that malfunctioned. Yet these were professional actors. They knew the problems needed to be discovered and solved, and they all pointed to what all this work was for: creating the world of the play for audiences.

PERFORMANCE ITSELF AS A CREATIVE PROCESS

In the Dressing Room

The date when the play was to be performed on stage for an audience had been set before the actors were cast in their roles. On that date, they had to perform, ready or not; these actors were. This did not prevent various degrees of apprehension as they contemplated being seen and judged by audiences. They were very much their everyday selves—actors wanting to be respected for their work. In the minutes before going on stage, they had developed ways of calming themselves. Smith and DeMarse joked around with the other actors. DeMarse also meditated or did body exercises. Brown's co-star, Ritchie Coster, balanced on an exercise ball and juggled.

Becoming their characters. The necessary preparations for going on stage helped them to leave their everyday selves and become their characters. As old Sol, the mad overseer, DeMarse had to put on dirty, ill-fitting clothes, and a wig of unkempt hair splaying out in all directions. On a following night, when he played Mr. Vaughn, DeMarse was freshly showered, put on an expensive suit, and made sure his hair was neatly combed. Brown described a step to becoming Simon this way: "Putting on the make-up…I would literally just transform…putting all the stuff on my eyes, aging myself a bit…dirty myself up…then I would just sit…and look until he came and was looking back at me."

Evoking their characters' feelings also became part of transforming into their characters. DeMarse, about to go on as Mr. Vaughn, the overprotective father, cradled his arm as he had for his newborn son, again allowing tenderness and the wish to protect his child to flood him. Brown intoned one of Simon's tragic lines in the South African accent which had now become second nature to him. That line said in that way always evoked Simon's world.

Performing on Stage

Awareness of the audience. On stage, Smith said, "the intent and the experience is to enter the world of the play and live there for the length of the play." Now though, the audience was part of the actor's experience, in a sense, collaborating with the actors—helpfully or not. Smith called the audience "the fuel of the evening." But she also said, she is not usually specifically aware of the audience. DeMarse, when he entered the stage, acknowledged his everyday identity as an actor performing for an audience. Then the awareness faded and he found himself in his character's circumstances, in the character's world. At least his actor identity faded from consciousness. He compared his changing awareness of the audience to driving a car. When driving was uneventful, his mind wandered away from the road to other things, but if something needed adjustment, such as a lane closure ahead, driving again became the center of consciousness. Smith described something similar. Though not usually aware of the audience, she implicitly sensed what was going on in the second row—audience attention, restlessness, laughter. Awareness of the audience and the centrality of the drama world had a relationship like the figure-ground relationship in perception (Rubin, 1921). The actor inhabited one experiential world, such as the drama world; it was in the center of awareness; another, such as the everyday world, was in the background with the possibility of figure-ground reversals when hearing candy wrappers rattling or cell phones going off.

Mishaps. Things sometimes went awry on stage. With these experienced actors, they became challenges to improvisation, part of responding spontaneously in the drama world. An actor skipped some lines and the other actor both continued the action and "reviewed" necessary information. When DeMarse's Sol shot at the hallucinated bear, the gun didn't go off as it was supposed to. At first, he remembered saying to himself, "The audience paid to see it… Why didn't they fix it?" But then almost immediately, back in Sol's character, he became terrified of the bear attacking him and conveyed that to the audience.

Keeping the performance fresh. The aim was to create the drama world anew, to live in their characters' lives, to be spontaneous in their actions and reactions. They wanted to do that every performance. Each was different depending on the audience, on how the actors were feeling that day. Two hazards they wanted to avoid as much as possible involved enacting their roles unfelt: one was performing their role mechanically, what the actors called "phoning in." The other was "indicating," imitating an emotion in an exaggerated way rather than feeling it, a hazard paradoxically called "acting" (in quotes).

To a large extent, these three actors in these three plays succeeded. They did as they explicitly continued to work on their plays. They reread or reviewed the playwright's words throughout the run, deepening their understanding of the plays and their characters. They evaluated their performances and worked on what they or the director felt needed improvement. Thus, the actors formed new intentions for their performances. They did not impose their new intentions—that would be "acting." Still the intention, primed[4] and perhaps still in the background of the drama world, implicitly affected their portrayals. For example, in the second run of the play, Smith, in a scene with the ticket agent, intended to listen to him more closely. When she did, her responses to him spontaneously became more specific.

Living in the drama world was not all or none; it was more or less vivid. "You aim for a range," said Brown, "from good to great." The three actors told of peak experiences when all the actors were fully "in the moment," the audience transported into the drama world as well. Brown described it as "Living in a different dimension...everything looks absolutely real. It's no longer a set, it's no longer words, no longer a play...and the words come out of you in ways you've never said them before and they are right."

SUMMARY AND REFLECTIONS: ON THE ACTORS' CREATIVE PROCESS

The creative process in acting began with a structured document to explore—the script. The actors worked on it independently before rehearsals, during the rehearsal period, and through the performance run. How they did this reflected both their training and their unique life experiences. Nevertheless, each was aware of other traditions and also pulled in their techniques, too. There was also convergence. They all analyzed their plays, scene by scene, explicitly or implicitly. They all embodied their characters.

They all came to feel their characters' emotions by drawing on prior experiences— for the inside-out actors by allowing spontaneous associations or sensory re-enactment. Brown, the outside-in actor, drew on people and pictures, but also said of feeling life, "It has to come inside." Psychologists have suggested how this might work: Seeing the intentional movements and emotional expressions of others excite mirror neurons, a brain foundation for empathy, for feeling as another (Keysers & Gazzola, 2009). Taking the shape of an emotion induces feeling to some extent as well (Ekman, 1993; Flack, 2006).

The independent work primed the actors to feel and to do, explicitly or implicitly, "waking up" possibilities without rigidly determining how the actor react once in the drama world. What the actor saw and heard triggered how they responded using the scripted words.

The three actors agreed the collaboration in rehearsal and performance was crucial. It happened as actors responded to one another spontaneously in the drama world. It was a collaboration with the director who led discussions about the play and whose instructions the actors took seriously, a challenge to try to carry out with integrity. In performance, it was also a collaboration with their audiences.

THE ACTORS' DIFFERENT EXPERIENTIAL WORLDS AND THEIR INTERACTIONS

The actors described their interactions with their fellow actors in ways that suggested three distinct psychological worlds (Schütz, 1945). Each experiential world brought a distinctive sense of self, a specific kind of sociality, a typical way of responding, its own sense of time, and of what is taken for granted. In different ways, each also contributed to role creation as well.

Together, the actors came to inhabit the drama world. The sense of self was that of their character in their character's circumstances with actions motivated by the character's goals. In terms of time, each scene had to reflect current feelings, objectives, and expectations. The actor, when in the everyday world, knew the whole play, but the character did not. The words and the blockings came to be taken for granted. The interactions were those of the characters who listened and reacted to one another spontaneously.

During breaks, the actors were their everyday selves in unscripted conversations about anything, but often supporting one another in their identities as actors. A third mode of experience had as its typical action reflection and analysis. Their everyday selves and personal goals faded into the background as actors and directors shared a focus on the play. Rather than living in the play, they talked about the play, discussing their characters' personalities, emotions, and objectives, perhaps leading to new acting intentions—a reflective, theoretical mode of experience.

The different worlds affected one another both successively and simultaneously. The support, trust, and laughter from everyday conversations relaxed the actors about their everyday selves and made them able to immerse themselves more fully in the drama world. The insights from the discussions of scenes and characters and comments from the director brought new intentions, perhaps lingering in the background when the drama world is the focus. Those intentions opened up, gave access to, new possibilities for acting in the drama world, one stream that could be integrated into what actors did as they listened and reacted to what was going on around them spontaneously. The audiences, at times part of the everyday world of the actor on the stage, at times to various degrees transported into the drama world, typically remained in the background, on the fringes of consciousness implicitly affecting the vividness of the drama world. Perception studies have shown the physical background of a figure can affect how it is perceived and that there can be figure-ground reversals. For the actor in rehearsal and on stage, the figure-ground structure and its possible reversals is between different psychological worlds.

The actors spoke of the effects having been in the play's drama world as their characters on their everyday worlds. Smith spoke of acting as visiting another life. DeMarse told of discovering new aspects of himself; Brown, of discovering new human possibilities. Experiences in the drama world enriched their everyday sense of what it is like to be human.

To bring a scripted play to life on the stage, the words were the same night after night, taken for granted. The playwright's words became the medium through which meanings could spontaneously emerge. The actors wanted to serve the play. Doing so involved allowing their everyday experiences and their prior preparations to flow into their embodiment of their characters and allowing themselves, in rehearsal and performance, to live in the character's world.

AFTER THE PERFORMANCE RUN

The three actors continued to perform on stage, screen, and television, with Smith and DeMarse turning to playwriting as well. All three looked back on their work in the plays discussed here with special fondness, a fortunate coming together of master playwrights, talented directors, and committed and generous fellow actors. Smith said this about her pleasure in her work in *Bountiful* and acting in general: "It's the play and the work on it… It's this little world that we make. It's each other and it's oneself and this part of oneself…it's this created and inhabited world."

NOTES

1 An earlier version of the material discussed here, with more details of the methodology, appears in Doyle (2016).
2 Schütz's multiple worlds framework was described in greater detail in Chapter 4.
3 The quotes in this chapter come from unpublished interviews conducted by the author in 2011 and 2012.
4 In psychological research, priming refers to presenting one stimulus to make related stimuli more available that usual. Thus they study how a stimulus presented first affects someone's response to a second stimulus (Hsu and Schütt, 2012). For example, if the word *table* is flashed on a screen first, the person will respond more quickly to the subsequently presented word *chair that* if the first word was *car*. In theatrical acting, intentions prior to performing a scene, such as looking at the stars, makes doing so more likely in the drama world.

REFERENCES

Doyle, C. L. (2016). Multiple realities: The changing life worlds of actors. *Journal of Phenomenological Psychology, 47*(2), 107–133. doi:10.1163/15691624-12341310

Ekman, P. (1993). Facial expression and emotion. *The American Psychologist, 48*(4), 384–392.

Flack, W. F., Jr. (2006). Peripheral feedback effects of facial expressions, bodily postures, and vocal expressions on emotional feelings. *Cognition and Emotion, 20*(2), 177–195. doi:10.1080/02699930500359617

Foote, H. (1989). *The Orphans' home cycle.* New York: Grove Press.

Hsu, N., & Schütt, Z. (Eds.) (2012). *Psychology of priming.* Hauppauge, NY: Nova Science.

Kazan, E., & Osborn, P. (1955). *East of Eden.* Warner Bros. Film.

Keysers, C., & Gazzola, V. (2009). Expanding the mirror: Vicarious activity for actions, emotions, and sensations. *Current Opinion in Neurobiology, 19*, 666–671. doi:10.1016/j.conb.2009.10.006

Olivier, L. (1986). *On acting.* New York: Simon and Schuster.

Rubin, E. (1921). *Visuell Wahrgenommene Figuren : Studien in psychologischer Analyse.* Kobenhaven: Gyldendalske boghandel.

Schütz, A. (1945). On multiple realities. *Philosophy and Phenomenological Research, 5,* 533–576.

Stanislavski, C. (1986). *An actor prepares.* E. R. Hapgood (Trans.). London: Methuen. (Original work published in 1936.)

Strasberg, L., & Morphos, E. (1987). *A dream of passion: The development of the method.* Boston, MA: Little, Brown.

PART III

Focus on Intuition and Embodied Creating

Music by Biscardi

Letting the Hands Go Someplace

Chester Biscardi is a contemporary American composer, one recognized as the creator of modern classics (Sjoerdsma, 2008). His works have been lauded for their honesty, their broad range, lyricism, and beauty (Cooman, 2011; Gimbel, 2011; Carl, 2012). They are said to inspire "wonderful performers, giving them music that satisfies and challenges" (Carl, 2012, para. 5).

Biscardi has written music in diverse styles and genres, including opera, instrumental solos, orchestral works, songs, and chamber music. This chapter explores the creation of two works: one for solo piano and another for piano quintet.[1] Amid differences, both works were created with respect for intuition,[2] by listening to what felt right in the body. He described one experience this way: "[I] push...and keep pushing...making more versions and sketches...and nothing is happening and I throw up my hands...and as soon as I get to the door, something in my body says, 'Go to the piano.' The answer is in my body proper. It's not in my brain" (Biscardi, 2020, unpublished interview).

BEFORE THE TWO COMPOSITIONS

Chester Biscardi, as a little boy, did not hear much classical music, but, as an altar boy, he listened to nuns singing Gregorian chants every week at church. His father, an immigrant, frequently sang Italian love songs to his mother, accompanying himself on the accordion. The public schools in Kenosha, Wisconsin had a well-developed music program, and they presented him with his first instrument, a French horn that was almost as tall as he was. One day he had a cold and couldn't get any sound out of his horn. Little Chet burst into tears. He asked for a violin and his father saved money in order to buy him one.

Biscardi had two adult cousins, better educated than his father, and his father put them in charge of his son's intellectual and moral development. They owned a piano and gave him his first piano lessons.

Little Biscardi, aged nine, decided that he needed to write music as well. An early piece was called "Happy and Sad." He continued to write occasional pieces and played in

DOI: 10.4324/9781003013860-10

orchestras all through high school. And, thanks to an anonymous patron, he took piano lessons from a well-known local teacher.

His adult cousins knew him to be a student leader, articulate in both speech and writing. They saw law as the perfect career for a second-generation immigrant boy. Biscardi yielded to their wishes. Though he still played and composed, music was not part of his academic program at the University of Wisconsin-Madison. He majored in English Literature and studied Italian as well, a language he didn't learn at home because the family wanted him to be a true American.

In 1969 he was already accepted to law school when the Italian faculty invited him to spend a year abroad in Bologna, Italy. He was also accepted at Bologna's great music school, the *Conservatorio di Musica G. B. Martini*. There he received a rigorous education in music theory.

When he returned to Madison, the Italian faculty convinced him to do graduate work in Italian Literature with offers of fellowships and teaching assistantships, his first experience mentoring on the college level. He told himself he could always go to law school later. He returned to composing with new vigor.

It was a period of major reassessment for Biscardi. He showed one of his compositions to the resident composer in the School of Music. The professor said something like, "What the **** are you doing in Italian Literature? You are a composer." That confirmed what Biscardi knew. Composing was what he wanted—needed—to do despite the wishes of his family. He was also realizing that he was gay and wanted to be open about that aspect of his identity. In 1972 he came out as a gay man and at the same time transferred to the Master's program in the School of Music. He later earned a doctorate from the Yale School of Music.

He began a teaching career at Sarah Lawrence College in 1977 and for many years was head of its music program—giving the leadership part of himself expression. At the same time, he wrote numerous compositions; literature was often a source of inspiration.

THE ERA IN MUSIC

It was a time of questioning, a rebellion against the dictates of the past. A single key, a single tempo, traditional structures such as the symphony were no longer seen as necessary or productive. Music was not considered autonomous, a separate aesthetic experience independent of culture and history. The conventional sense of beauty was no longer a requirement; consonance needed to live with dissonance. Each of the twelve tones of the chromatic scale could be given equal weight. The music could quote from both classical music and popular forms, as well as from the music of different cultures. A single piece could consist of a mix of styles. It was as if all the previous strictures that had made music a unified, well-structured, aesthetically pleasing experience could be and should be violated.

In the 1970s many composers in academic institutions felt the pull of what is now viewed as "late modernism" even as minimalism, neo-romanticism, and electronic and other experimental music started to take hold. As a student, Biscardi "absorbed the principles of complex organization and largely chromatic language that characterized late modernism… But in the course of about a decade, he took this grounding and enlarged his expressive vocabulary to encompass far more lyrical and tonal materials" (Zagorski, 1995).

BISCARDI'S CREATIVE PROCESS

The Clues

Biscardi participated in over seven hours of interviews in his studio, the interviews punctuated with illustrations on the piano. The interviews focused on his telling the story of creating works in two different genres: a commissioned work for solo piano and a chamber quintet. In addition, he shared diaries, musical sketches, his own writings on his music, and his interview in the *Oral History of American Music* series (Biscardi & Valenti, 2013). He also responded to further email questions and commented on early drafts of this chapter.[3]

The Making of *In Time's Unfolding*

In February of 2000, Biscardi was given a challenge by the president of the Music Library Association: compose a piano solo that would "look forward to the future while at the same time reflect backward on the past." The work was to celebrate that organization's 70th anniversary in 2001.

Biscardi was an especially appropriate choice for such a task. He loves to play the piano and always composes on it, whether for a piano piece or for full orchestra. He also is fascinated by the different ways in which composers of the past affect contemporary composers and their musical thinking. He distinguishes between two kinds of effects: By *influence* he means a brief quotation from an earlier work as homage. *Resonance* is more subtle. It reflects the kind of music a past composer produced without quoting it directly, incorporating their sounds in a new work. Looking to the past had been a part of his composing and his thoughts about composing before the commission came to him.

Beginning with reflecting. First came some reflective questions: "What don't I want to do? I don't want to compete with classical composers. So, who do I want to go back to?" He made a conscious decision: to allow himself to draw on composers he loved as a youth, Gershwin, Copland, and Schumann in particular. The piece turned out to be a look at his own past as well.

Let the hands play. Biscardi sat down at the piano and "let his hands go someplace." They played a two-chord sequence, a rising major second. The chords resonated with a two-chord sequence in Keith Jarrett's recording of the song "Something to Remember You By," a track on a recording Biscardi had recently listened to. Only those two chords were Jarrett-like, and, in reflection, Schumann-like as well. Biscardi loved them.

Sketching at the piano. One chord led to another. Then he "sketched" at the piano, playing around until his body and his ear told him something felt right. "It's visceral," Biscardi said.

Listening. After he found a section that felt right, he recorded it, then walked across the room and listened, sometimes continuing to walk around. He wanted to evaluate with the perspective of distance, asking himself how this would strike other listeners. Still, he was not analyzing or reflecting; again, it was visceral, how did it feel in the body?

Heuristic variation. If it didn't feel right, he had heuristics—strategies for varying the sketch: "Should it be faster or slower? Played backwards?" Does it "need something between those two chords?" Should he "take a note from inside the chord and put it on top?"

"Did you think those questions in words first or did your hands try those possibilities out first?" asked the interviewer. The answer, though the question was asked in several different ways, was always, "it's simultaneous." The conscious craft part of his brain and his hands on the piano were so connected, they worked in synchrony. His creative process exemplified *embodied mental processes*, processes which engaged not only the brain but his whole body—arms and hands on the piano, the ear, the legs as he paced as he listened, the sensed vibrations, the cascade of emotions as a body experience.

Discovering as he went along. The first chords led to a lyrical idea, next reprised the opening, and then it needed to open up, become more rhythmic and dynamic. His hands moved up, got faster, played something that reminded him of a piece he had written, a companion piece to a work by Morton Feldman.

Playing earlier works. He pulled out the Feldman sheet music, listened, allowed it to fill him, and then went back to his new composition and let his hands play. Something in it reminded him of Schumann's chords, time to play Schumann and allow Schumann's music to resonate with the next sketch.

Going back to prepare. Once he knew what a given section was saying, he sometimes needed to go back and figure out ways to prepare for it. The process was the same: playing around until something felt right, recording it, listening to it, revising it if it still didn't feel right in his body.

No underlying vision of structure. Biscardi felt his way, section by section. He did not begin with an underlying vision of the whole work. He discovered as he went along. Each section evoked emotion and so part of the discovery was which emotions emerged, to be found by playing, playing with variations, recording, listening—feeling his way with his hands and his ear intuitively. No theory explicitly guided the process. Again and again, Biscardi said, "It's a question of what it feels like in my body. My ear says, 'that's the right chord.'"

Were there nevertheless implicit guidelines underlying what felt right? Biscardi knew that structure emerged from repetition with and without variation. But he didn't impose. "It's the idea itself that begs to be repeated or varied as I go along. It gives me that path," Biscardi wrote in an email. One of Biscardi's earlier works was analyzed in a former student's master's thesis and found that its structure could be captured by mathematical set theory. Biscardi thought this had nothing to do with how he composed, but, on reflection wrote, "perhaps it's justified in that he's used an analytical system to recreate mathematically what my brain/heart/soul were doing." Perhaps here implicit structure was intuitively guiding his composing.

The process of writing the piano piece went on, quoting the beginning of Schumann's *Carnival* here, resonating with Gershwin and Copland there, "stealing," as he put it, from his own past work which also had been affected by composers he loved.

The parts in the whole. The functions and meanings of the musical phrases in this unfolding work were different from their role in the sources that inspired them—an illustration of the Gestalt principle: the whole is different than the sum of its parts (Wertheimer, 1923/1958). Biscardi was drawing on the past, in the present, allowing himself to be affected by the works of earlier composers, but doing it in a way that was making the piece *his* music as a contemporary composer.

Creative visitations. During the period when Biscardi was composing this piece, living in the world of music, there were, of course, times when he was doing other things. Still, once he was fully engaged, the piece he was working on was always with him in the background, "in his bones" (Doyle, 2003), intermittently appearing amid other activities—creative visitations. He carried a notebook so that he could sketch the musical ideas that came to mind. Amid the world of dreams, musical ideas sometimes woke him up; at times the dreamed music was no good at all; at others, it solved musical problems.

Biscardi loved all the arts, so all the while he was attending the theater, visiting museums, reading philosophy, fiction, and poetry. These influenced and resonated with him as well.

One day, while he was in the middle of composing his commissioned piece, he came across a poem by Galway Kinnell, "When One Has Lived a Long Time Alone." Biscardi was struck by these lines:[4]

> and as the conscious one among those others
> uttering their compulsory cries of being here...
> all of them in time's unfolding
> trying to cry themselves into self-knowing—
> one knows one is here to hear them into shining

(Kinnell, 1990, p. 65)

Biscardi knew he had found the title of his work: *In Time's Unfolding.*

Complicated musical problems, loneliness, and self-doubt. The difficulties of "Trying to cry oneself into self-knowing" described Biscardi's experience intermittently. Sometimes it was a musical problem he had to solve. As he needed to weave together specific influences, he had to find ways to move from the resonances with one composer to those of another. Then the focus was on the musical problem, writing the transition. But there were other times when self-doubt took him out of the world of music and led him to reflect on his everyday self. At one point he wrote in his diary, "I choose to be alone—and the loneliness and solitude at times is unbearable." He wondered whether he was a failure.

A meaningful incomplete task, even if blocked for a time, pushes for completion (Lewin, 1926/1951), a phenomenon named after one of Lewin's students, now known as the Zeigarnik Effect.[5] Though loneliness and self-doubt floored Biscardi from time to time, he persevered, brought himself back to composing the piano piece, and allowed his body to once again lead him ahead.

The sense of direction and flow. There was a point in the piece when he said to himself, "okay, let's see where this is going to go," when he felt, yes, it was going in the right direction, a time when he found the climax and its resolution. He knew the piece should end with some kind of reprise of the opening. But again, he was up to a transition. Biscardi sat down at the piano and his hands created the transition in an effortless flow leading right into a restatement and subtle variation of the opening chords.

At completion. Biscardi was content. The piece had done what it needed to do. Drawing on other composers and his own work, time was unfolding over a musical landscape that was poignant and painful, lonely, angry, lyrical, tender, and heroic, celebrating the past in the modalities of the present with a final note pointing toward the future.

How the Quintet Came Together

Biscardi worked on his piano quintet for over 17 years. The first sustained composing occurred between 1987 and 1990; he refined some sections occasionally till 2002. The next two years again brought sustained work. In the latter period, he wrote detailed diary entries which gave voice to his experience day to day in a way that remembering in an interview could not.

The seed. The idea of dealing with his relationship with his father in music first came to him when he read a 1987 article by Stanley Kunitz entitled "The Poet's Quest for the Father." It led Biscardi to Shinder's 1983 anthology, *Divided Light: Fathers and Sons Poems*, works by poets about their relationships with their fathers. One poem, about Telemakhos, the son of Odysseus, made a deep impression on Biscardi and sent him back to *The Odyssey*. These lines held special meaning for him: "I am the father your boyhood lacked/and suffered pain for lack of. I am he" (Homer/Fitzgerald, 1998, p. 295).[6]

Biscardi had felt his boyhood lacked his father. He had experienced his father as distant, as abandoning him to his better-educated cousins. Then, when Biscardi was twelve years old, his father died, which can feel like another abandonment. But in 1978, his mother told him something that made him see his father differently. She said, "You know your father always wanted you to be a musician." The father, unbeknownst to the son, supported the life he had chosen.

Starting. Biscardi wrote a poem about his feelings about his own father, but they were still jumbled. He needed to speak about father and son in music. In 1987 he began work on an orchestral work based on the story of Telemakhos and Odysseus. The narrative suggested characters and part of the process was assigning musical equivalents. The piano would be Odysseus. His son would be played by Biscardi's childhood instrument, the violin. He sketched out some musical scenes—a requiem, a recognition scene as the son finds the father.

Possible collaborations. In 1990, the Ohio Ballet became interested in commissioning a work. He decided to try the material as music for a ballet. Biscardi made notes for an embellished scenario, adding new events and characters, and sketched out more music as well. The Ohio Ballet did not receive the hoped-for funding. Then the prospect of an opera came up. His mind moved to a three-part opera, each part dealing in some way with manhood. A shortened version of the Telemakhos scenario could serve as the third part. The opera did not materialize when differences in vision between Biscardi and the librettist made them agree to drop the project. The fate of collaboration depends on shared goals.

Putting the Telemakhos project aside. The sketches related to these early attempts were put in a folder as other projects emerged. Biscardi always had many ideas for music. When one project came to a dead end, he put it aside and worked on others. Between 1990 and 2002, Biscardi composed works for saxophone, for a guitar duo, for four-handed piano, for chamber groups, and for mixed ensembles. From the 1990s until 2002 he also turned to writing songs and other choral works, including setting some poems he loved to music. *In Time's Unfolding* was written in 2000. The different musical genres fascinated him and Biscardi was ready to see what he had to say in several.

But the Telemakhos project never completely left him. Whenever he was between works, Biscardi looked back at old sketches and might work on them a little, and then put them aside as a new work captured his attention.

A second seed. What brought him back to the Greek epic was a concert that included Schumann's (1842) *Piano Quintet in E-flat Major*. Biscardi was moved by its emotional expressiveness, by the intimacy of chamber music, by how much could be said with only five instruments. This seemed the perfect genre for the Telemakhos project.

Uninterrupted work. Biscardi has been awarded a number of prizes, fellowships, and residencies over his career. The one he received now gave him time to devote to his quintet. He was to be the resident composer at Copland House, an award that went to one composer each year. On July 19, 2002, he picked up the folder with all the sketches as he had worked on them over the years and took it to the home of the composer Biscardi loved, to the very studio in which Copland had composed. Here is how the work went.

Sorting. First a little intimidated, he soon settled into a selection process, playing the sketches on Copland's piano and intuiting which were promising for the quintet: this spiky piece did not feel right, these as refined over the years did. The requiem as already written was fine as it was.

A musical web. The requiem had started the unfinished orchestra piece of 1987. Now that did not feel right. Then, he asked himself reflective questions: What should start it? What sends Telemakhos off to look for his father? It turned out to be a who—of course, Athena. But what is her music? Earlier Biscardi had thought of her as creating a mist; now perhaps a web. He sat down at the piano and played some notes. He recognized that each pitch was different from the others. That particular grouping of notes reminded him of twelve-tone music, a musical technique in which a row or series of notes is ordered from the chromatic scale, each note played only once until all of the others have been played, each given the same weight. Then come prescribed variations, playing the notes backward, reversing the direction of the intervals between the notes, doing both. Biscardi had rarely used this technique, yet his deep grasp of all of the possible elements of music made them available to him. His hands and his ear told him to make explicit what had been suggested implicitly. Twelve-tone music did seem like the musical equivalent of a web. No single note was more important than the others, moving in one direction and circling back in different ways. He wrote out all of the rows, a conscious, mechanical task of assembling possible permutations of the original sequence. Then he let his hand and ear chose some to use. He recorded his selection then got up and moved around the studio listening, "feeling the length of threads in Athena's web…interweaving…surrounding Telemakhos, convincing him to leave the comfort of the familiar and go forth on a hero's path."

Back and forth and discovery. But should Athena start the quintet? No, the piano should assert itself. The first three measures should belong to the heroic Odysseus. A little over a week later, the order was reversed. No, she should start the piece after all. The bold piano phrases occasionally broke into the requiem. The requiem developed into anger in the violin. Yes, Biscardi was angry at his father for abandoning him to his cousins (and perhaps for dying as well); the anger music emerged. It's interesting to note that in a much later sketch he decided that it should be the piano alone that quietly begins weaving the web out of which the strings emerge. And at the very end of the work, the piano—Odysseus—restates the web in its original form, this time intertwined with his son.

Interruption and return. In September of 2002, it was time to go back to teaching, an activity he also loved and took very seriously. The everyday world called as family illness required his attention. Not until September of 2003 did he return to his quintet.

Fixity and release. In his diary, Biscardi reflected, "I couldn't figure out how to get out of the anger… One of the reasons I couldn't figure out what to do next…(I was) sticking in musical gestures from the aborted 1987 orchestral sketches that just didn't work… I'm hitting my head against the wall."

In the interview, Biscardi described himself as obstinate, doing this kind of pushing for days. This is an experience many creative problem solvers describe, persisting in a direction that isn't working, what Duncker (1945) called a fixity; the usual "cure" is incubation. Biscardi sometimes had a different experience. When he, in frustration, gave up upon his fixated direction, he often started to leave the studio for another, any other activity. Within seconds something in his body said, "Go back." His body knew there was an answer, but he only found it with the piano under his hands—the intuited intimation that the solution was coming but needed body action to realize it.[5]

On the morning of November 4, after a brief push, he gave up trying to write himself out of anger. Without physically leaving the studio for another activity—again no incubation period as in the classic problem solving account, Biscardi simply gave himself permission to stop trying. His hands found a moment from his 1987 *Traverso* for flute and piano. A finger touched high B, which was in the Athena row. Of course, she needed to come back, reminding the angry son to remember his quest. Again and again, Biscardi said, after days of struggle with a musical problem, he gave up, let go and without his trying to impose a solution, his mind, his hands, and his ear found the answer without imperious self-interference, an insight or a flow in the form of music.

Slow progress and a poem. Till June 10, 2004 other commitments intervened but now his piano hands found the father coming back with one more "burst of boldness." Yes, a quote from his own *Mestiere* (1979) fit perfectly here bringing a transition, "painful poignant music from the strings." July brought wispy ethereal violin solos and the piano drifting into nothingness. It also brought a new poem about his father. The last stanza said,

> What I'm finding, now that I'm older than he ever had a chance to be,
> Is that I love him for who and what he was.
> He lives in the details of my music.
> And I've stopped asking myself
> What sort of man I would have been
> If my father hadn't died when I was twelve.

Could setting the poem to music replace the need for the quintet? No, Biscardi decided, he would not make the poem a song. He needed to give voice to the search for and reunion with the father in music alone. It was his medium for finding form for complicated feelings and new understandings.

Two emotional trajectories. Biscardi was awarded a residency at the MacDowell Colony to start in late August 2004, more uninterrupted time to work on his quintet. He also made a change in how he wrote his diary. His new laptop computer invited more extensive entries than his handwritten diaries of the past. They now told of cascades of feeling in two senses: the feelings over time as they emerged in the music and the feelings of the composer reflecting on the day's work and on himself as a composer.

On the morning of September 2, he chastised himself with the words "A week already. Yesterday was molasses." But by 4pm, "Struggling with details and difficult transitions. Over and over again. But when I look forward, whatever that might be—I move. I let go. I find. It has been seven hours straight." The same cycle began on the morning of September 8: "Yesterday was a bust. Self-esteem bottomed out...I feel like I write what's equivalent to a sentence for a writer in a month." Then the very next day, reflecting on his progress the day before: "Yesterday was an intense day, beginning early and moving on in the quintet. Some beautiful stuff."

The diary confirmed that some of the work continued to be stripping away the unnecessary fragmentary sketches from the past. Transitions continued to be difficult. By September 14, though, he was up to the transition to the meeting of father and son, but he needed to know what it was a transition to.

Ambivalence to acceptance. Biscardi had always had mixed feelings about the musical sketch he wrote for the meeting of father and son in 1987. It was blatantly romantic, expressing emotion nakedly; he thought that he, a modernist composer, should leave that kind of music behind. So, he decided to add a muted trio to the piano-violin duet. But then:

> Sept 21. Almost noon, realizing and accepting the emotional impact of a musical moment instead of denying it. Why mask the meeting of father and son—so longed for—by having a ghost trio intervene? Go for it. Step by step.

The next day was unforgettable—an imagined visitation from the past:

> I am working through the father music, the recognition scene, and I hear this voice that is so distinctly my father's voice as I remember it as a child... And he's saying, "Do it, Little Chet. Let this music be as beautiful and as emotional as it really is."

Biscardi added, "I am speechless and overwhelmed."

A visitation in a dream. A few days later, Biscardi had a dream. "Everything in my apartment is gone... A reconstruction of the interior is clearly underway." Biscardi's affective life and his sense of what he was allowed to do in music were both undergoing reconstruction. The father Biscardi met as he was finishing the recognition section, was not the distant father as the child saw him. It was the father who, the son imagined, sat on the porch listening with delight to the strains of his son's violin, the father who yearned for his son to be a musician, the father who would have encouraged his son to be himself. The music openly expressed the father's love for his son and the son's for the father, unashamedly, in a duet of piano and violin.

The need for craft. The piece still needed work. He needed to find out what came next, trying things out, reflecting, revising what was promising. By September 27 he was writing, "I never worked so hard to reclaim my right to be a composer. Today was...a painstaking refining of ideas that then lead to new places." The work was moving to its conclusion.

Finishing. On October 6 the first draft came to completion, bringing a different feeling. "While writing the final pages, I fell into an unexpectedly quiet, dream-like state." Once again, a musical flow.

Titling. He named the piece *Piano Quintet, for piano and violin, with violin, viola and violoncello.* Though the Telemakhos story provided a narrative structure, he felt that "ultimately the form, music, soul of it came on their own accord." He told of the framework in the liner notes, for those who wanted to know more, but the music with its feelings, journeys, and arrivals had inherent meaning.

SUMMARY AND REFLECTIONS: COMPARING BISCARDI'S TWO CREATIVE EPISODES

Two different musical works by the same composer: one stretched over seventeen years with a thick folder of possible sketches to sort through in the last two years; the other, a commission with a deadline of less than a year. *In Time's Unfolding* required thinking in only one instrument. *Piano Quintet* involved thinking for five instruments still composing all the parts simultaneously on the piano. In his mind's ear he sometimes heard the different instruments making the music together; at other times, he divided up the chords among the instruments after.

Each musical work drew on poetry but in different ways: a poem which then sent him to the *Odyssey* was the seed for the quintet. As he was in the process of writing the piano solo, a poem gave him the title. In the quintet, he was ambivalent about a beautiful duet which he judged unseemly for a modern composer and perhaps also because he was not ready to acknowledge the feelings the music was insisting on. No such concerns marked the piano work. The quintet had a narrative frame, giving him a sense of the emotional trajectory at the outset. In *In Time's Unfolding*, the structure emerged gradually.

Nevertheless, many basic features of the composing process were the same and echoed the creative process in other arts. He was affected by his domain and field, both reflecting its trends and moving against them. Writing music in the era of post-modernism, he gave up classic forms, harmonies, and tempos. He drew on the post-modern technique of quoting phrases from earlier works of his own and others. Yet the functions of the quotes and resonances in Biscardi's music were different from their sources, demonstrating again the Gestalt principle that the same element in a different structure acquired new meaning. In both, he rebelled against the dismissal of beauty as important in composing, showing once again that both working within the context of an era and insisting on straying from some of its dictates are dual features of the creative process in the arts and sciences.

Intermittent self-doubt was overcome as meaning-laden incomplete tasks tugged at him. Transitions were the most troublesome in both works. No classical form provided structure; yet structure emerged from repetitions and variations amid other passages and in different ways, the final notes reprised the beginning. Implicit rather than explicit guidelines steered the process intuitively. Consciously exploring different variations in mind and hand often helped. Once he was committed to a project, the music world was always with him in the background, emerging as creative visitations amidst other activities. Strong motivation sometimes led to a fixity, the repetitive pursuit of an unproductive direction. Consciously letting go of the problem allowed the intrinsic organizational processes of the "mind, body, and soul" to bring progress. However, the classic account, the insightful solution rising to consciousness, is not what Biscardi experienced. Instead, he had intimations.[7] Go to the piano. With the piano under his hands, his body knew how the music had to go even if he didn't. And these were times of flow, discovery, and surprise.

He needed the piano to discover. In a sense, it was not an external object. It became part of his body, connected to his mind, as much as the vocal system is the part of the body that allows a person to speak and sing.[8] The piano was essential to his embodied composing.

Biscardi's composing drew repeatedly on intuition which he experienced as in his body. The initial explorations, the evaluation of a sketch, the intimation of a flow coming, the sense of completion—all were guided by what his body told him. Music theory, music history, the musical knowledge of his domain had been internalized (Csikszentmihalyi, 1996), were now in his body. So was the music he loved. Both were available as his work unfolded intuitively. He often struggled, trying this variation and that. Sometimes the struggling allowed him to move ahead; sometimes the struggle had to be let go. Then he needed to let his body lead till at last he knew that he had said what he needed to say.

For Biscardi, these two compositions were a special kind of meaning-making, composing what could make musical sense for an audience, but also discovering personal meaning, exploring music history in the piano solo but also the course of his own work; exploring musical relationships between violin and piano in the quintet but also his changing emotions as his vision of his father had been changing.

From the time Biscardi was a little boy, music was, for him, the natural language of feeling and thinking. Guided by his body intuitions, the process of composing was finding the phrases which both expressed feeling and led to new understanding. He continues to compose to this day.

NOTES

1 Both works are available on CD (Biscardi, 2011). The piano piece can also be retrieved from https://www.youtube.com/results?search_query=biscardi+in+time%27s+unfolding and the quintet from https://www.youtube.com/results?search_query=biscardi+quintet.

2 Hogarth (2010) noted the psychologists had defined intuition in 17 different ways, but he also found common ground which he summarized as "the essence of intuition or intuitive responses is that they are reached with little apparent effort and typically without conscious awareness...little or no conscious deliberation."

3 Unless otherwise indicated, all the quotes come from unpublished interviews conducted by the author and other material provided by Biscardi. The material was analyzed by the methods described in Doyle (2016).

4 "When One Has Lived a Long Time Alone" from *When One Has Lived a Long Time Alone* by Galway Kinnell, © 1990 by Galway Kinnell. Used by permission of Alfred A. Knopf, an imprint of the Knopf Doubleday Publishing Group, a division of Penguin Random House LLC. All rights reserved.

5 The motive to complete an incomplete task, known as the Zeigarnik Effect, was introduced in Chapter 1.

6 From Homer (1998). *The odyssey* (R. Fitzgerald, Trans.). Farrar, Straus, and Giroux. Permission to reprint granted by copyright holders Farrar, Straus, and Giroux and by Benedict Fitzgerald for the Fitzgerald Estate.

7 Intimation as a possible feature of the creative process was introduced in Chapter 1.
8 Sudnow (1979) makes a similar point.

REFERENCES

Biscardi, C. (2011). *Chester Biscardi: In time's unfolding*, Naxos 8.559639, Hong Kong.

Biscardi, C., & Valenti, M. (2013). Major figures in American music: Chester Biscardi. *Oral History of American Musicians*. OHV 454. Yale University Archive.

Brickman, S. (1991). Compositional craft in Chester Biscardi's Mestiere, 1991, unpublished paper.

Carl, R. (2012). Fanfare: *The magazine for serious record collectors* (January 2012). Retrieved August 28, 2019 from https://chesterbiscardi.com/press/chester-biscardi-times-unfolding/.

Cooman, C. (2011 Dec). Fanfare: The magazine for serious record collectors. Retrieved April 26, 2020 from https://chesterbiscardi.com/press/chester-biscardi-times-unfolding/.

Csikszentmihalyi, M. (1996). *Creativity: Flow and the psychology of discovery and invention*. New York, NY: HarperCollins.

Doyle, C. L. (2003). On writing for children and psychology: Getting the words to flow. *Bulletin of Psychology and the Arts*, 42–45.

Doyle, C. L. (2016). Multiple realities: The changing life worlds of actors. *Journal of Phenomenological Psychology, 47*(2), 107–133. doi:10.1163/15691624-12341310

Duncker, K. (1945). On problem-solving. *Psychological Monographs, 58*(5), 113. doi:10.1037/h0093599.

Gimbel, A. (2011). Biscardi chamber pieces. *American Record Guide, 74*(6), 67.

Hogarth, R. M. (2010). Intuition: A challenge for psychological research on decision making. *Psychological Inquiry, 21*(4), 338–353.

Homer. (1998). *The odyssey*. R. Fitzgerald (Trans.). New York: Farrar, Straus, and Giroux.

Kinnell, G. (1990). When one has lived a long time alone. In *When one has lived a long time alone*. New York: Knopf.

Kunitz, S. (1987). The poet's quest for the father. *New York Times*, Section 7. 136 (47, 208). Retrieved March 4, 2020 from https://www.nytimes.com/1987/02/22/books/the-poet-s-quest-for-the-father.html.

Lewin, K. (1926/1951). Intention, will, and need. In D. Rapaport (1951). *The organization and pathology of thought* (pp. 95–153). (Translated from the original German published in 1926 by D. Rapaport.) New York: Columbia University Press.

Shinder, J. (1983). *Divided light: Father and son poems: A twentieth century American anthology*. Syracuse, NY: Sheep Meadow Press.

Sjoerdsma, R. (2008). Chester Biscardi—A voice for our time. *Journal of Singing, 64*(5), 625–633.

Sudnow, D. (1979). *Talk's body: A meditation between two keyboards*. New York: Alfred A. Knopf.

Wertheimer, M. (1923/1958). Principles of perceptual organization. M. Wertheimer (Trans.) in D. C. Beardsley & M. Wertheimer (Eds.), *Readings in perception*. New York: Von Nostrand. (Originally published in German in 1923.)

Zagorski, W. (1995). The gift of life. Retrieved April 26, 2020 from https://chesterbiscardi.com/press/still-point-cri-cd-686/.

CHAPTER 7

Sendak's Search
Finding and Taming the *Wild Things*

When Maurice Sendak (1928–2012) entered the field of children's picture books, they were not taken very seriously. No one spoke of them as art. Its authors and illustrators were not valued as true artists. They were not even invited to publishers' parties. Nor were children typically portrayed as having intense negative emotions. Sendak's *Where the Wild Things Are* heralded a change in both the content and the respect for children's picture books (Nordstrom, 1998).

The title by which we know the book was not the original title. He had been given a contract for a book entitled *Where the Wild Horses Are*. A few months later, he came to his editor telling her he could not draw horses. She was not pleased.

How the horses became things, how text and illustration changed over time, and the reasons he spoke of *Wild Things* as "more myself" than anything he had done before—these are all part of this chapter's story.

Sendak, in his lifetime, was recognized as a pioneering author-illustrator of picture books. He was interviewed many times and several books have been written about him. His preliminary manuscripts and sketches have been preserved. Together these provide valuable clues to his creation of *Where the Wild Things Are*.

SENDAK BEFORE *WILD THINGS*

Maurice Sendak does not remember his childhood as a happy time. His parents were immigrants somewhat bewildered by the culture in which they found themselves. His father, a dressmaker, worked very hard; he was also a storyteller, amusing his children with engaging, surprisingly dark stories. His mother had emotional problems and sometimes found her children difficult to cope with. Now and again, she called little Maurice the Yiddish equivalent of "wild beast." His older brother and sister doted on him and they, in a way, were not only playmates but also his "good" parents.

Sendak was a sickly child, so he rarely played outdoors. Instead, he spent time, looking out a bedroom window observing the children's games below. And he made

DOI: 10.4324/9781003013860-11

art. He drew, often sketching the children playing outside. He and his older brother Jack created books and constructions together. They built an entire wax model of the 1939 world's fair.

As a boy, little Maurice was obsessed with Disney characters in film and comic books. Some early drawings are tracings of his favorite, Mickey Mouse from coloring books. Art class was the only one that interested him in school and he drew a comic strip for his high school newspaper. He even got a job after school, filling in the backgrounds of Mutt and Jeff cartoons for a comic book.

As young adults, Maurice and his brother Jack created toys with moving parts based on fairy tales. They took them to FAO Schwarz, the most famous toy store in the US, to see if there would be interest in manufacturing and selling them. The answer was no; they could not be made economically. Maurice had carved the figures, and based on the skill shown by them, he was hired as an assistant to the window designer. His job was to create pictures from children's books for the windows. So he got to know the director of the children's book department, Frances Chrystie, and spent hours studying the children's books she had selected (Cott, 1976).

Chrystie recognized Sendak's talent and interest. She arranged for her favorite children's book editor, Ursula Nordstrom, to "drop in" for a visit to Sendak's studio. The next day, Nordstrom invited Sendak to illustrate a children's book. He accepted immediately. Between 1950, when Sendak was 22, and 1955, Sendak illustrated 17 books for Nordstrom. After his third illustration project he earned enough to be able to leave his job.

At the same time, Sendak was visiting art museums, studying at the Art Student League, listening to music, and reading widely—a self-designed post-high school education. He also underwent psychoanalysis during this period, a way of coming to terms with the emotional toll of his childhood (Hentoff, 1966). In 1957, he met Eugene Glynn, a psychoanalyst who worked with adolescents. Glynn became Sendak's partner for the next 50 years—until Glynn's death (Cohen, 2008).

Sendak Becomes a Writer-Illustrator

In 1955, Sendak created the first book that he both wrote and illustrated. *Kenny's Window* (Sendak, 1956) has a sprawling, imaginative text with Kenny dreaming of a magic garden he wishes to live in. He is given a paper with seven questions which are still with him when he awakens. He searches for answers to the questions, a challenge he has to meet in order to get his wishes. With the help of his toys, he finds unexpected answers—at the same time learning lessons in interpersonal relations. The last question is, "Do you always want what you think you want?" And the answer is no, because Kenny no longer wished to live in the magic garden. This desire to live in a magical place met a different fate in what Sendak created next: a dummy, a mockup of the words and pictures for a potential book. Its title was *Where the Wild Horses Are*.

THE CREATION OF *WHERE THE WILD THINGS ARE*

The First Attempt: The 1955 Dummy

Sendak's wild horses dummy (Sendak, 1955) had an unusual format. Instead of common picture book dimensions, the dummy was 7 inches long but only ¾ of an inch high, emphasizing the linear quality of the narrative. Pictures told the story with a series of vignettes; there were very few words, and these mostly on signs. A little boy follows instructions on a series of signs that direct him to the wild horse place, asking him to slow down and to hide. Peeking out from behind a tree, the nameless little boy sees three horses frolicking. He pulls a horse's tail; the horse breaks loose, and kicks the boy out of his clothes. He sees another sign warning him to beware. Then he is chased successively by a monster, a predatory bird, and a wolf. The boy escapes by diving nude into open waters and climbing into a boat that conveniently appears. There's even a yellow captain's suit aboard, so fully clothed, he sails to an island. There he mounts a tame horse who takes the boy to a house with a sign indicating the house is his and he finds a bride in white waiting for him.

Sendak knew the dummy needed work. Sendak spoke of his ideas welling up in him like a dream (Lanes, 1980). Intuition told him he was not yet ready to live in this one. Sendak called the eight years following his 1955 dummy an apprenticeship (Sendak, 1964). He needed time to sharpen his skills and deepen his writing before going back to the horses. He, like other artists, reflect on their own creative process and organize their lives to support it.

Years of Apprenticeship and Perhaps Incubation

During the eight-year gap, Sendak illustrated 34 books by other authors, finding ways to adapt the art styles he had been studying when they fit the feel of the text. (He illustrated several E. H. Minarik "bear" books starting with *Little Bear* (Minarik & Sendak, 1957), its art resembling 19th century engravings. The illustrations for *Charlotte and the White Horse* (Krauss & Sendak, 1955) were influenced by the art of Blake and Chagall.

Sendak was also the author and illustrator of six books between 1956 and 1963. In them, we can see his developing skill in story-telling, his sensitivity to the realities of childhood, and his ability to surprise the reader with unexpected associations.

Very Far Away (Sendak, 1957) was a less sprawling, more coherent story than his first attempt. The book focused on a single question, "Where is very far away?" and the answer turned out to be around the corner (if you walk around the block many times). Getting there ended up being disappointing and the boy and his animal friends went home. In *The Sign on Rosie's Door*, Sendak (1960) drew on his boyhood experiences of looking down at children at play from his window and portrayed a plucky girl's resilience in the face of being deserted by her friends before she can perform a song—a child thwarted but able to cope. And Sendak played with the possibilities of language, with the rhythm and rhyme, in four little books that became the *Nutshell Library* (1962b). The books are full of unusual associations. For example, *Chicken Soup with Rice* (1962a) has a series of rollicking verses, one for each month.

There is a whale spouting chicken soup as it breaches, a bird stirring soup in a nest, and a Christmas tree decorated with bowls of soup. Many psychologists see thinking up unusual associations, which they call divergent thinking, as a key to the creative process (see, for example, Guilford, 1950).

The *Nutshell Library* sold many more copies than Sendak expected, perhaps giving Sendak the confidence to return to his wild horses.

How Sendak Worked: Routine and Rhythm

Sendak had by now developed a very regular routine, often seven days a week: worktime, dog walking time, lunch, rest, worktime, dog walking time. At work in his studio, he surrounded himself with books, original fine art, Mickey Mouse paraphernalia, and mementos.

He also surrounded himself with music. For each project, he experimented till he found the music that he felt had the right rhythm and "color" for what he was working on. He pointed out that children's books share some qualities with music: rhythm created with repetition and pauses, loudness and softness, long and short phrases. He spoke of children's books as moving with the rhythm of word-picture, word-picture as pages are turned. The characters he drew were often in motion, sometimes almost dancing off the page. They had expressive faces and dynamic body poses (Hentoff, 1966).

Sendak Returns to *Wild Horses*

On April 14, 1963, Sendak began jotting down notes for the wild horses book he had committed himself to write. They were little more than unrelated associations. For example, it began with a boy asking where the wild horses are. One answer was to go fly a kite, so he flew a kite which lifted him to the sky with other kite flyers who were off to different places. One told the boy to jump in the lake, which he did (Cech, 1995).

Sendak, in reflection, knew he was not on the right path, that he needed to rest from the project. On April 24, he reviewed the 1955 dummy and started again, this time with a story.

In this draft, the little boy found that the way to the wild horses was through his own room and there were signs pointing to where they were. Four days later, Sendak added to the story, picturing the boy's room, its transformation into a forest, losing his way, and how, ignoring signs, he finds himself in a magic garden. No wild horses were there; only a woman who claimed to be his mother, though she didn't look like her and the real mother was at home. The fake mother turned into a wolf who chased the boy through the forest. This version ended with

> In a moment the boy grew to an old man and frightened the wolf away. I am now an old man, said the boy, and I still have not come to where the wild horses are. And besides, I am tired.
>
> *(Sendak Foundation quoted in Lanes, 1980, p. 92)*

Again a question begins the action. Words on the signs give instructions. The search is for wild horses. What is new is that the way to the desired place is through his room, which becomes a forest. Earlier works intertwined reality and fantasy, here we have a transition in the transformation of the boy's room.

The fiction world Sendak dreamed up here made a connection to childhood in a psychologically sophisticated way. Psychoanalytic theory points out that a common children's fantasy is that their parents are not their real parents. Another psychoanalytic idea is that fairy tales help children to cope with a mother who is sometimes nurturing, sometimes beastly angry with the fantasy that there are two mother-like figures: the good mother—fairy god-mother and the bad mother—wicked witch (e.g., Bettelheim, 1976). In this draft, Sendak came up with a fake mother who turns into a dangerous wolf who chases him out of the magic garden while the real mother is at home. As in the 1955 dummy, the magical place is a scary place.

Sendak, now in his 30s, valued the insights he had gained from his earlier psychoanalysis. He said, though, that he never applied psychoanalytic theory when he was writing (Cott, 1976). He worked intuitively. Images came to him.

This early attempt took neither his character nor Sendak to the wild horses. Nevertheless, it yielded one image that remained with him throughout the drafts: a boy's bedroom (everyday world) can become the path into a fantasy world. A draft that in reflection seems unsatisfactory can still provide key material.

The End of April to the May Dummy: Finding Max, the Story, and the Things

There are 44 pages of preliminary manuscripts at the Sendak Foundation, many not dated, so the order is not clear. Here are some of the highlights.

Evaluation and incubation. In his manuscripts, marginal comments tell of Sendak's evaluation of his day's work. In the margins of one page of an early attempt, Sendak chided himself for forcing rather than allowing words to come to him and told himself to stop working on the project for a while. Again, knowing how his creative process worked, Sendak realized that he was not fully inhabiting the world of the book and needed to rest from it, another self-chosen incubation period.

We don't know how long he rested from the project but it couldn't have been for long, because in about a month, Sendak was close to the final story and had created another dummy. In it, he abandoned many of the elements of the April 24–28 draft. Gone were the signs, the fake mother transformed into a wolf, the boy changing into an old man.

Max and mischief. Progress came from trying out variations and allowing intuition tell him when he found the right one. He wanted to give the boy a name. He tried past names: Kenny, from *Very Far Away*, Johnny from one of the *Nutshell Library* books. Those names didn't work. Then the name Max came to him and Sendak knew that was it (Rodgers, 2013). He must have liked the sound, that one syllable with its sharp ending. Max's first letter was the same as his beloved Mickey Mouse and the same as Maurice Sendak's own. Perhaps the name Max reminded him of the word *maximum*, from the Latin root meaning "greatest." Most important, the name must have reminded him of a favorite author-illustrator, Wilhelm Busch (1865), and his classic children's book, *Max und Moritz*. In it, two boys make serious mischief to their peril. The name Max implicitly captured multiple associations.[1] Of course, Sendak did not reason this out; he recognized the name as right.

We do not know whether the name Max came to Sendak before or after the book opens with the little boy making mischief. We do know that Sendak recognized that the boy's name had to be Max and that by May 1963, the first scenes are of Max misbehaving.

Discovering that the story should begin with Max and mischief was a transforming one. The story now came to be about a child whose destructive behavior angers the mother, making the child even angrier and out of control, the mother banishing Max to his room—the impetus for the journey to the wild place. The mischief-anger-fantasy combination gave Sendak the best-formed story he had written so far, one that was motivated and kept moving scene by scene.

No horses after all. Sendak must have been sketching, too, because he came to the conclusion that he could not draw horses. Yet earlier works were full of horses. They were frolicking in three panels in the 1955 dummy. One had a starring role in *Charlotte and the White Horse* (Krauss & Sendak, 1955). There was a flying horse in *Kenny's Window* (Sendak, 1955) and a talking horse in *Very Far Away* (Sendak, 1956). As Jonathon Weinberg pointed out in a personal communication (2020), if Sendak wanted to draw something, he kept at it, learning what he needed to learn until he succeeded.

When Nordstrom heard Sendak say he couldn't draw horses, she asked him acidly what he could draw. Things, he answered, he could draw things. Sendak had no idea of what the wild things would look like at this point, but the word gave him maximum freedom. And the sound of the word fit (Sendak & Moyers, 2004).

The text had to come first; each word had to be right in sound and meaning, each phrase with the right rhythm. For Sendak now, a picture book text needed to be like a poem, with sound and rhythm as well as content conveying meaning. He even experimented with telling the story in rhyme, but then wrote to himself, "ALL BAD" in the margins (Morgan Library, 2009, para. 4). The final text was poetic, mostly free verse with a rhyme occasionally sneaking in.

Sendak generally put off working on illustrations until he had a satisfactory version of the story. By the middle of May, Sendak had a "good enough" version: Max makes mischief and is called a wild thing by his mother. He tells her he will eat her and is sent to bed without supper. A forest grows in his room, an ocean rolls by, and Max sails to land of the wild things. He tames them with his stare, they crown him king and teach him to do more wild things. For various reasons, he sails back to his bedroom where he finds his supper.

It was time to let illustrations tell their part of the story.

From May Dummy to the Final Book

After having played with preliminary sketches, Sendak completed the dummy in May, 1963. The relation between text and illustration was new. In the past, he saw his work as an illustrator to do just that, to illustrate the story as written. With the text that went into this dummy, the words allowed the illustrations to tell part of the story, making each aspect dependent on the other to form an organic whole.

There was the mischief Max made; two pages called for illustrations of it. The dummy's first mischief had Max with arms raised, one foot in the air, coming at a cat with hunched back, menacing it with a fork. The second finds Max on a table, a piece of tablecloth in his mouth. In post-dummy sketches, he varied these basic themes, for example, having Max eating from a huge bowl of spaghetti, having Max terrorize a cowering cat and dog hugging each other for safety. The *Wild Things* book has more interesting mischief. First, a completely different antic—An angry Max hammers a twisted bed sheet into the wall, the sheet holding a quilt to create a tent, with a stuffed animal suspended from the sheet as well. The second mischief was a livelier version of Max terrorizing an animal. Fork in hand, Max is going at his dog, now fleeing toward the gutter of the book. The mischief in the book is visually much more animated and more destructive than Sendak's first conceptions. Max, in a wolf suit, is really being a wild thing.

But what did the wild things from the wild place look like? Sendak allowed the sketches his hands drew to tell him. The dummy shows that, at this point, he was in transition on their appearance. Some of the wild ones were recognizable animals—a horse, a dog, a wolf, and a lion. Maybe he was considering a menagerie of different species. Yet one figure was clearly a human female and others were totally imagined creatures with mixed animal features such as being four-footed and having horns and tails. But his hand also drew humanoid faces on some of the creatures. They appeared on the page as he was sketching. That's just the way Sendak told it to Terry Gross (Sendak & Gross, 1986).

Sendak recognized those faces. They were caricatures of his mother's relatives. In later interviews, he talked about those relatives and an incident that may have awakened memories, priming[2] him for the sketches. He, his brother, and sister were reminiscing and laughing about the Sundays of their childhoods. Back then, they hated those Sundays. Aunts and uncles and cousins join them for dinner and loom over the children, exposing their bad teeth and the hair curling out of their noses. They pinched the children's cheeks and said, "I could eat you up." And because dinner was always delayed because of the mother's slowness in cooking, little Maurice had the fantasy that they really could eat him up if dinner was delayed much longer.

The relatives appeared on Sendak's drawing paper first, created by his drawing hand, before he reflectively decided, yes, all the wild thing faces should all resemble relatives transformed into hybrid animals (Sendak & Gross, 1986; Sendak & Stewart, 2000). It was intuitive embodied creation leading to reflection and new intention. In addition, in their final proportions, they resembled human babies with big heads, big eyes, and roly-poly bodies. The look was right. They must have made him laugh when he realized what he had drawn, because they were funny as well as scary. Sendak's pictures as well as his words evoked multiple meanings.

As the text was reaching its final version, he also clarified Max's feelings in the illustrations. For example, facing a wild thing sea creature from his boat, in the dummy he shies away, frightened. In the book, Max confronts it. He also simplified some illustrations for the final book, removing the dog from the page showing Max's return home for example.

Text Changes

Sendak had most of the final words in the dummy, but he made several major word changes for the book that was published. In the dummy, once Max tamed the wild things, they became his teachers, teaching him new wild ways. Sendak intuited that was wrong. In reflection, he realized he was losing his focus on Max. The wild things should not be teachers. It was Max's fantasy and he was the king. Max needed to control what happened next. Reflection stimulated the search for a word. What came to Sendak was the idea that Max gives the things permission to let loose, to go wild, to create some kind of pandemonium with him joining in. Pandemonium was what he meant, but the wrong word. The right one eluded him. Every word mattered.

He shared his frustration with a friend, Crockett Johnson, the author-illustrator of *Harold and the Purple Crayon* (1955). Johnson made a suggestion which Sendak immediately recognized as right. Though creating a book was a solitary occupation for Sendak most of the time, at certain points, talking a problem over with a trusted friend gave him just what he needed.

The word Johnson suggested was *rumpus* (Nel, 2012). It was a synonym for pandemonium. It had the right rhythm. It also included the word "romp" which suggested playfulness; "rump," which suggested naughtiness. Not that Sendak made a list in his mind. He just knew it was the right word.

So Max, now in control of the activities of the wild things, gives permission for the wild rumpus to start. Sendak already had a good idea of what the rumpus would look like in the 1963 dummy. Two sketches he had made for the lessons the wild things taught did nicely for the rumpus. The animals and Max shouted and bayed at the moon as they danced and stamped; they swung from trees—a joyous letting loose of feeling without restriction. The dummy's second dancing double spread was deleted in the final book. Instead, there was a parade with King Max on the back of one of the wild things. Taking out unnecessary redundancy was part of Sendak's process.

Editor's suggestions. Two words in the dummy became the subject of discussion. The last word of the book, referring to the dinner waiting for Max, was "hot." Some in the editorial office thought hot implied that Max might burn himself and suggested the word "warm" instead. Sendak said no. Hot was the stronger word to end on.

A young editor had the courage to call Sendak and to discuss the word "quick." When Max met the wild things, at first, "he tamed them quick with a magic trick," possibly a remnant of the rhymed version. The editor felt "quick" weakened the rhythm and the rhyme distracted. After a 15-minute discussion, Sendak agreed (Lanes, 1980). Every word counted both to author and editors. Sendak was willing to change a word when he was convinced, but refused when he wasn't.

Deleting the wrong words. Between the 1963 dummy and the final book, Sendak made two other major changes in the text: one was the reason why Max decided to leave the wild things. In the dummy he realizes that the wild things don't love him best. They don't let him eat from grown-up plates or teach him how to call long-distance. About love, yes, but also about the pleasures of adult things in this preliminary version. The plates and long-distance calls are gone from the final book. So is the statement about who doesn't love him best. There is one clear statement about why he wants to leave the wild things. He wants to be where someone loves him best. Ideas that distracted from the most important message needed to be pared away. And the message needed to be stated positively. Max wanted to be where someone loved him best. The reminder of that love comes from the smell of good things to eat from afar, love expressed by providing sustenance.

In the dummy, sailing back, Max denies the value of his fantasy adventure, telling himself, with internal rhyme, "Wild things are child things." In the final book, he does not deny the pleasure or the value of the trip to the wild things. Nor, Sendak told Hentoff (1966), has Max necessarily abandoned the wild things forever. Max knows he can go back whenever he needs to. In taking out the "wild things are child things" line, Sendak took out the suggestion that it was childish to fantasize, a preachy statement that actually went against what Sendak believed. We don't know how the statement got there—another remnant of the rhyming version? We do know he knew to take it out.

SENDAK'S CREATIVE PROCESS: SUMMARY AND REFLECTIONS

The journey from wild horses to wild things shows that Sendak was not deterred when the early starts were recognized as terrible. Even they provided material for the final book. He had a sense of when he should rest and when he should keep going. The most creative work came from allowing words to come to his hands or voice intuitively, not forcing. Sources from his childhood were drawn into the book, but put in a new context with new meaning. The crucial discovery of the name, Max, with its multiple resonances, led to a better-formed, more dynamic story. In working on parts, he played with variations until one he recognized as right intuitively appeared, often one with multiple resonances. In perfecting text, every word mattered in sound and meaning. Talking to a trusted friend gave him an important word. One editorial suggestion was rejected, another accepted. The rhythm of the text mattered. Rhyme, which had been so successful in the *Nutshell Library* books, didn't sound right here. In reflecting on his writing, he noticed and pared away material that distracted from a central meaning. He replaced a negative statement with a stronger positive one. He edited out a preachy generality that weakened meaning.

Some of the same features were seen in his work on illustrations. He played with variations in trying to find his wild things. Allowing was better than forcing: when his hands drew his relatives' faces, he recognized their rightness. They gave the wild things yet another layer of meaning—again stumbling on multiple resonances. He replaced a redundant image with a new one. He simplified illustrations that took away from what was most important. He clarified the cascade of Max's emotions. He replaced static images with more dynamic ones.

Most of the words and illustrations came to him as he was writing and sketching—embodied creation. Some led to reflection and new intentions. Words and images jointly conveyed meaning—mischief, wild things, rumpus.

A MILESTONE BOOK FOR SENDAK

Sendak referred to his work prior to *Wild Things* as an apprenticeship, calling wild things "more myself" than anything he had done before (Sendak, 1964). In the past, for each book, he had chosen recognizable artists to model his illustrations on. With *Wild Things*, he drew on several artists and blended them into a unique style (Hentoff, 1966).

In the past, Sendak, the writer, and Sendak, the illustrator, could be at odds. The writer called for concrete details, the illustrator wanted to convey emotions. The two selves fused in *Wild Things* (Hentoff, 1966).

Sendak the writer had also matured and discovered his personal style. No longer wordy sprawling narratives, the text had the economy, rhythm, and richness of a poem; the content, a well-formed story.

In *Wild Things*, Sendak said, he had gone deeper into the emotional life of childhood than ever had before. If we look at some of his earlier writings, each with their own virtues, the fantasy worlds were disappointing. There was a magic garden in *Kenny's Window*, but Kenny chose not to live there. *Very Far Away* was only a block away and didn't do for any of the travelers what they had hoped. In the 1955 dummy, the boy got to the wild horses, but they kicked him away and then he was confronted with monsters from whom he had to escape. An early attempt in 1963 didn't take him to wild horses, but to a fake mother who turns into a wolf.

Wild Things was different. Sendak knew children weren't always well-behaved and could at times be cruel. When Max and his mischief emerged, Sendak put Max in a wolf suit, acting out anger destructively. Being sent to to his room made him even angrier, but also perhaps frightened by his mother's anger and anxious about losing her love. No longer turning away from emotions that potentially threatened to overwhelm him, Sendak's Max confronted them, allowed the emotions to be expressed, but under his control. In the process, Sendak, through Max's journey, got to that wild, faraway place he had been trying to get to in previous books.

Was Sendak mirroring what happened in his psychoanalysis, in a safe situation "sailing," as the book said, "back over the years" to revisit the emotions of his own childhood? Perhaps. But more importantly, he was giving mythical shape to a major developmental achievement: the need to get control of emotions that threaten to overwhelm, or as the wild things say, "eat you up." A healthy resolution is allowing them to play out in fantasy. Then reality beckons. It sets limits against which children may push; it also provides what is essential to nurture the inner forces for growth: food for the body, love for the soul.

Sendak has acknowledged that this was the deep meaning, but not because he put it in intentionally. Only after he finished the book did he recognize its meanings (Hentoff, 1966). While he was in the process of creating *Wild Things*, he was in Max's world, living Max's adventure, allowing intuition to tell him when the sound or look of the story was going off course, then allowing other variations to come to him. Though his intuition may have been informed by psychoanalysis, intuition, not psychological ideas, guided him.

THE STORY IN PAGE LAYOUT

Sendak used every aspect of children's book-making to resonate with the feeling life of the story—even page layout. In both the 1963 dummy and the final book, the amount of white space on a double page spread embodied the proportion of the real, verbal-dominated world in relation to emotional experience. In the first pages, there were a few words on the white left-hand pages and illustrations with wide margins on the right-hand pages, the real world pressing down on feeling. As the garden grows in Max's room, the right-hand illustrations take up more of the page. As he sails to the wild things, the illustrations bleed more and more onto the-left hand pages. By rumpus time, there is no white space at all on three double-page spreads. And not a single word. The rumpus is preverbal. Max was unleashing primitive emotions—joyously without limits. Words on white margins returned only when Max stops the rumpus and sends the wild things to bed. Thereafter, the illustrations gradually recede from taking up almost all of the double page spread. When Max gets back to his room, there is a perfect balance. The page on the left side is white and has words; on the right is Max in his bedroom with no white margins. The world Max had returned to has more space for feeling life in the everyday world than at the book's opening. The words are given equal weight—a balance between inner emotions and outer reality. Every aspect of the picture book—words, illustrations, layout—contributed to the whole.

A FINAL COMMENT

With *Wild Things*, Sendak found himself as an artist. Sendak's development is reminiscent of the three beginnings Franklin (1994) distinguished in her study of visual artists: the attraction to a medium in childhood, the later commitment to an artistic domain, and finding one's voice with content and ways of working with materials that feel unique. In *Wild Things* Sendak had found his theme, the sound of his texts, the way he handled illustration and layout, his power as a picture book artist.

Sendak insisted that he was not Max. He said, he as a child, was not as brave; his mother, not as loving (Sendak & Moyers, 2004). Yet, there is a sense in which 34-year-old Maurice was a bit like Max. Sendak tamed all the aspects of the medium which often pulled in different directions and brought them into a harmonious whole. He relived and tamed childhood emotions. With intuition as a guide, the play of variation, recognizing the rightness of a possibility, evaluation, and integration, Sendak found what he had been searching for so many years.

Generations of children continue to delight in their own journeys to the world of *Where the Wild Things Are*.

NOTES

1   Freud (1899/1999), in his *The Interpretation of Dreams*, wrote of over-determination, how, in a dream, a single word or image may contain layers of emotionally relevant meanings.
2   Priming as a psychological concept is defined in Chapter 5.

REFERENCES

Bettelheim, B. (1976). *The uses of enchantment: The meaning and importance of fairy tales*. London: Thames and Hudson.

Busch, W. (1865). *Max und Moritz: Eine bubengeschichten in sieben streichen*. Munich: Braun and Schneider.

Cech, J. (1995). *Angels and wild things: The archetypal poetics of Maurice Sendak*. University Park, PA: Pennsylvania State University Press.

Cohen, P. (2008). Concerns beyond where the wild things are. *New York Times*. Retrieved May 21, 2020 from https://www.nytimes.com/2008/09/10/arts/design/10sendak.html?_r=1&oref=slog.

Cott, J. (1976). Maurice Sendak: King of the wild things. *Rolling Stone*. Retrieved May 21, 2020 from https://www.rollingstone.com/culture/culture-news/maurice-sendak-king-of-all-wild-things-235862/.

Franklin, M. B. (1994). Narratives of change and continuity: Women artists reflect on their work. In M. B. Franklin & B. Kaplan (Eds.), *Development and the arts: Critical perspectives; development and the arts: Critical perspectives* (pp. 165–191). Lawrence Erlbaum Associates.

Freud, S. (1899/1999). *The interpretation of dreams*. (J. Crick, Trans.). Oxford University Press. (Originally published in German in 1899.)

Guilford, J. P. (1950). Creativity. *American Psychologist, 5*(9), 444–454. doi:10.1037/h0063487

Hentoff, N. (1966). Among the wild things: Sendak's fantastic imagination. *New Yorker*. Retrieved May 21, 2020 from https://www.newyorker.com/magazine/1966/01/22/among-the-wild-things.

Holland, B. (1987). The paternal pride of Maurice Sendak. *New York Times*. Retrieved May 21, 2020 from https://www.nytimes.com/1987/11/08/books/the-paternal-pride-of-maurice-sendak.html.

Krauss, R., & Sendak, M. (1955). *Charlotte and the white horse*. New York: Harper & Brothers.

Lanes, S. G. (1980). *The art of Maurice Sendak*. London: Bodley Head.

Minarik, E. H., & Sendak, M. (1957). *Little bear*. New York: Harper.

Morgan Library (2009). *Where the wild things are: Original drawings by Maurice Sendak*. Retrieved May 20, 2020 from https://www.themorgan.org/exhibitions/where-the-wild-things-are.

Nel, P. (2012). *Crockett Johnson and Ruth Krauss: How an unlikely couple found love, dodged the FBI, and transformed children's literature*. Jackson, MS: University Press of Mississippi.

Nordstrom, U. (1998). *Dear genius: The letters of Ursula Nordstrom*. (L. S. Marcus, Ed.). New York: HarperCollins.

Rodgers, P. (2013). Mad Max: Three preliminary drawings for *Where the Wild Things Are*. In J. G. Schiller, D. M. V. David, & M. Sendak (2013). *Maurice Sendak: A celebration of the artist and his work*. (L. S. Marcus, Ed.). New York: Abrams.

Sendak, M. (1955). Dummy for *Where the wild horses are*. The Maurice Sendak Collection. Archives & Special Collections at the Thomas J. Dodd Research Center, University of Connecticut Library.

Sendak, M. (1956). *Kenny's window*. New York: Harper & Row.

Sendak, M. (1957). *Very far away*. New York: Harper & Bros.

Sendak, M. (1960). *The sign on Rosie's door*. New York: Harper & Row.

Sendak, M. (1962a). *Chicken soup with rice*. New York: Harper & Row (a little book from *Nutshell Library*).

Sendak, M. (1962b). *Nutshell library*. New York: Harper & Row (4 little books).

Sendak, M. (1963, April) Wild Horses. First new draft. Sendak Foundation. Reprinted in Lanes *op. cit.*

Sendak, M. (1963, May). *Where the wild things are* (dummy). The Maurice Sendak Collection. Archives & Special Collections at the Thomas J. Dodd Research Center, University of Connecticut Library.

Sendak, M. (1964). 1964 Caldecott acceptance speech. American Library Association Institutional Repository. Retrieved May 23, 2020 from https://alair.ala.org/handle/11213/8111.

Sendak, M., & Gross, T. (1986). Sendak on childhood. Fresh Air with Terry Gross. Retrieved June 1, 2020 from https://freshairarchive.org/segments/sendak-childhood.

Sendak, M., & Moyers, B. (2004). Maurice Sendak. Retrieved June 1, 2020 from http://www.pbs.org/now/arts/sendak.html.

Sendak, M., & Stewart, M. (2000). Author Maurice Sendak's favorite books. Martha Stewart Living Television. Retrieved June 1, 2020 from https://www.youtube.com/watch?v=ed5vR7F8N3g.

PART IV

Writers as Phenomenologists

Discoveries from Exploring the Inner Landscape

Tolstoy's *Anna Karenina*

From Condemnation to Understanding

Anna Karenina (Tolstoy, 1878/2000) is one of the most honored novels in world literature. Its characters seem so human, they become people we feel we know. The emotional worlds of the characters as they encounter dramatic events are so sensitively portrayed that we experience them along with the characters.

The first drafts did not have these qualities. Anna, one of the two major protagonists, was described by a satirical narrator as socially coarse, sexually provocative, and unattractive; her kind, devoted husband, a tragic victim of his wife's adultery. The second major protagonist and second major plot in the final manuscript do not appear at all in the early drafts. By the final manuscript, Anna is beautiful, socially gracious, and rich in human understanding. Stuck in a loveless marriage, and pursued by the passionate, loving attentions of a very persistent admirer, she finally yields. A second plot enlarged the book and allowed Tolstoy to explore various kinds of relationships between men and women. As the book developed, it came to consider another issue: what, for different characters, gives life meaning. The path to these remarkable changes is this chapter's story.

Our clues to Tolstoy's process come from translations of excerpts of Tolstoy's drafts (Turner, 1993; Šklovskij & Avagyan, 2011; Blaisdell, 2020), and the accounts of Tolstoy scholars and biographers who had access to letters and diaries (Bartlett, 2011; Wilson, 1988; Zweers, 1969). Some of the drafts are not complete; rather they contain just a scene or two with notes on the rest. The available drafts deal mainly with the novel's beginning. Comparing them to the final manuscript, they tell their own story of how the characters first appeared and changed as Tolstoy worked.

THE ERA IN LITERATURE AND CULTURE

One of *Anna Karenina*'s two major plots had the same bare outline from the beginning: an adulteress ends up committing suicide. This plot appeared in earlier 18th century novels as well: e.g. *Madame Bovary* (Flaubert, 1957) and *Thérèse Raquin* (Zola, 1868). And the issue of what to do about an adulterous wife was also a subject that engaged

DOI: 10.4324/9781003013860-13

intellectuals as part of the "woman question." The murder of an adulterous wife was considered justifiable homicide in France and was supported by an Alexandre Dumas 1872 work which Tolstoy admired.

Suicide was sometimes considered a romantic solution to unrealized love. In the German novel by Goethe (1774), *Die Leiden des jungen Werthers* (The Sorrows of Young Werther), a young man takes his own life in the face of a hopeless passion for a married woman. That book was said to inspire a rash of young men's suicides (Alvarez, 1990). And there was in Tolstoy's time an epidemic of suicides in Russia (Bartlett, 2011). Even in his first thoughts of his novel, Tolstoy was entering familiar literary and cultural territory.

TOLSTOY BEFORE *ANNA KARENINA*

As Bartlett (2011) pointed out, Tolstoy already was a celebrated writer when he sat down to write *Anna Karenina*. In his early years he had been a dissolute young man who gambled, slept around, and fathered an illegitimate child with a servant girl on his estate. In the same period, he was already writing works that announced a major writer had entered the field of literature; his first was a fictionalized memoir of his childhood (Tolstoy, 1852/1964). When he settled down and married Sofia Bers, he condemned his earlier life as immoral. Thereafter he spent five years, steadily working from autumn through spring, studying Russian history around the time of the Napoleonic wars, and then writing the novel immediately recognized as a classic, *War and Peace* (Tolstoy, 2007).

As an aristocrat with empathy for those around him, he was aware of the tremendous inequality in his society. The serfs who had worked his land had been freed, but remained poor and uneducated. He saw education as the key to improving their lot. He established a school on his estate and developed an educational philosophy based on nurturing the children's natural creativity and individuality. To teach reading, he looked for material that would delight as well as educate children. When he could not find what he was looking for, he decided to put together his own book, his *Azbuka* (Tolstoy, 1872/1957), one which would introduce the alphabet and provide a graded series of short pieces including *Aesop's Fables*, Russian folk stories, and stories he wrote himself. This book and his promotion of his educational philosophy began before he started *Anna Karenina*, but also overlapped with it (Bartlett, 2011).

Still, he was also eager to return to fiction and, with the bicentenary of Peter the Great's birth, decided Peter should be the hero of his next novel. He surrounded himself with historical accounts along with material relating to the times and places of Peter's era. It didn't go well. Tolstoy tried to write the opening again and again, 33 starts in all, but abandoned each one. The more he learned, the less he respected Peter, coming to know him as an alcoholic and a sadistic torturer (Bartlett, 2011). Late in 1870, he interrupted the Peter work and began a story of a landowner who murders his unfaithful wife. Tolstoy then went back to Peter, but his disappointment in Peter's character made progress difficult (Turner, 1993). Neither the Peter project nor the short story was ever completed—unless one considers the aborted short story a precursor to *Anna Karenina*.

THE DISPUTED SEEDS OF THE BOOK

When did the idea of an adultery novel come to Tolstoy? Some point to Sofia Tolstoy's diary entry dated 1870 (S. Tolstoy, 1978/2010). She wrote that her husband was thinking of writing about an adulteress from high society who is more to be pitied than condemned. Blaisdell (2020) questions this because the entry was written separately from other chronological entries and may have come from memory rather than a current happening.

Even earlier, Tolstoy's sister had been mired in a loveless marriage. She abandoned her husband, fled the country, became the mistress of a Swedish diplomat, and bore him an illegitimate child. Tolstoy was sympathetic and supported her, even going to her husband and asking him for a divorce. Her lover abandoned her and her husband died, so she returned to Russia, but feared bringing her daughter with her. She regretted her folly and became a nun (Bartlett, 2011). If we look at the early drafts, we see nothing of the sympathy for the adulteress. It developed as he wrote. If Tolstoy's experience with his sister seeped into his novel, it was later in the writing.

Almost all scholars (Bartlett, 2011; Turner, 1993; Wilson, 1988; Blaisdell, 2020) point to an event involving a neighbor as an immediate seed for the novel. On January 4, 1872, a woman, who Tolstoy knew, killed herself. Anna Pirogova was the housekeeper and mistress of a neighborhood friend. Sofia described Anna as "a tall, stout woman…a brunette with grey eyes, not beautiful but attractive" (S. Tolstoy, 1960, p. 93). When the neighbor took up with a family governess, a heated quarrel with Anna P. ensued. She wrote her faithless lover a note calling him a murderer. Then she ran off and threw herself under the wheels of an oncoming train. Sofia's diary told of Tolstoy's going to the autopsy and, on seeing the crushed head and the naked mangled body, becoming visibly upset (S. Tolstoy, 1978/2010). Over a year later, he began the novel that became *Anna Karenina*. Thus, cultural issues, earlier adultery fiction by others, an aborted short story, and the suicide of a mistress came together. Rather than a single seed, multiple sources pointed to a single subject.

TOLSTOY'S HELPERS

Creative work typically takes place with the support of others (Gardner, 1993). Two people were of major help with the writing of *Anna Karenina*. One was his wife, Sofia, who copied his scrawl into legible writing for all his work; she also occasionally raised questions and made suggestions. The other was the philosopher and literary critic Strakhov. *War and Peace* had overwhelmed him and he gave voice to his admiration in a very positive review. Thereafter, he became a close friend and assisted Tolstoy by commenting on drafts and helping with proofreading, happy to facilitate the work of the man he recognized as the greatest writer in Russia. Sofia and, soon after, Strakhov were the first to know that Tolstoy had begun a novel that had nothing to do with Peter. Sofia wrote in her diary on March 18, 1873 that her husband suddenly began a new work, one on contemporary life (S. Tolstoy, 1978/2010). She was delighted. When Tolstoy was at work on fiction, she became a valued partner and being her husband's copyist gave her great aesthetic pleasure as well (Bartlett, 2011).

Tolstoy's account of the genesis of his novel was in an unsent letter to Strakhov. Tolstoy must have recognized that it greatly underestimated the time the novel would take, but let Strakhov know soon after. Strakhov, too, was thrilled that Tolstoy was excited about a new work of fiction. The encouragement and eager anticipation of wife and friend helped to nudge Tolstoy back to the novel at times when he was having great difficulty resuming the writing.

THE BEGINNINGS OF *ANNA*

In that unsent letter, to Strakhov, Tolstoy described the events that led to a flow experience, a vision of a new fiction world.

> After work, I happened to pick up…a book by Pushkin… And there is a line, "The guests were getting ready to leave for the country house." Involuntarily, unexpectedly, without knowing myself why or what would come of it, I thought up characters and events, began to continue it, then, of course, altered it, and suddenly it came together so neatly and nicely that there emerged a novel, which I have today finished in rough, a very lively, ardent and finished novel, with which I am very pleased and which will be ready…in two weeks, and it has nothing in common with the piece I have been struggling to write in the past year…I have been working happily all morning.
>
> *(Tolstoy, 1873, translated and quoted in Šklovskij & Avagyan, 2011, p. 217)*

Over the next two months, there were five drafts of the beginning. Tolstoy kept changing the names of the characters; here they will be named only when they win their final names.

The First Vision of Anna: A Beautiful But Coarse Woman

Tolstoy began, as the Pushkin excerpt did, with a social event, an after-opera party at the home of an aristocrat. The guests are chattering about a scandal; the wife of a high government official is having an affair with a handsome young officer. Husband and scandalous wife themselves appear. Tolstoy's first picture of her was as beautiful, with big black eyes, but she was inappropriately seductive. The guests note her low-cut neckline, her chewing on her necklace, taking it in and out of her mouth. She seats herself next to the officer allowing her shoulder to bulge out of her dress. Even her talk is inappropriate, said so loud everyone can hear.

Most of the scene is narrated by a satirical third-person voice, with some parts told from the point of view of the gossipy guests (Turner, 1993).

The Second Draft

Scene one: Anna less attractive. In the second try at the scene, Tolstoy wrote a different Anna: "a bit fat. So fat that just a little more and she would have been ugly." She did have a kind smile but, "No one could argue with a young person who called her unattractive…with her much too much squinting of her not-big narrow eyes… Narrow, very narrow forehead, small eyes, big lips and nose of an unattractive form" (Zhdanov and Zaidenshnur, 1970, p. 721, translated and quoted in Blaisdell, 2020, p. 41 with slight editing). Blaisdell suggests that she now resembled Anna P. whose autopsy Tolstoy viewed.

Scene two: What does it feel like to be the husband?. Now we get to know and enter the mind of the husband. He is aware that something is happening which threatens their marriage. He is crushed by what he has seen, and pleads with his wife to think about what she is doing, to honor her sacred marriage vows. It was for him as if she has been taken over by the devil. He can see she is unmoved. Her eyes are laughing at him (Zweers, 1969; Turner, 1993). Tolstoy was picturing with compassion the world of the husband, a man somewhat like himself, a sensitive, intelligent, socially awkward, kindly man. Years earlier he had described himself in his diary similarly, as clumsy, shy, and awkward, as not knowing how to behave in society (Šklovskij & Avagyan, 2011).

A Plan for the Book

Further chapters were also sketched out in conjunction with these two drafts. Some events are the same as those of the final novel. Yet their meanings are different because both the characters and the ways of telling the story are different. The tragedy in these first drafts is the husband's. The generous and sensitive husband, a true Christian, sees suffering as what is demanded of him and "turns the other cheek" (Bartlett, 2011; Blaisdell, 2020).

An early draft of Anna's suicide does not take us into her world either. Anna tells her husband he won't be suffering for long and writes him a note saying she is crazy and bids him be happy (Baisdell, 2020).

The Third Draft: The Cast of Characters Expands

The third draft suggests that Tolstoy asked himself the question, what was going on before the lover met the married woman he fell passionately in love with? In the process, Tolstoy introduced two new characters: the lover-to-be tells his mother of a young woman, Kitty, he has been courting, and speaks of an intention to propose to her. Later, he meets a friend, an eccentric landowner, who has come from the country to show his animals at a livestock fair (Turner, 1993; Blaisdell, 2020; Bartlett, 2011). Here we have the first mention of the character who will become the hero of the second plot later on.

The Fourth Draft: Broadening the Theme

From the second draft notes, we know that the erring wife had a brother, the one who proposed divorce to the husband. The fourth "draft" consisted of a single scene, one which, with revisions, became the opening scene of the novel. Anna's brother had a wife who discovered her husband was having an affair with the governess of their children.

The adultery theme is expanding. Here was a second adultery with two differences. The married perpetrator is a man and it is a lightly taken affair rather than being an irresistible passion that breaks up a marriage. The book was becoming an exploration of marriages and other relationships between men and women.

PUTTING THE PIECES TOGETHER (BUT NOT BY TOLSTOY)

What has been called the fifth draft has also been given the name "The first completed redaction of Anna Karenina." It is a bit of a patchwork quilt sewn together by Zhdanov and Zaidenshnur (1970) from various drafts preserved by Sofia. It begins with the scene at the cattle show from the third draft, puts in the second draft scenes of seductive, less than beautiful Anna at the party and her conversation with her concerned, sensitive, suffering husband. They have a child, but it is the husband who is the loving parent. The bumbling, sensitive landowner is in love with Kitty and proposes. She at first turns him down, hoping to marry Vronsky,[1] the new and final name of the lover. A second proposal to Kitty from the landowner is accepted and their marriage becomes another relationship to contrast with Anna and Vronsky. In this version, Anna gets her divorce and marries Vronsky, but the relationship deteriorates quickly, ending in the suicide. Here, in different drafts, both the husband and the landowner somewhat reflect how Tolstoy saw himself, but since this is a patched together version by others, we only know that, in various fragments, there were two possible Tolstoy avatars. Much of the story is told by a narrator, often sarcastic about the erring Anna. At this point, the tragedy continued to be that of a sensitive husband with a faithless wife (Turner, 1993; Blaisdell, 2020).

THE NOVEL PUT ASIDE

Tolstoy spent two months, from mid-March to mid-May, working on his new novel. Then, for the first of several times, work on the novel stopped as other concerns took center stage. Tolstoy had to live through two deaths in late spring. One was caused by the goring of a peasant by one of Tolstoy's bulls. Though Tolstoy nursed him, the injured man died a few days later. The other was of a beloved five-year-old niece (Bartlett, 2011).

Writing commitments called. A new edition of Tolstoy's collected works was about to be printed, an occasion which led him to re-edit *War and Peace* with the help of Strakhov. Summers were always vacation times for Tolstoy, and the family went to a second estate in Samaria. A drought destroyed the harvest of the farms in the district, and the farmers' families were going hungry. Tolstoy shared what food he had, but also did a survey of the effects of a famine, set up an aid fund, and wrote a letter to a newspaper soliciting and receiving help for his starving neighbors.

He continued to promote his educational ideas. He hosted teachers to explain and demonstrate his methods. He reluctantly agreed to have his portrait painted and spent days sitting for it. And then, once again, death struck, this time one of his own young sons (Bartlett, 2011).

THE FIRST (ABORTED) PRINTING

Late in the year, Tolstoy returned to writing. He liked his draft well enough to give Sofia this draft to copy. In March of 1874 he took Sofia's recopied draft of the first 37 chapters to a printer, for a book. The manuscript was markedly different from the earlier drafts.

Here, Tolstoy had discovered the narrative voice of the novel, how Tolstoy told the story. Earlier, much of the story had been told by a narrator, sometimes with a satirical voice. Now, more of the story was told by the narrator's entering the perspectives of the characters. For example, we learn of the casually straying husband from his point of view, waking up on the couch rather than in his bed, recalling a merry dream of dancing girls. Then, when he reached for his usual robe in its usual place and found his hand coming up empty, he remembered his wife's discovery of his unfaithfulness. The ball, where Kitty had assumed Vronsky would propose, is told from her point of view. She had taken as given that he would ask her for the final dance. Instead, she looks on with horror as he chooses Anna as his partner, dancing with her with a look of humble adoration on his face (Turner, 1993).

With this method of telling the story, Tolstoy allowed himself to experience the perspectives and feelings of the different characters. The characters also changed. Anna was now beautiful, also highly respected, socially gracious, and rich in human understanding. Her husband no longer resembled the author in any way. He was unfeeling, rigid, and hypocritical, an ambitious man who saw empathy as weakness and adhering rigidly to society's rules and voicing popular opinions as essential to his goals. He was 12 years older than she, and little things about him were annoying—his big ears, the way he cracked his knuckles. A handsome noble army officer and occasional poet, overwhelmed by Anna's beauty, intelligence, and vitality, pursued her, time and again. Though he awoke her suppressed, passionate inner being, making her feel alive in a new way, she resisted his overtures until…finally, she succumbed.

The landowner became a more important character. From the consideration of both the husband and the landowner as his avatars in the patchwork of possible scenes, Tolstoy now chose the landowner as the character to embody major aspects of himself. He even signaled this to the reader by the name he gave the landowner. Lev Tolstoy gave the landowner the surname Levin.

Conjecture. Perhaps choosing the landowner as his avatar was what allowed Tolstoy to portray Anna, her husband, and her adultery in a new way. Perhaps Tolstoy had been repelled by a fiction world where a sensitive, if bumbling, husband somewhat like himself had to deal with an out-of-control, socially coarse, sinful, marriage-wrecking wife. (Tolstoy tended to be jealous of any friendliness his wife showed to visiting men.) With Levin as his avatar destined to marry the lovely Kitty, Tolstoy could now allow himself to enter Anna's world and allow her character and her marriage to develop in new directions in his imagination. As Blaisdell (2020) pointed out, Anna changed from someone to satirize and condemn to someone we care about. In fact, it has been suggested that the story of the writing of *Anna Karenina* is the story of Tolstoy falling in love with Anna (Šklovsky & Avagyan, 2011). He now experienced her world as he was writing, and she developed into one of the great tragic characters of literature.

CANCELING THE PRINTING

Strakhov was deeply disappointed by what happened next. Tolstoy wrote to Strakhov that he no longer liked what he had written. In May, Tolstoy halted the publication.

His mind was on what he considered more important other things. The Literacy Committee had agreed to test his educational methods against current practice. When the results were inconclusive, he did not give up and wrote an article on education for a major journal. He was revising his *Azbuka*. His fifth child was born. In June a devastating death— his beloved aunt, the woman who raised him like a mother, died (Bartlett, 2011).

Strakhov visited Tolstoy in July and, in person and in letters, tried to convince him of the value, of the absolute originality of the novel as it was developing. Tolstoy wrote to his friend that "thanks to him he felt the novel might be worth finishing." He even told Strakhov of the changes he was considering—"to redo from the start everything concerning Levin and Vronsky" (Donskov, 2003, pp. 171–172; translated and cited in Blaisdell, 2020, p. 137). But did he go to work on it then? No.

There were distractions aplenty—the need to find a new tutor for his children, a daughter's serious accident requiring a trip to Moscow for medical care, continuing to work on the revision of his ABC and reader, his *Azbuka* (Bartlett, 2011).

WORK ON *ANNA* RESUMES

What made him finally resume work on the novel? Several authors (Bartlett, 2011; Blaisdell, 2020; Turner, 1993) agree that Tolstoy went back to his novel for money. He needed it for another passion of his, to buy more land—extrinsic motivation. But human action rarely has single causes; the incomplete project for which he already had new ideas must also have exerted some intrinsic pull. So might have the enthusiasm and encouragement of Sofia and Strakhov.

Tolstoy knew his commercial value as an author and drove a hard bargain. He and the editor of *The Russian Messenger* agreed that *Anna Karenina* would be published in his journal in segments. Tolstoy was to receive an advance generous enough to buy the land he wanted and payment for the submission of each installment.

But much of the final manuscript had not yet been written beyond the first third of the book. Nevertheless, the pattern of starts and stops with long delays between working on the book continued. Summer vacations, housefuls of guests, the death of another old aunt, a child with a severe injury, Sophia gravely ill, deaths of a premature child and of a ten-month-old son interrupted Tolstoy's time and attention for long periods. Tolstoy himself became depressed at one point, obsessed with death, and feeling his life to be empty. The journal editor had to apologize for long delays in the installments, leaving enthusiastic readers hungry to know what happened next for months. Winter and early spring remained the times when Tolstoy returned to the writing and *The Russian Messenger* published installments in the early months of 1875, 1876, and 1877 (Bartlett, 2011).

THE FINAL MANUSCRIPT

Redoing Levin and Vronsky

The new Vronsky is not a bad fellow, but less noble, more ordinary than the earlier versions. No longer a poet, he had considered his interactions with Kitty a casual flirtation befitting officers, never realizing that his attentions led her to expect a proposal. His passion for Anna is sincere and takes over his life. He even gives up his military career for her. When he and Anna spend time in Italy, he takes up painting to relieve his boredom, but has no concept of the true nature of art. As he makes a new life with Anna in Russia, he is able to take his place in the community, often leaving home for various activities. Anna is ostracized from society so has to remain at home. Every time he goes off, she fears his love for her was weakening. She becomes increasingly demanding of his time and attention—a vicious cycle and a developing tragedy.

And what of the new Levin? Sofia is said to have declared, "Levin is you, Lyova, minus the talent" (Pevear, 2000, p. xiii). True, Levin was not a celebrated writer, but he did have the same position in society, lived on a similar estate, and had similar opinions about education, agriculture, politics, and morality. The book now opened up. It was no longer just an adultery story like those other 19th century novels nor a portrayal of different man–woman relationships alone. Now Tolstoy could use the book to test out his opinions through Levin's conversations with other characters. He could portray his feelings as events unfolded. The new Levin's dreamy elation when his proposal was accepted and the happy early years of his marriage to Kitty reflected Tolstoy's. Levin's feelings of vulnerability when he looked at his first newborn child echoed those of Tolstoy's as well. Levin became as prominent as Anna in the book and elements of Tolstoy's life became a parallel plot to the adultery story.

Tolstoy achieved a new freedom in the writing, allowing the many streams of his everyday life to flow into his fiction world. Perhaps his idea that writing novels was not of great import contributed to that new freedom. All the while, Anna continued to become herself, and, in the process, embodied Tolstoy's passionate nature which he was trying to suppress as he tried to live according to a strict moral code. As Pevear (2000) pointed out, the artist in Tolstoy was kept in balance with the moralist and the characters ended up at times saying and doing things that surprised the author. Furthermore, attention to structure, to repeated images such as that of the train, and the ultimate unity of the book emerged as the artist wrote, and rewrote, and rewrote.

THE SEARCH FOR MEANING

Writing in installments, the Levin sections took the place of his diary which he did not keep during this period; the novel reflected current thoughts and feelings. At one point, the story began to reflect Tolstoy's own dark mood. Levin asked himself, why would a man with a prosperous estate, a happy marriage, and a growing family have such dark moods? He saw his moods as related to his struggle to understand the purpose of his life in the face of death. He had to know the *why* before he could figure out *how* to live. And being unable to find meaning made life unbearable. Levin's brooding was almost identical to Tolstoy's description of himself in *A Confession* (1983), completed soon after the novel. In both, in almost the same words, he wrote of fearing he would succumb to suicide. He hid ropes that he could use to hang himself and no longer carried a gun when hunting for fear he would turn it on himself. The Levin story came to reflect Tolstoy's struggle and became a man's agonized search for meaning.

Psychiatrist Victor Frankl (1963) would see Levin/Tolstoy as experiencing existential anxiety, the inner void when life feels empty of meaning. Finding meaning, Frankl said, is a major human motivation. Though it was emotionally difficult, writing *Anna Karenina* became part of Tolstoy's search for the meaning of his own life—at different points temporarily finding it in managing his estate and in his marriage. In the pages of the book, the need and search for meaning became a major theme. In fact, the adultery theme can be seen as an example of the search.

Meaning in life—finding it, losing it, searching for it, finding another—was an implicit theme in the book even before Levin's existential crisis took center stage. In developing each of the characters through conveying their inner worlds, Tolstoy showed what gave meaning to their lives. For Anna's brother, the casual adulterer, it was pleasure in the moment—sensuous pleasure from delicious food and from erotic dalliances, social pleasure from having a jolly time with others. His wife, after a visit to Anna, realized that it was her children that gave her life meaning. Kitty too found meaning in family and in the mutual love she shared with her husband. For Anna's husband, his ambition to rise in the bureaucracy outfoxing his rivals and to be respected as an exceptionally able civil servant was central. Thus, when he was shamed as a cuckold, he felt lost till a society matron brought a shallow version of Christianity to him along with her love, soothing him. Anna and Vronsky thought their deep passion for one another was the only meaning their lives needed, even without the support of society. When that failed to be enough, Vronsky was able to find additional meaning in being a philanthropic landowner and in his success in local politics. That solution was closed to Anna. Her fear of losing the only meaning she had left panicked her. She was unable to stop herself from creating terrible scenes which she knew had to weaken the very bond she depended on. And finally, the horror of contemplating the loss of Vronsky's love led to depression, with suicide seen as the only way to get relief. Tolstoy knew the world of depression and could write the devastating pages describing what her world was like as she rode through the streets, took a train one stop, and threw herself to her death. At that point, Tolstoy became Anna and imaginatively experienced the day that ended with her suicide. Still, Tolstoy did not take his own life nor did Levin. Levin was spared that fate, finding meaning in living according to "the good," revealed not by reason where he had searched for it, but by intuition.

Tolstoy started with the standard adultery story, broadened it by portraying different relationships among men and women, and found an inclusive theme that was profound. Tolstoy found it more and more as he applied his method: telling the story from the points of view of different characters, as he wrote, experiencing their perspectives, their emotions, and their search for loss, and discovery of meaning.

The Novel Complete

When Tolstoy corrected the final pages of his Anna, he wrote to Strakhov of being sad and lonely, but free, the letdown many writers feel when they have to say goodbye to the fiction worlds they have been living in. He was to go through an argument with his publisher who had refused to publish the epilogue's suggested pacifism with Levin's opposition to Russians getting involved in the Serbo–Turkish War. The epilogue was printed as a separate short book.

TOLSTOY AFTER *ANNA KARENINA*

The publication of the novel as installments and later as a book led to Tolstoy's recognition as one of the greatest writers of all times. His response was to spend time at a monastery. Tolstoy's own search for meaning went on. Though he continued to write some fiction and to promote his views of education, that search brought him to thinking about, writing about, and finally living a more radical change. He wanted to live as a true Christian based on the Sermon on the Mount. This meant giving away wealth, living modestly, and practicing and promoting non-violence. In the end, Tolstoy made important contributions to three domains: literature, education, and moral philosophy. His revised *Azbuka* (*New ABC*) is still available (Tolstoy, 1874/2018). His writings on non-violence led to a correspondence with Gandhi, who in turn inspired Martin Luther King.

TOLSTOY'S CREATIVE PROCESS: SUMMARY AND REFLECTIONS

Tolstoy's process of creating *Anna Karenina* was a torturous process, one he avoided and at times denigrated. Once he was able to allow his writing to take him into the inner worlds of each of his characters, he found himself experiencing the varieties and universalities, the pleasures and horrors, of being human. Perhaps he could not bear living in the world of a husband, somewhat like himself, having to face the adultery of an evil, unrepentant wife. So his first vision of the adultery story underwent radical reorganization. The characters changed—Anna, her husband, and Levin. Tolstoy's Anna was free to transform from an evil woman possessed by the devil into an admirable person whose thwarted passions and desire to live without hypocrisy we understand. From a simple story condemning adultery, the strict morality Tolstoy believed in, the book became more compassionate, enlarged to portray man–woman relationships in which we can empathize with both parties, and finally to understand how each character sought to make life worthwhile. The change in method was central. It allowed Tolstoy's writing to lead him far from the ideas he started with and away from what he thought he believed.

Fiction writers say that their aim in writing is telling how life is (Chapter 4). Tolstoy's way of doing so anticipated one of the great themes of the 20th century, the psychological void of a meaningless life and the ongoing search for meaning. Like some other writers, his first writings on the novel started out with one theme, one cast of characters, one writing style, and by writing and rewriting, found each of these changing in interaction with one another as the novel finally took shape. He went through long periods in which he did not write, periods when other activities took over his time and perhaps served as incubation periods as well. As the method of the book came to convey characters' inner worlds, he developed into one of the first phenomenologists in fiction writing. His descriptions of his characters' psychological worlds—for example, how elation colored Levin's world after Kitty accepted his second proposal, how Anna's world darkened as depression led to suicide—are contributions to phenomenological psychology as well as fiction. As the creative process allowed Tolstoy to give fictional form to his lived experience, the writing became part of his own existential and spiritual search.

NOTE

1 The names of the characters kept changing from draft to draft.

REFERENCES

Alvarez, A. (1990). *The savage god: A study of suicide.* New York: W.W. Norton

Bartlett, R. (2011). *Tolstoy: A Russian life.* Boston, MA: Houghton Mifflin Harcourt.

Blaisdell, B. (2020). *Creating Anna Karenina: Tolstoy and the birth of literature's most enigmatic heroine.* New York: Pegasus Books.

Donskov, A. (2003). Л. Н. Толстой—Н. Н. Страхов. Полное собрание переписки [L. N. Tolstoy – N. N. Strakhov. Complete Correspondence]. (vol. 1). Ottawa: University of Ottawa.

Dumas, A. (1872). *L'Homme-Femme.* Paris: Librairie Nouvelle.

Flaubert, G. (1957). *Madame Bovary: Patterns of provincial life.* (F. Steegmuller, Trans.) New York: Modern Library.

Frankl, V. E. (1963). *Man's search for meaning: An introduction to logotherapy.* (I. Lasch, Trans.). New York: Beacon Press.

Gardner, H. (1993). *Creating minds: An anatomy of creativity seen through the lives of Freud, Einstein, Picasso, Stravinsky, Eliot, Graham, and Gandhi.* New York, NY: Basic Books.

Goethe, W. (1774). *Die Leiden des jungen Werthers* (The Sorrows of Young Werther). Leipzig: Weygand'sche Buchhandlung.

Pevear, R. (2000). Introduction. In L. Tolstoy, *Anna Karenina.* (R. Pevear & L. Volokhonsky, Trans.). New York: Penguin.

Šklovskij, V. B., & Avagyan, S. (2011). *Energy of delusion: A book on plot.* Champaign-Urbana, IL: Dalkey Archive Press

Tolstoy, L., & Edmonds, R. (1964). *Childhood, boyhood, youth.* New York: Penguin Books. (*Childhood* first published in Russian in 1852.)

Tolstoy, L. (1983). *A confession.* (D. Patterson, Trans.). New York: W.W. Norton. (First published in Russian in 1884.)

Tolstoy, L. (2000). *Anna Karenina.* (R. Pevear & L. Volokhonsky, Trans.). New York: Penguin. (First published in Russian in 1878.)

Tolstoy, L. (2007). *War and peace.* (R. Pevear & L. Volokhonsky, Trans.) (1st ed.). New York: Alfred A. Knopf. (First published Russian in 1869.)

Tolstoy, L. N. (1872/1957). Azbuka. In *Polnoe sobranie sochinenii.* [Complete Works] 1957 (vol. 22, pp. 6–787). Moscow: Khudozhestvennaia literatura.

Tolstoy, L. N. (1873). Letter to Strakov. In *Polnoe sobranie sochinenii* [The Complete Works of Count Tolstoy] (vol. 62, p. 16). (V. G. Chertkov, Ed.). Moscow: Khudozhestvennaia literatura.

Tolstoy, L. N. (1874/2018). *New ABC.* Book on Demand Ltd. (First published in Russian in 1874.)

Tolstoy, S. (1960). Diary. In *Reminiscences of Lev Tolstoi by his contemporaries* (M. Wettlin, Trans.). Moscow: Foreign Languages Pub. House.

Tolstoy, S. (1978/2010). *The diaries of Sofia Tolstoy.* (D. Lessing & C. Porter, Trans.) Alma Books. Retrieved August 1, 2020 from https://archive.org/details/diariesofsofiato0000tols_h2t5/page/32/mode/2up?q=novel. (Originally published in Russian in 1978.)

Turner, C. J. G. (1993). *A Karenina companion.* Waterloo, ON: Wilfrid Laurier University Press.

Wilson, A. N. (1988). *Tolstoy* (1st American). New York: Norton.

Zhdanov, V. A., & E. E. Zaidenshnur (Eds.) (1970). *L. N. Tolstoy, Anna Karenina.* Moscow: Literaturnye Pamyatniki.

Zola, É., & Nelson, B. (1868/1993). *Thérèse Raquin.* London: Bristol Classical Press. (Originally published in French in 1868.)

Zweers, A. F. (1969). Is there only one Anna Karenina? *Canadian Slavonic Papers, 11,* 272–281.

CHAPTER 9

Woolf's *To the Lighthouse*

Revelations from Streams of Consciousness

In a memoir, Virginia Woolf (1985, p. 81) wrote, "My mother…obsessed me in spite of the fact that she died when I was thirteen, until I was 44." When Woolf was 44, she wrote *To the Lighthouse* (Woolf, 1927). Nevertheless, *Lighthouse* is not an account of her childhood as she remembered it. The book is a modernist novel. It stretches time by describing long streams of consciousness as experienced by multiple characters; the first 124 pages are devoted to less than a day. Then the novel condenses time; ten years go by in the next 18 pages, conveying the numbness of grief. Though the book drew on childhood events and characters, the book is fiction, with some events and characters completely imagined. Still, at the same time as Woolf created a major work of literature, she found that writing it eased her psychological pain.

This chapter will look closely at the process of creating *To the Lighthouse*, how it began, what gave her difficulty, and what she achieved. We will also explore why the process of writing a fictional work may have freed her of her obsession. The clues come from Woolf's diaries and notes and her reminiscences of the past. Virginia's husband, Leonard, wrote an autobiographical account of the time during which she wrote the novel (L. Woolf, 1967).[1] There are several excellent studies of her life and work (Bell, 1972; Lee, 1997; Briggs, 2006). And the book itself suggests what Woolf's experience of the creative process was like.

VIRGINIA WOOLF BEFORE *LIGHTHOUSE*

Virginia Woolf née Stephen (1882–1941) was born in London, into a blended family; both father and mother had previous marriages and children. Woolf described herself as "born not of rich parents, but of well-to-do parents, born into a very communicative, literate, letter writing, visiting, articulate, late nineteenth century world" (Woolf, 1985, p. 65). Her father, Leslie, was an essayist, historian, biographer, mountaineer, and some-time philosopher subject to occasional rages but who enchanted his children as he read to them and cut animal shapes out of paper. Her mother, Julia, was known both for her great beauty and her charitable works. She was the children's teacher and wrote stories

DOI: 10.4324/9781003013860-14

just for them. The blended family consisted of eight children including two stepbrothers, who, at different times, sexually abused her. Summers were spent on St. Ives, a seacoast town in Cornwall with a view of Godrevy Lighthouse.

Reading, making up stories, and writing were attractive to Woolf from the time she was very young. Little Virginia was five when she wrote her first letters. She was allowed to read any of the books in her father's library. Her interest in books and writing fostered a bond with her intellectual father and she remembered favoring her father over her mother as a child. In fact, she wrote of rarely being alone with her mother, the mother of eight children, a hostess who enjoyed having house guests, and someone who devoted considerable time to helping the needy. Woolf felt she never really knew her mother (Woolf, 1985). Nevertheless, the mother's death precipitated a mental health crisis, episodes she would be plagued by intermittently for the rest of her life. Today she would probably be diagnosed as bipolar, an underlying condition for which in her day there was no way to control; several episodes of her depression coincided with the deaths of her parents, suggesting an interaction between a hereditary predisposition and environmental events. Her life ended in suicide as London was being bombed in World War Two. Yet in her lifetime, she became a very productive writer—a frequent book reviewer, essayist, memoirist, short story writer, and author of nine novels (Bell, 1972; Lee, 1997; Briggs, 2006).

In 1912, Virginia married Leonard Woolf, a former civil administrator in Ceylon. A prolific writer himself, he wrote two novels, articles, and books on political and economic topics, and five autobiographical volumes. Leonard had met Virginia as a part of the Bloomsbury Group, an assemblage of intellectuals, writers, and artists who met regularly to discuss society and the arts. Together Leonard and Virginia established Hogarth Press which published many of her works including *To the Lighthouse*. Leonard, who suffered through several of her mental episodes, noted that the 1920s and 1930s were relatively healthy compared to earlier times; though she was still subject to disabling mood swings, those years were her most productive. She and her husband knew that headaches were a warning sign that the pressures were beginning to become overwhelming and they used that as a signal to leave London to rest and recuperate (L. Woolf, 1967). *To the Lighthouse* was published in 1927.

THE ERA IN THE ARTS

The early 20th century was a time of experimentation in the arts, in particular, different ways to convey reality. In painting, Seurat was intrigued with what scientists were saying about color perception, that the eye had only three or four color receptors and the rainbow of colors emerged by the proportions of primary color receptors activated. He was inspired to create the surface of a painting through adjacent dabs of color which viewers' eyes rather than the painter's brush combined to create hue and form. The effect was a shimmering surface from which structure emerged. Picasso and Braque had invented cubism, portraying several perspectives of the same object simultaneously.

In fiction writing rather than having an objective narrator tell the story as was the tradition, authors such as Richardson, Proust, and Joyce were using a stream of consciousness method to tell their stories, usually from the viewpoint of a single character. Woolf admired the work of Tolstoy, and his ability to read the minds of multiple characters as they encountered events. Woolf, in the writing of two novels before *Lighthouse, Jacob's Room* (Woolf, 1923) and *Mrs. Dalloway* (Woolf, 1925a), added her own innovation: developing the story almost entirely by presenting the streams of thought of *multiple* characters, moving from one to another often in the same scene with only occasional third-person narration. Much of *Lighthouse* is written in the same way.

WOOLF AT WORK

When Woolf wasn't on vacation or felled by physical or emotional illness, she spent her days writing. Her husband (L. Woolf, 1967) wrote that she kept the schedule of a stockbroker who goes to work daily. She began the day with a warm-up—exercise in the air and reading literature, priming herself to spend the morning writing fiction. Afternoons were spent working on other projects such as reading manuscripts for Hogarth Press and writing essays, lectures, book reviews, and letters. These other projects provided important family income and gave her imaginative mind a rest while still working with words and literature. Between teatime and dinner, she typed up the morning's work, editing as she did, and then took walks, allowing her mind to wander back to fiction. Here we see a serious writer at work, one committed both to the enterprises of both fiction and non-fiction, working steadily day after day.

Wallace (1985) pointed out that creative people who take on and fulfill extensive projects organize their lives in ways that allow them to work steadily. Woolf (1929) herself wrote of the need for women who want to write to have an income and a room of her own. Woolf had, as well, the loving encouragement of her husband—again showing the support of a significant other as a common feature of people who devote their lives to creative work (Gardner, 1993).

Woolf's work was sometimes interrupted by visitors; she was known as an interesting and witty conversationalist and enjoyed sociality. Yet, at times, she resented them. She wrote explicitly of her change in consciousness when writing fiction. When visitors came, she wrote, she was Virginia, but when writing, Virginia was gone and she was all sensibility, receptive to what her imagination brought to her—a different mode of being with a different sense of self. She noted that she liked both states, but not having to be Virginia when she was interrupted amid writing (Woolf, 1953).

Woolf was very sensitive to the criticism of literary friends and reviewers. Both her fiction and non-fiction books were generally received positively and commissions for non-fiction essays kept coming in. Still, Woolf was stung by even a hint of a negative comment (Woolf, 1953). Though we often idealize the creativity of those devoted to the arts as producing art only for art's sake, intrinsic motivation alone, the reality is that most artists do care about how their work is received, Woolf especially so. Intrinsic motivation has to be strong enough to continue, even when the work is criticized. For Woolf, it was.

THE JOURNEY TO *LIGHTHOUSE*

The diary entry which first hinted at the novel came in June 1923, in the midst of writing *Mrs. Dalloway*. Woolf recorded a general sense of excitement about the poetry of existence somehow related to the sea and St. Ives. Thereafter she did not make notes for a St. Ives book for almost two years. In January 1925, having finished the first draft of *Mrs. Dalloway*, the idea came to her of writing "The Old Man," a story with a character based on her father, but fictionalized as a professor specializing in Milton. Nevertheless, as her revisions on Mrs. Dalloway came to an end, she foresaw a series of short stories branching out from the Dalloway characters and expected that two of those characters would lead to her next novel (Woolf, 1953).

Instead, an unexpected flow[2] experience:

> one day walking round Tavistock Square I made up, as I sometimes make up my books, *To the Lighthouse*; in a great, apparently involuntary, rush. One thing burst into another. Blowing bubbles out of a pipe gives the feeling of the rapid crowd of ideas and scenes which blew out of my mind, so that my lips seemed syllabling of their own accord as I walked.
>
> *(Woolf, 1985, p. 81)*

She then recorded notes of what the flow produced: first, a diagram, an H made up of two long rectangles connected by a short narrow bridge (Woolf, 1983). That structure with minor modifications became the structure of the book. She probably knew at this point that Part 1 would draw on her childhood at a sea resort like St. Ives, the narrow bridge would relate to her mother's death, and the last part would be a trip to the lighthouse. At a later point, she wondered in her diary whether she wasn't thinking out the book too clearly. This comment was probably related to an earlier diary entry about the process of writing *Mrs. Dalloway*: groping for something to deepen the characters and then touching a hidden spring, portraying the pasts of her characters in the present as the characters reminisced—an innovation she had not thought out consciously but came to her in the writing (Woolf, 1953).

Her subsequent notes included *metafictional statements*: reflections, often intentions for the book's content rather than writing the text itself. The sea was to be heard throughout the book. Knowing that she was breaking the implicit rules for writing fiction, she suggested that the book shouldn't be called a novel, perhaps, instead, an elegy (a lament for the dead). She knew she wanted to deal with her late parents through fiction. She went back and forth over who should be the book's most important character. Though her very first idea of the book was to base it on her father, a later note emphasized the beauty of the character who came to be called Mrs. Ramsey (henceforth, Mrs. R.) (Woolf, 1983). Still further on, a diary entry described a scene: the book's center was to be the father, sitting in a boat reciting a line from a Cowper poem, "'We perish each alone' and crushing a dying fish" (Woolf, 1953, p. 77). Here she was fictionalizing the father's love of reciting poetry, his self-centeredness, and his hurtful crushing of his children's hopes. In another diary entry she asked herself whether she should do a concentrated intense study of the father or a slower, wider book (Woolf, 1953).

Only writing scenes in the world of the book could settle this. So she began to improvise text, but judged what she was writing illiterate. Like the writers in Chapter 4, she could tell she was moving in the wrong direction. Woolf decided to let the book simmer—an incubation period for the new novel while she completed the short stories she began. If ideas came to her as she took walks between tea time and dinner, she made notes, sometimes picturing scenes, sometimes reflections about the book. Otherwise she would allow the book to lie fallow (Woolf, 1953).

Finally, on August 6, she again laid out her plan for the book and pictured the opening scene: Mrs. R. sitting at a window with her son, as Mr. Ramsey (henceforth, Mr. R.) appears and disappears as he walks up and down outside. Woolf knew the scene would include the boy's eager expectation of going to the lighthouse. It is likely that she already had pictured how James would be shattered and enraged by his father's declaration that bad weather would prevent the trip. Mrs. R. would try to soften the blow by saying the weather *might* be good even though she knew it wouldn't be. In addition to envisioning scenes, Woolf reflected on what she intended the part to convey: expectation, a display of Mrs. R.'s character in conjunction with Mr. R.'s. The note's last line made clear who would be central in Part 1: "the dominating impression would be of Mrs. R.'s character" (Woolf, 1925b, para. 4).

Was it picturing the scene that led Woolf to decide that the emphasis should be on the mother in Part 1 rather than the father or was it a more reflective decision? We do not know, but in the plan, we see both imagining scenes and making notes on more general reflections, complementary processes that alternated throughout the making of the book.

Woolf (1983) also made briefer notes for Part 2. In earlier notes, she had labeled Part 2 "the death" (echoing the death of Woolf's mother). Now she called it "the passing of time." This short bridge was to convey ten years passing. She was not yet sure how. It was to be an experiment in style. Woolf wrote of relishing new challenges (such as this) that kept her writing fresh (Woolf, 1953).

The early notes for Part 3, the trip to the lighthouse, showed she had already decided on some characters for Part 1. She noted that some would be brought back in the third part.

Starts and Stops

Woolf was now ready to write. By September 5, she had written out 22 pages much as her earlier plan suggested. Still, there was change. Lily, a new adult character appeared, an unmarried modernist painter (Woolf, 1983).

Woolf marveled at how much easier the process went compared to writing earlier novels, but then it came to a stop. Several bouts of physical and emotional illness felled her and her commitment to writing essays and book reviews delayed her as well. A passionate friendship with Vita Sackville-West blossomed, bringing pleasure but also distraction. Only 18 additional pages were completed by December (Briggs, 2006).

It was mid-January before she returned to the book and realized that her concept had grown in the interim, a partially unchosen incubation period. In particular, she envisioned two final scenes for Part 1: a dinner scene and one between husband and wife. In her diary, she noted she was living totally in the book, sensing she was on the right path, writing freely (Woolf, 1953). She completed the first draft of Part 1 on April 29, 1926, and though there were later revisions, the basic content was in the published work.

Some Highlights of Part 1

After the scene in which the father quashes the boy's dream of sailing to the lighthouse, we meet the stream of thought of other characters as events unfold: Lily the artist is hurt as Mr. R.'s young protégé proclaims that women can't write or paint; nevertheless, she begins but cannot finish a painting of Mrs. R. and her son in the window. Old Mr. Carmichael disappoints Mrs. R. because he doesn't need anything from her. Two young people please Mrs. R. by becoming engaged as she planned, but upset her by coming late to dinner; six children play and run freely all day. All the characters come together for dinner. At first, the dinner party is awkward as each feels isolated, and they chafe against one another. But, as darkness falls, Mrs. R. has the children light candles, she serves a special dish, and somehow the atmosphere changes. Mrs. R. transforms the dinner, which began with isolation and irritation, into a memorable feast with a sense of unity among the guests. Later, Mrs. R. settles an argument between James, who wants a skull to remain on the bedroom shelf, and Cam, his sister, a year older, who it frightens. Mrs. R. hides the skull with her shawl. Thus it remains unmoved for James and she softly talks Cam to sleep by imagining all kinds of benign things the shape could be. Mr. and Mrs. R., who have been at odds during the day, come together in Part 1's final moments in which without either saying it, they are aware of their love for each other (Woolf, 1927).

The Writing and Highlights of Part 2

Woolf wrote the draft of Part 2 in a month. She first made quick notes for the section: the passing of time through the seasons, wind, and sea, the decay of everything, but also "hopeless gulfs of misery," "the war," and "slept through life" (Woolf, 1925c, paras 8, 10, 22). This suggests that Part 2 would reflect the depression and emotional numbness that followed Mrs. R.'s death as well as the horror of World War One. Woolf's diary prescribed the method: "Empty house, no people's characters, abstract, all eyeless and featureless" (Woolf, 1953, p. 88). She improvised two pages and asked herself of her own experiment, whether it was "nonsense or brilliant" (Woolf, 1953, p. 89). Again, intermittent evaluation and uncertainty are part of the experience of many artists, no matter how experienced and celebrated.

Woolf's style met the challenge she set for herself. Part 2 is a complete contrast to what came before. Most of the section is impersonal, an objective third-person voice telling of the deterioration of a house mostly empty of people, interrupted at places in parentheses with three-line impersonal pronouncements of the fate of various characters: Mrs. R.'s death, a daughter's marriage, the wartime death of a Ramsey son, the married daughter's death in childbirth, the surprising success of Old Carmichael's poetry. Though told in a third-person voice about what happened to the house, most of the passages are lyrical, with nature personified. Yet the images of the house—decaying, infested with vermin, and invaded by weeds—are devastating. The house, with only a housekeeper occasionally present, is mainly without life. As the part concludes, life again breaks through in the form of two valiant housekeepers who arrange for the clean-up of the property, making it ready for the Ramseys' return. Guests have been invited. The part ends with the arrival of Lily, the artist. Woolf wrote a draft of Part 2 in a month and it is substantially like the final manuscript (Woolf, 1983).

The Writing and Selected Highlights of Part 3

Part 3 was the most troublesome. Her plan was to alternate chapters between Lily on the lawn, trying to paint the picture she had been unable to complete ten years earlier, and the sail to the lighthouse by Mr. R. with his youngest children, now adolescents, Cam and James. Woolf started in June, but, in July, she had what she called "a nervous breakdown in miniature." In her diary, Woolf (1953) described her depression, how she could not read or write. The first sign she was getting better was reading Dante, without understanding, but with pleasure. Then she began writing notes and, soon after, returned to work.

By September, she saw the end in sight. She thought of ending in the boat, but realized that she left Lily on the lawn. How could she make the two events simultaneous? She had confidence that she would solve it somehow and she did. Woolf finished the first draft of *Lighthouse* and, like her characters, with mixed feelings: relief at finishing, disappointment—could it be better?—and triumph (Woolf, 1953).

Rewriting. For Woolf, as for many writers, an important stage of writing is rewriting. She found her first draft sketchy, full of incomplete sentences, and in need of cutting. She improvised by filling out, making the language throughout more rhythmic, and deleting material that felt unnecessary. At a pace of six pages a day it took her almost three months, finishing on January 14. Part 3, which had given her the most problems in the first draft was the one that was most altered in revision. She edited out much of the material on religion, social class, and illustrations of the tyranny of the father after Mrs. R.'s death (Dick, 1983, Woolf, 1953).

Part 3. Part 3 takes place on a single morning. Mr. Ramsey has ordered his two adolescent children to return to the summerhouse for an excursion to the lighthouse. Mr. R. does what Mrs. R. would have done—bring presents for the lighthouse keeper and his son. The adolescents see him as a tyrant, are reluctant to go, and plot to show their resistance through silence. At the same time, Lily, the artist, and old Mr. Carmichael wait on the shore—he, reading, she at work at the picture she was trying to paint ten years before. As the trip proceeds, Mr. Ramsey gives his 16-year-old son what he had withheld all through childhood, recognition—a compliment, here on his steering. The daughter, Cam, now remembers a tender time with her father and rediscovers her love for him. The children relent and forgive, now ready to give their father the sympathy he often craved. When they arrive, Mr. R. jumps out of the boat as if he were a young man. Meanwhile, Lily, as she is painting, remembers Mrs. R., feels anger at her abandonment and contempt for her old-fashioned ideas about women. Then, as more scenes from the past come to her, Lily acknowledges her love and longing for Mrs. R., and calls out her name. As if in response, Mrs. R. appears in the window before Lily as in the earlier scene Lily was trying to paint. The book ends with Lily finding the balance she had been searching for in her painting. After adding a final stroke to it, she puts down her brush and says to herself, "I have had my vision" (Woolf, 1927, p. 209).

WOOLF AS PHENOMENOLOGIST

There is a sense in which every novelist is an implicit psychological theorist; in portraying human life, embodying the ways in which people respond to the events and people around them. Woolf was like a phenomenological psychologist, giving voice and shape to the stream of consciousness as different characters experience it. In fact, she explicitly studied her own stream of consciousness and how it changed moment to moment. In conveying the subjective experience of her characters, she showed it to be as changeable as the weather and the sea. Mrs. R.'s wondering how she could ever have loved her husband early in the dinner was followed by a scene between them in which each recognized love for the other. Yet beneath the ever-changing surface there was shape; Mrs. R.'s support of all the characters when she sees them as needy, the loving bond between the Ramseys despite momentary annoyance and ambivalence.

Amid the transitory changes that come and go, Woolf saw some events rising above the ever-changing stream to become more permanent in a person's consciousness—moments of vision (Woolf, 1953): an experience never forgotten and the crystallization of a vision in art and poetry were two examples in the novel. Mrs. R. transformed a dinner at which no one seemed to be communicating with anyone else into a communion of harmony, an event that would be remembered by all present. Lily the artist and Old Carmichael the poet, by creating art, made their visions permanent.

Woolf captured the grieving process in ways that psychologists have later identified as possible phases: depression, emotional numbness, anger, and acceptance. In the character of Mr. R., probably without knowing it, she even incorporated the Freudian idea that one way of coping with grief is identifying with the lost person, making the lost person a part of oneself (Freud, 1917). Mr. R., in the trip to the lighthouse, did what his wife would have done—bringing presents to the lighthouse keeper's family and supporting his children.

In the character of Lily, Woolf also portrayed the phenomenology of the creative process. Her portrayal embodied features that have appeared in psychologists' and creative artists' descriptions ever since. Many have reported the felt trepidation at facing a blank sheet or canvas. The commitment to a project brings the work to mind at odd moments, sometimes with an insight, creative visitations. Plans, reflections on how the work should proceed, sometimes don't work out when tested in the medium. The loss of consciousness of the surroundings and the work unfolding rhythmically are characteristics of flow. The work may feel unbalanced bringing reflection. A sense when the work has found completion brings with it a sense of relief, fulfillment, and yet also uncertainty.

A NOVEL, NOT AUTOBIOGRAPHY

Though the book drew on Woolf's experiences as a child, *Lighthouse* was neither a biography of her parents nor autobiography. In an essay on biography, she distinguished between biography and fiction by citing Henry James: Biographers are limited by facts. Novelists are free to imagine and rearrange (Woolf, 1939).

There was no trip to the lighthouse with her father ten years after her mother's death. The house on St. Ives was sold soon after Julia died; Parts 2 and 3 were completely invented. Though children appear in Part 1, with the exception of James, they, till Cam in Part 3, are minor characters. And though the portrait of the Ramsey family patriarch resembled Woolf's father in his neediness and regret over not doing more original work in philosophy, Mr. R. was a philosopher rather than the prominent biographer, mountaineer, editor, and sometime philosopher her father was. Nor do we see all of the father of Woolf's childhood, her favorite, the one who encouraged Little Virginia's reading and writing, who amused children by reading stories and cutting out paper animals. We do see Mrs. R. interacting with her children in creative ways in a few scenes, but not in her role as the teacher of the children.

Nor do we get much impression of the relationships among the siblings. Much of the book consists of the interactions among the adults and how they see themselves and each other, especially Mrs. R. So it was an exploration of her childhood experience from different perspectives. Like the era's painters who found form by combining dabs and portraying several points of view simultaneously, Woolf, by her empathetic imaginings, allowed a vision of the mother, the father, and their relationship to emerge from the partial views of various characters.

Because she was improvising scenes, inevitably, her current feelings and understandings as well as her memories imbued her rendering of the subjective lives of the characters, a convergence of streams. When she gave Mr. R. her father's sense that he had not become a major thinker, she was also giving voice to her own uncertainties of her capacities as a writer which she expressed in her diary. Perhaps Woolf's surprise at the commercial success of *Mrs. Dalloway* was one element that entered into Mr. Carmichael's surprising success as a poet. Lee (1997) pointed out that there was a bit of Virginia at various ages in the portrayal of all the Ramsey sisters, though it was only Cam who had the same position in the Ramsey family that Virginia had among the Stephen children. Woolf herself recognized that observations of her sister as a mother flowed into her portrayal of Mrs. R. (Woolf, Nicolson, & Trautman, 1977).

Avatars

The thoughts and feelings of many of the characters in part reflect Woolf's as she "inhabited" them. Still, some more directly reflected essential characteristics of Woolf and her family and could be considered fictional avatars—characters who display defining characteristics of the author or other living people. *To the Lighthouse* has several that are easy to identify. Mr. and Mrs. R. for Woolf's parents, James for her younger brother Adrian. One unusual feature of the novel is that Woolf used two avatars of herself. One is Cam both at 7 and 17; the other is the artist, Lily. Lily's thoughts and feelings as she paints and her meditations on the role of women in society reflect Woolf's own.

THE PSYCHOLOGICAL WORK

Again, the book is a work of art, neither a memoir, nor an account of traumatic experiences. So why did it free her from her obsessive thinking about her parents? What was the psychological work that Woolf herself compared to psychoanalysis? She theorized she had expressed long buried feelings and thus somehow explained them, but then asked what does "explain" mean? (Woolf, 1985). Here are some possibilities for the psychic work that the writing did for her.

First, Woolf was haunted with the idea that she did not really know her mother. Not knowing her, she could not properly mourn her. Through her imagination she got to know her mother, not only as she was seen from the bits and pieces experienced by a child who was rarely alone with her, but from the viewpoint of various adults and from her empathetic entering into the very consciousness of her mother, experiencing how her mother might have seen life, her relationships, and her responsibilities.

Yet the scenes were invented. How could this help? Woolf tells us in the reflections of her avatar, Lily.

> As she dipped her brush into the blue paint she was also dipping into the past, making up scenes about people she knew. Not a word of it was true…but it was what she knew them by all the same.
>
> *(Woolf, 1927, p. 173)*

By making up scenes and entering into each character's vision of Mrs. R., Woolf came to know a mother Woolf herself had created, as she emerged from multiple viewpoints, much as some contemporaneous painters portrayed reality.

Now knowing the mother of her imagination, Woolf was finally able to mourn Julia's death. She also found ways to express the changing emotions psychologists have suggested for the grieving process: the emotional numbness and the sense of everything falling apart from Part 2. Woolf had the most difficulty in portraying more of the mourning process in Part 3, but she finally found it as she pictured Lily's changing emotions as she was painting: anger at Mrs. R. for dying, annoyance at her manipulation of others, contempt for her traditional views of women's roles, but finally acknowledging and accepting longing and love for Mrs. R. Through the process, Lily was now able to summon Mrs. R. to appear at the window, calmly knitting, an image that she could bring to herself when she needed to—a moment of vision. Through her avatar, Woolf was able to create an image of a mother by imagining scenes and so got to know her. Not the actual past, but the constructed past, created by allowing memory and imagination to merge.

But the book was as unbalanced as Lily's painting. What of the lighthouse trip of Mr. R. and his teenaged children? There was no such trip. Four of the grown-up children visited St. Ives a year after their father's death and walked in the garden, perhaps one source of the lighthouse trip idea for the book. The imagined trip was psychically necessary. The difficult adolescent period with her needy father whose unquenchable grief and tyrannical demands had to be put in perspective. In imagination Woolf could give expression to her love for him, remembering him tenderly asking her if she needed anything.

Like Paley in Chapter 4, Woolf did not want to leave a character, her father, without resolving his grief. On reaching the lighthouse, Mr. Ramsey emerged from the boat like a young man. He, too, in enacting what his wife would have done, completed the grieving process by supporting his son, and doing charitable works—healing through identifying with the lost person as Freud (1917/1957) suggested.

WOOLF'S CREATIVE PROCESS: SUMMARY AND REFLECTIONS

The process of writing *Lighthouse* had characteristics we have seen in the fiction writers who came from a different era and in other examples of creative episodes as well. The era, the state of the domain, and the creator's earlier work put the present episode in perspective. A network of enterprises and the support of Leonard facilitated the work. The process itself was marked by a continual interaction between living in the world of the novel and reflecting—here clearly documented in her metafictional statements in her diary and notes. Innovations, characters, and scenes emerged spontaneously in the writing. She sensed when the writing wasn't working and when it was on the right track. She benefited from incubation periods. She gained perspective from writing from different points of view. She drew on characters she knew and had avatars of herself at different points in her life, but imagination drew on other streams too as characters interacted in scenes. She enjoyed challenges and was intrinsically motivated, but also experienced frustration and doubt.

Yet as Gruber (1981) pointed out, every creative episode is also unique. Yes, there was a facilitating network of enterprises but they also sometimes interfered with her work. Yes, incubation sometimes led to new understanding, but sometimes it was enforced incubation due to illness, which prevented her from doing the writing she wanted to do. Unlike some other writers, her early inspiration was of structure as well as content rather than discovering the structure in the writing. Certainly not all fiction writers are manic-depressive and she had to wait till depressions lifted to get back to work. Most creative work requires courage, a dive into the unknown. For Woolf, it required the special courage of going on in the face of recurrent illness. But, when healthy, she as writer relished challenges.

In her diary, Woolf wrote that the book had to be told the way it was told. It was her multiple stream of consciousness method that allowed a representation of her mother to emerge from multiple points of view and so became subjectively real. It was imagining tender moments between husband and wife and remembering others with her father that allowed her to forgive her father for tormenting her adolescence and to rediscover her love for him. Her experiment in Part 2 allowed her to give poetic shape to her grief and emotional numbness at the family deaths and the horror of war. Though giving form to problems, conflicts, and feelings are features of expressive therapies, rarely we do hear so clearly from an author how the process of writing a well-structured, innovative, beautifully written book did psychic work for her. Her experiments in style made that possible. Woolf had invented a new way to convey reality as she explored the nature of our inner worlds. Here again we see an outstanding example of the interaction of form and content in creating a work of art.

NOTES

1 In this chapter, citations of Woolf refer to Virginia. Leonard Woolf will be cited as L. Woolf.
2 The concept of flow was introduced in Chapter 1.

REFERENCES

Bell, Q. (1972). *Virginia Woolf: A biography*. London: Hogarth Press.

Briggs, J. (2006). *Virginia Woolf: An inner life* (1st Harvest). Orlando, FL: Harcourt, Inc..

Dick, S. (1983). Introduction. In V. Woolf (1983). *To the lighthouse: The original holograph draft* (S. Dick, Ed.). (pp. 11–35). London: Hogarth Press.

Freud, S. (1917). Mourning and melancholia. In S. Freud & J. Rickman (1957). *A general selection from the works of Sigmund Freud*. New York: Doubleday Anchor Books.

Gardner, H. (1993). *Creating minds: An anatomy of creativity seen through the lives of Freud, Einstein, Picasso, Stravinsky, Eliot, Graham, and Gandhi*. New York: Basic Books.

Gruber, H. E. (1981). *Darwin on man* (2nd edn). Chicago: University of Chicago Press.

Lee, H. (1997). *Virginia Woolf*. New York: Alfred A. Knopf.

Wallace, D. (1985). Giftedness and the construction of a creative life. In F. Horowitz & M. O'Brian (Eds.), *The gifted and talented* (pp. 363–385). Washington, DC: American Psychological Association.

Woolf, L. (1967). *Downhill all the way: An autobiography of the years 1919–1939*. Hogarth.

Woolf, V. (1923). *Jacob's room*. New York: Harcourt Brace and Company.

Woolf, V. (1925a). *Mrs. Dalloway*. New York: Harcourt, Brace.

Woolf, V. (1925b). Aug. 6, 1925. Retrieved February 12, 2020 from http://www.woolfonline.com/?node=content/text/transcriptions&project=1&parent=6&taxa=13&content=4522.

Woolf, V. (1925c). To the Lighthouse ten chapters. Retrieved February 10, 2020 from http://www.woolfonline.com/?node=content/text/transcriptions&project=1&parent=6&taxa=29&content=5552&pos=0.

Woolf, V. (1927). *To the lighthouse*. London: Hogarth Press.

Woolf, V. (1929). *A room of one's own*. London: Hogarth Press.

Woolf, V. (1939). The art of biography. *Atlantic Monthly*, April, 1939. Reprinted in Woolf, V. (1966). *Collected essays: vol. 4*. London: Hogarth.

Woolf, V. (1953). *A writer's diary* (L. Woolf, Ed.). London: Hogarth.

Woolf, V. (1983). *To the lighthouse: The original holograph draft* (S. Dick, Ed.). (Ser. Bloomsbury studies). London: Hogarth Press.

Woolf, V. (1985). *Moments of being* (J. Schulkind, Ed.). San Diego, CA: Harcourt Brace Jovanovich.

Woolf, V., Nicolson, N., & Trautmann, J. (1977). *The letters of Virginia Woolf: 1923–1928* (Vol. 3, A change of perspective). London: Hogarth Press.

PART V

Creating Collaborations in Science and Art

Blackburn and Company

Unraveling the Telomere Mysteries

Elizabeth Blackburn, a Nobel Prize winning scientist, once began a lecture by saying, "My career started with pond scum" (Blackburn, 2017, loc. 00.23). Blackburn's pond scum was actually a clump of tiny one-celled critters that biologists call *Tetrahymena thermophila*. When she peered at it through a microscope she said she "fell in love at first sight" (Brady, 2007, p. 46). It had all sorts of odd features, with seven different sexes and, like other one-celled creatures with cilia, each critter's single cell had two nuclei. *Tetrahymena* has been called a quirky little creature, so different from multiple-celled animals, so different from mammals.

Then why study it? Blackburn had the faith that learning about its chromosomes would teach us about their functioning up and down the evolutionary scale. And for her, the study of chromosomes would bring her closer to a goal she had set for herself. When she was in graduate school, a mentor asked each of his students, "What do you want?" Her answer was, "I want to understand how living things work" (Brady, 2007, p. 17). What *Tetrahymena* taught Blackburn and company about how living things work and their experiences in learning it is this chapter's story.

Scientists communicate their work in journals for their scientific peers. They've developed a technical vocabulary, and, because they strive for objectivity, tend to report their findings only in terms of hypotheses, methods, results, and conclusions. Sharing the human experience of scientific work is not typically part of technical articles. Still, technical *Tetrahymena* articles give important clues to the time course of the Tetrahymena discoveries. Other clues came from lectures, and writings. A major source was an excellent Blackburn biography in which the author, Catherine Brady (2007), reported on her extensive interviews with Blackburn, her collaborators, and other associates.

The telomere story has chapters and its sequels are still being written. The plot mainly takes place in the world of molecular biology and so some technical material is included in telling its story. The human side of the creative process is central here and shines through.

The story involves several chapters and more than one character. It begins with Elizabeth Blackburn, who was chiefly responsible for its first chapter. Then her collaborations with other researchers advanced the plot.

DOI: 10.4324/9781003013860-16

BLACKBURN BEFORE TELOMERES

Elizabeth Blackburn was born in Tasmania, Australia, near a beach. Little Elizabeth loved animals and was endlessly curious about them. She picked up jellyfish on the beach and ants in her backyard. She kept tadpoles in "soon-to-become" smelly jars in the living room (Blackburn, 2009a). In her teenage years, she was attracted to illustrated science books. The structure of amino acids fascinated her and, from tracings she made, amino acid diagrams became the pinups on her walls. Finally, it was molecular biology that called to her when she attended the University of Melbourne for both a Bachelor's and a Master's Degree (Brady, 2007).

It was an exciting time in molecular biology. Watson and Crick (1953), with the unacknowledged work of Rosalind Franklin, had determined the structure of the chromosome molecules responsible for our genetic inheritance. It was DNA, shaped like a spiraling ladder; with its rungs various arrangements of four bases: Adenine (A), Thymine (T), Guanine (G), and Cytosine (C). Furthermore, if a rung has an A, its rung partner will be a T. If a rung has a C, its partner will be G. But determining their order and their significance in any particular organism was work to be done.

In Fred Sanger's lab at Cambridge University, he and his students were pioneers in developing various ways to identify specific DNA and protein sequences. This was the place one of Blackburn's mentors recommended for doctoral work. So she sailed off from Australia to England and joined the laboratory, one of the most respected in the field. She found herself amid excellent scientists and worked long hours as they all did. This did not preclude romance. There she met her future husband, John Sedat, a post-doc, who would prove to be a helpmate in science and in life.

Sedat was scheduled to be a researcher at Yale and Blackburn's post-doctoral work was to be supported by a fellowship. Blackburn found a lab there headed by Joseph Gall. As she told it, "love brought me to a most fortunate and influential choice" (Blackburn, 2009b). Gall was a pioneering scientist and proved to be a supportive mentor, one who did not, as many in the field did, discriminate against women, and so she enjoyed having talented women as well as men as lab colleagues (Brady, 2007).

THE TELOMERE EPISODE BEGINS

For her post-doctoral work, she was ready to piece together different methods to do some sequencing herself. But what to sequence in who? Gall introduced her to *Tetrahymena*, the little one-celled critter with the quirky features.

She and *Tetrahymena* turned out to be a perfect match. She had become interested in telomeres, the specialized DNA segments that make up the end regions of chromosomes. Earlier work had determined that telomeres had the same function as the stiff end pieces that cap shoelaces. As the caps do for shoelaces—keeping them from unraveling, the telomeres keep the chromosome from unraveling. And *Tetrahymena* had thousands of minichromosomes with exceptionally long telomeres. But what were the telomeres made of? No one knew. Gall had invented ways to purify *Tetrahymena*'s minichromosomes, so Blackburn was ready to go.

Today, DNA sequencing has set procedures. In those days a sequencer was like a detective with methods for uncovering clues that had be to put together to come to a conclusion. Blackburn was ready. She told Brady, "I was fresh from a world where we'd found all these new methods for sequencing DNA and here were all these juicy molecules their end regions ripe for picking" (Brady, 2007, p. 45).

A large knowledge base matters; training matters; mentors matter; and attitudes matter in doing creative scientific research. The textbook account of scientific research says that the planning of an experiment begins with a hypothesis to test. Her mentor at Cambridge gave her a different attitude: You don't have to test a hypothesis. It's fine just to go into the lab and explore.

So Blackburn did what explorers do; she visited the territory to see what she could see. That territory was minuscule—the tiny telomeric ends of tiny minichromosomes of tiny one-celled creatures. Now she explored by putting to work all the sequencing methods she had learned: electrophoresis to separate fragments of DNA according to size, various chemical ways of cutting up the DNA to reveal its constituents, radioactive labeling of specific components so she could see their distribution on x-ray film. Each procedure had to be carried out carefully with full concentration on carrying out the steps.

She never knew ahead of time what the results would be. She found coming to the lab was an exciting adventure to see what new clues turned up. When all the clues were in, it was time to use her visual imagination, to create a telomere sketch by bringing together what the various clues told her. She drew diagram after diagram but one after another did not account for all the clues. Keeping at it, varying this and that, like a child playing with a construction set, she finally found a solution she was able to confirm.

Her results were a surprise. The end segments of the minichromosomes were complex and unlike any DNA structures that were previously described. She found a repeating pattern. Like the beads of a double-stranded necklace, she found the same pattern repeated again and again: four Cs and two As on one strand coupled with four Gs and two Ts on the other. She could see the bands on the x-ray films after she had radioactively labeled the C bases. Then another surprise: after cell division, each new cell's chromosomes were thought to be a carbon copy of the old. But this was not the case for the telomeric ends of the chromosomes. Some had 20 copies of the CCCCAA-GGGGTT pattern, others had up to 70 (Blackburn and Gall, 1978)! Why?

When cells divide, all the DNA which holds the genetic inheritance is copied completely, but, for an unknown reason, the telomeres are not copied to the very end. What did that have to do with the variety in telomere length in different little *Tetrahymena*? Blackburn always tried to see if existing principles could account for what she had seen, but her findings on telomeres did not easily fit into existing frameworks. Time to explore some more.

TRUSTING INTUITION: TELOMERES SEEMINGLY OUT OF NOWHERE

Every biological species is unique. But some are more different than others. One of *Tetrahymena*'s quirks is that this single-cell organism, like some other protozoans with cilia, has two nuclei: one for reproduction—the germ cell nucleus—for both sexual and asexual reproduction, and another, the somatic nucleus, whose DNA contains the blueprints for making all the proteins the cell needs. At this particular stage in *Tetrahymena*'s life cycle, something strange happens in the somatic nucleus. The longer chromosomes get chopped up into the minichromosomes. That's where the minichromosomes come from. But at first, they are naked; no telomeres are attached. They acquire telomeres soon after. How did that happen? Were they somehow created by recombining with existing telomere fragments produced by the chopping up process? That would be the explanation drawing on known principles.

Somehow, this explanation did not feel right to Blackburn. She couldn't say why, but her intuition told her that these were new telomeres, manufactured by an active substance, an unknown enzyme in the cell. She trusted her intuition; now the challenge was to find evidence. An unexpected adventure provided it.

A COLLABORATIVE, COCKAMAMIE, "WHAT IF" EXPERIMENT

Scientists get together at meetings and share their results even before they publish them. And that leads to discussions in both formal question and answer periods and more informal conversations. In 1980, Blackburn told of her telomere work in a presentation at a Gordon Research Conference on Nucleic Acid.

Jack Szostak, a Canadian researcher at an institute connected to Harvard Medical School, was also at the conference. His work centered on yeast genetics. He was particularly interested in DNA recombination, the process by which, after fertilization, some DNA from one parent may be exchanged with a segment of the DNA of the other. This creates a chromosome different from those of either parent. Sometimes it isn't an exchange; just a fragment of one chromosome was integrated into another. Both are examples of recombination.

Szostak had studied the recombination process by constructing and playing with segments of yeast DNA called plasmids. The cut plasmid ends were very active and repaired themselves by joining their ends, making the DNA fragment circular. The circular plasmids had another intriguing quality—they were able to replicate themselves so he could grow lots of them. And if he made a cut in the plasmid rings with chemical scissors and the conditions were exactly right, the now linear plasmids integrated themselves into yeast chromosomes—a perfect set-up for studying recombination. Otherwise, and this was the more typical outcome, the linear yeast plasmids were likely to degrade. Plasmids with bare ends did not typically survive on their own.

Szostak was fascinated by Blackburn's talk of those long repeated patterns of telomeres and the mystery of where those long sequences came from. As they walked together from one meeting to another, he and Blackburn began what turned out to be a series of conversations, talking science. He guessed that the long chains of telomeres might have gotten there by his favorite process, recombination. Blackburn had other ideas. The conversation intrigued them both.

Designing an experiment in science sometimes raises a question something like fiction writers ask themselves: I wonder what would happen if… For the fiction writer, the action takes place in the fiction world.[1] For the scientist, the action takes place in the laboratory.

Szostak asked, what would happen if we mixed *Tetrahymena* telomeres with yeast DNA plasmids. He could take circular yeast plasmids, and cut them with chemical scissors, producing a linear segment of DNA. Would the *Tetrahymena* telomeres attach themselves to the ends of the yeast DNA fragment? Would they protect the linear plasmid from degrading?

It was a wild experiment, a long shot. Yeast is a fungus, now its own kingdom but once classified as a plant. *Tetrahymena* is a protozoan, which is now also classified as its own kingdom, but once was called a one-celled animal. Such distant species do not usually invite pieces of one another to become part of them. It was, Blackburn told Brady, a "cockamamie idea" (Brady, 2007, p. 75).

Blackburn added, "There's a tension between being very rational and being prepared to do things simply because it might work—they're far out, but if the experiment works it provides rich information" (Brady, p. 75). If it did work using these very different organisms, it would suggest that there may be something universal about the workings of telomeres. No one could say that what she had found was limited to that quirky little one-celled *Tetrahymena*. Besides, it would be fun to try and not too difficult.

Neither researcher could have done this experiment alone. But it was possible when two scientists coming with different expertise and different lab skills worked together. Collaboration among colleagues, who bring different perspectives, can be very generative for scientific work.[2]

Blackburn provided purified *Tetrahymena* telomeres. Szostak put the *Tetrahymena* telomeres together with yeast plasmids with cuts in their rings. Once the two substances made contact with one another, he added chemical glue to stitch the two together. Then he observed what would happen if he introduced these yeast DNA segments capped with *Tetrahymena* telomeres into yeast cells. Would the plasmids "live?" Would they function as linear chromosomes?

The cockamamie experiment worked. More of the linear yeast plasmids, capped by *Tetrahymena* telomeres, lived. The telomeres had made the yeast plasmids into minichromosomes. They were even replicated by cell division. Telomeres functioned in yeast as they did in that distant quirky species *Tetrahymena*.

Now Szostak went fishing for yeast telomeres which had never been sequenced. What he did was to chemically cut the *Tetrahymena* telomere off one end of the yeast DNA and added all sorts of yeast DNA fragments to the concoction. He figured there must be a few yeast telomeres among the fragments and that they would find the DNA with the missing ends. They did and he was able to sequence them. The yeast telomeres were similar, but not identical to those of *Tetrahymena*. And they weren't all the same. Some of the repeated bands had one C, others two Cs, and some three Cs. Nevertheless, here was evidence that telomeres consist of similar compositions in very different organisms.

Every revelation seemed to raise new questions. Back in Blackburn's lab, she and her students asked, what did the telomere ends of the cut-plasmid yeast fragments look like? The telomere chains had gotten longer! New telomere chains must have been added by something in the yeast cells. But what was added?

Janice Shampay, a graduate student, took on the task of sequencing the now longer telomere chains. The *Tetrahymena* telomeres that had been stitched onto the yeast DNA were still there. What was added was an even longer chain of yeast telomeres. Something in the yeast cell was building yeast telomeres. Szostak admitted that the experiment suggested that Blackburn's intuitive leap was supported: an active process, through the working of an enzyme in the yeast, had added yeast telomeres to those of the stitched on *Tetrahymena* telomeres (Shampay, Szostak, & Blackburn, 1984).

Part of the creative process in science is sharing the work through publications in journals, both the results and the authors' interpretations. Then, other experts in the field chime in. Many were not convinced by the paper Szostak and Blackburn wrote. Some microbiologists put forward different models of where those added yeast telomeres could have come from. The dominant view still held to a well-known, well-studied past principle, that recombination was somehow responsible.

A DETERMINED GRADUATE STUDENT JOINS THE FRAY

Competing hypotheses are a stimulant to further research and Blackburn's lab was ready for the challenge. Carol Greider, a graduate student, was especially eager to help write the next chapter of the telomere story.

Greider had applied to ten graduate schools and eight of them rejected her. The only two that accepted her were the California Institute of Technology (Cal Tech) and the University of California at Berkeley. That unusual outcome resulted from something that had plagued Greider much of her life. She was dyslexic. Her spelling was awful. As a child, she had trouble learning to read and thought she was stupid. She was not particularly drawn to any domain in high school. It was in college that she discovered the attractions of biology when she had the opportunity to do research in her first year. She found she loved the research process. By the time she was ready for graduate school, she had become fascinated by chromosomes. She had already done some experiments on them and knew that continuing to study them was the opportunity she wanted in graduate school.

Gatekeepers determine who will enter a field (Csikszentmihalyi, 1996) and a major gate for research scientists is admittance to graduate school. Many graduate schools begin by sorting out student applications based on tests. Given her dyslexia, Greider's scores were not impressive and her application typically went to the reject pile automatically. Ironically, it was two of the top-rated schools that took a closer look. The actual work she had done *was* impressive and both schools offered her interviews before making a decision. She was all set to go to Cal Tech after a visit there. Then she interviewed at Berkeley and met Blackburn. They talked chromosomes and telomeres and then talked some more. The world of molecular biology was the common ground on which they became acquainted. After, it was clear to Greider that she belonged in Blackburn's lab and Blackburn thought so as well. Greider even knew what she wanted to work on. She wanted to prove that a previously unknown substance was actively building telomeres on the ends of the gene-containing DNA (Greider, 2009).

Blackburn and her other graduate students had done preliminary work on the problem. They found they could grow new telomeres with various solutions in the test tube and had promising results. The problem was separating out the enzymes that built telomeres from all the other enzymes in *Tetrahymena*.

This was a genuine collaboration. Blackburn's lab was not hierarchical; graduate students were genuine partners. Blackburn and Greider talked together about how to go about it. Greider expressed her pleasure in the planning process this way:

> There was no established protocol for finding an unknown enzyme, so we had fun and made one up. In fact, more precisely, we continually made up new protocols. It was…biochemical improvisation: we started with one concept of an assay that might allow detection of addition onto telomeres, but kept modifying the assay after each set of experiments.
>
> *(Greider, 2009, p. 302)*

With each plan, Greider did what molecular biologists called the bench work, carrying out the experiments: radioactively labeling the bases that would be built into telomeres, preparing DNA fragments with a short telomere at the end for the new telomeres to hook onto, trying different solutions to see if they contained the enzymes needed to build telomeres. All this was exacting work requiring concentration and solving problems that turned up along the way.

Greider started in May 1984. Weeks went by with no get clear results. For example, in one experiment the radioactive labeled bases showed up weakly on the telomere end but also in the gene-containing DNA, no proof that a unique enzyme was building telomeres. More weeks went by. They tried new variations. They kept changing the conditions over a period of nine months without finding what they were looking for. Even Greider wondered how long she would keep going before she gave up. Part of the creative process in science is facing failure and knowing when to give up and when to go on. Greider kept going.

Late in December, Blackburn suggested an approach that Greider had been wondering about as well. Maybe the problem was that there were too few of the *Tetrahymena* fragments with telomeres at the ends. Suppose instead of using a fragment of gene-containing DNA with a short telomere to bait the enzyme into building more telomeres, they used artificially constructed chains with the same structure as a natural *Tetrahymena* telomere? They could create a much larger number. That idea made them hopeful of a new outcome.

Earlier work had shown that the G strand rather than the C strand was synthesized first. So Greider created artificial telomere chains with 18 repeats of the GGGGTT chain—many of them. And they could study what happened without gene-containing DNA in the bait. To give the hypothesized enzyme some building blocks to work with, she added T bases, radioactively labeled G bases, ATP for energy, and a preservative. Then, *Tetrahymena* extract went in, made from the developmental stage when telomeres were added to the chopped-up minichromosomes in living cells. If an enzyme built telomeres, getting *Tetrahymena* extract from that period of development should be rich in it. Could they finally prove a previously unknown enzyme was there and building telomeres or convince themselves it wasn't?

At last, after all those weeks of failure, late in December, the film showed the characteristic bands of the repeated telomere pattern. Long chains of GGGGTT segments had been added to the bait. It was a result that made Greider dance and thrilled Blackburn when she saw the autoradiogram the next day (Brady, 2007).

Ah yes, but could there be another logical explanation for the result? When they calmed down, Greider and Blackburn played devil's advocate to their own interpretation of their results, challenging each other with possible alternate explanations. Each alternate explanation needed an experiment to rule it out. Six months of questioning their conclusion along with six months of experiments to rule out alternative explanations took place before evidence-based reasoning convinced them that it had to be a unique enzyme that had built telomeres. Later, they named the enzyme *telomerase* (Greider, 2009).

Not so fast, said the reviewers, the gatekeepers who determine which papers will be published in a journal. They were skeptical and suggested further experiments to eliminate other explanations (Brady, 2007).

The review process is fraught and article authors often have a frustrating time first waiting for reviews and then responding to them. Blackburn and Greider had to carry out the suggested studies whether or not they felt they were needed. The new studies did not change the result and the paper was finally published in 1985 (Greider & Blackburn, 1985).

When Blackburn first saw the result, she knew it was an important finding, on a par with the most cutting-edge discoveries in the field. And she was as ambitious for recognition as most scientists. Yet, the finding did not cause a stir in the field. After all, it was about pond scum.

Nevertheless, Greider and Blackburn did not lose focus. The result raised new questions which piqued their curiosity. Yes, there was this mysterious enzyme, telomerase, which built chains of bases at the tips of chromosomes, preventing them from falling apart. How does the enzyme "know" what to build? There was more work to do.

MOTHER IS A SCIENTIST

In the middle of 1986, it seemed as if Blackburn's collaboration with Greider and her other graduate students would be interrupted. She was pregnant. Blackburn was delighted that she was to have a child. She was equally determined to continue her work.

Life made it even harder. Four months into her pregnancy, she went into premature labor, and she was told she needed five months of complete bed rest. She refused to give up on research or her baby. Her body had to be still, but not her mind. She kept in continual conversation with her graduate students as their jointly designed studies proceeded. After her son was born, she reorganized her time. She shortened her presence in her laboratory somewhat, cutting out her evening hours, but taking advantage of excellent child care during the day. So she was able to have the satisfactions (and frustrations) of both motherhood and research (Brady, 2007).

TOPPLING A DOGMA

Those prebirth and postbirth discussions between Greider and Blackburn centered on the question of what in the enzyme made possible the building of those telomere repeats. And given the various models, how could they be tested? They came up with three models. The one that Greider intuited as most likely and so tested first was that the enzyme contained an RNA component. Perhaps one of its attractions was that the result would move against what was commonly accepted in the field.

Biologists had assumed that each kind of substance in a cell was specialized for a different kind of work. The received dogma in all the textbooks was that DNA carried the genetic inheritance; DNA and its blueprints are copied into RNA; RNA uses the blueprints for making the molecules which control and regulate all sorts of cell processes.

Simple models need revision. As Greider put it, biology is "messy." The first crack in the received model occurred when two researchers independently showed that one of the most primitive living creatures of all, a particular kind of virus, begins life with only RNA which then builds DNA (Baltimore, 1970; Temin, 1970). The AIDS virus is such a virus.

An intriguing and surprising finding it was, but not enough to give up the clear, simple model. After all, a virus is little more than a packet of either DNA or RNA. It is a parasite and all it can do to survive is infect a more complex organism. It takes over the genetic material in its host's cells so it can multiply itself again and again. No one had suggested or shown that RNA can make DNA in an organism that has a nucleus and can reproduce itself without bothering a host.

But RNA is a structure with blueprints for building. Could telomerase contain RNA? Could there be an RNA blueprint in telomerase responsible for building telomere DNA? Wouldn't that be an amazing unexpected finding? It would have to be done carefully. The field of molecular biology would be skeptical. And it would be revolutionary because, by now, researchers had shown that telomerase built telomeres in several different species.

Greider and Blackburn knew a logical way to design an experiment to probe the role of RNA in telomere building: Disable RNA and see what happens. Back to bench work.

Greider again assembled the concoction that proved an enzyme was building telomeres. She made only one addition to the mix: chemical scissors known to cut the backbone of RNA but left DNA intact. If they were right, the broken RNA could no longer do its work. There wouldn't be much, if any, telomere building.

When Greider developed the film derived from the mixture, the usual multiple chains added to the artificial telomeres were missing. The cuts in RNA had prevented the usual building process from taking place. RNA had to be part of the telomere building substance.

Again, Greider and Blackburn argued back and forth with their own interpretation. They designed experiments that might disprove it, and were unable to. Their paper proposing that telomerase contained RNA was published in 1987 (Greider & Blackburn, 1987). Here was a revolutionary finding that exploded the earlier consensus: RNA can build DNA in organisms that have nuclei. RNA builds telomeric DNA. This time the field took notice.

TELOMERE CHAPTERS CONTINUE TO BE WRITTEN

Greider completed her Ph.D. research and received a postdoctoral fellowship at Cold Spring Harbor Laboratory. Nevertheless she continued to collaborate with Blackburn, now using all sorts of techniques to determine exactly what telomerase consisted of. They discovered it consisted of two elements: a protein and RNA containing a CAACCCCAA string, the rung partners of the strings that are synthesized first as telomeres are built, the blueprint for the GGGGTT string (Greider & Blackburn, 1989).

Thereafter Blackburn and Greider each developed independent programs to study telomerase further. Both, in different ways, studied the role of telomerase in human aging and cancer (Greider and Blackburn, 1996; Blackburn, Greider, and Szostak, 2006). Blackburn and her students are currently studying what other cell functions are affected by telomerase. Greider found the gene in mouse DNA responsible for the RNA blueprint and was able to study its mutations. That turned out to be the key to a rare human genetic disorder (Mary et. al., 2005). An intriguing new direction for cross-disciplinary study came to Blackburn when a psychology researcher came to see her with a proposal. How about collaborating on a study that looked at the relation between chronic stress and telomere length? Their cross-disciplinary research showed that severe, continual stress, such as having to take care of a chronically ill child, tended to go with shortened telomeres compared to a similar group of mothers who did not have that burden (Epel et al., 2010; Blackburn & Epel, 2012, 2018).

From the 1990s on, other molecular biologists took on telomere-telomerase studies and it has become a lively research area within molecular biology. In 2009, Blackburn, Szostak,[3] and Greider were awarded the Nobel Prize for their work on telomeres and telomerase.

THE CREATIVE PROCESS OF BLACKBURN AND HER COLLABORATORS: SUMMARY AND REFLECTIONS

The scientific method as described in textbooks gives only a skeleton of the contemporary scientific research process as it often is carried out. Make a hypothesis based on an observation or a theory. Design an experiment to test it. Conduct it. Compare the results with the hypothesis. If it is not supported, refine the hypothesis and repeat.

This barebones description leaves out the variety, the sociality, the fun, the tedium, the frustration, the excitement, and the passion with which the telomere episode was lived. Though most of the experiments did start with a hypothesis, Blackburn's first telomere study began simply with exploring, looking for the composition of telomeres with no idea of what she would find. The Blackburn-Szostak experiment began with competing hypotheses from the two investigators. The alternate models suggested by other scientists became a challenge to Blackburn and Greider. Some hypotheses began with intuitions. Blackburn and Greider trusted their intuitions to guide experimentation.

Looking at an episode consisting of chapters revealed another feature of creative work in science: asking questions. Each result brought up new questions: What's there? What would happen if? What could be causing this? How could it be proved? What other explanation could there be? How does it do it?

Another feature of the telomere work is typical of the creative process in modern science: it was a highly social enterprise and not only in the sense of its dependence on its base of domain knowledge and technology created by others. It depended as well on the opportunities presented by the field and the gatekeepers who accept some and not others to the possibilities of education, mentorship, and publication. Both Blackburn and Greider were fortunate in finding opportunities and ways to deal with obstacles. The sheer excellence of their work and the luck of finding sympathetic mentors made them able to get by the obstacle of low expectations of women in science. Blackburn had to navigate the complexities of combining research science and motherhood. Greider had to overcome dyslexia and the assumptions made about her as a result. Since modern scientific research depends on funding, Blackburn had to convince the selection committees of granting agencies like the National Institute of Health to fund her research and later, so did Greider.

The telomere episode also depended on face-to-face relationships. Blackburn was a post-doctoral fellow in Joseph Gall's laboratory who introduced her to *Tetrahymena*, had purified its DNA, and guided her in other ways as her mentor. Even her husband contributed as she used one of the methods he had devised as part of her search for the telomere composition. And it depended centrally on the collaboration between Blackburn and Greider.

Face-to-face collaboration means conversation and conversation has the features of improvisation. What each participant says affects what the next reply will be and the conversational flow is emergent—different from what each party might think alone (Sawyer & DeZutter, 2009). Greider termed the back and forth of inventing a way to find an unknown enzyme biochemical improvisation. Blackburn's conversations with Szostak and later with Epel demonstrated the richness of conversations across domains and subdomains, resulting in experiments neither co-investigator could have done alone. All these conversations, conversations based in the world of science, depended on a shared basic knowledge but with each party also having unique perspectives to contribute.

Science seeks objectivity. But the experience of scientific research, as all human experience, is imbued with feeling. The telomere research began with a sense of adventure. Along the way was the fun of thinking up possibilities, the determined focus in doing bench work, the eager wait to see the outcome of an experiment, the mounting frustration in the face of failure, the thrill of discovery. Writing and submitting results to a journal came with a cascade of feeling as well: ambitious hopes, anxiety about possible rejection, anger, disappointment, and elation depending on the outcome. A powerful emotion sustained the entire creative process: passionate curiosity about "how life works."

NOTES

1 Chapter 4 introduced Schütz's ideas of multiple modes of experience. The fiction world is one example; the science world, another.

2 Earlier the term *convergence of streams* as a possible feature of the creative process referred to two streams in a single person's mind—such as the political stream and the aesthetic stream that came together in *Guernica* (Chapter 3). Here, too, is a convergence of streams, but in two different minds working together—a reason why diversity often enhances the creativity of groups.

3   Szostak did not continue working on telomere research for long, but has made several other ground-breaking discoveries in other areas of microbiology.

REFERENCES

Blackburn, E. H. (2009a). Biographical. Retrieved on June 29, 2020 from https://www.nobelprize.org/prizes/medicine/2009/blackburn/biographical.

Blackburn, E. H. (2009b). Telomeres and telomerase: Their implication in human age-related diseases. *Experimental Gerontology, 44*(1–2), 123–123. doi:10.1016/j.exger.2008.08.011

Blackburn, E. H. (2017) The science of cells that never get old (Ted talk). Retrieved October 2020 from https://www.ted.com/talks/elizabeth_blackburn_the_science_of_cells_that_never_get_old#t-24913.

Blackburn, E. H., & Epel, E. (2018). *The telomere effect: A revolutionary approach to living younger, healthier, longer.* London: Orion Spring.

Blackburn, E. H., & Epel E. S. (2012). Telomeres and adversity: Too toxic to ignore. *Nature, 490*(7419), 169–171. doi:10.1038/490169a.

Blackburn, E. H., Greider, C. W., & Szostak, J. W. (2006). Telomeres and telomerase: The path from maize, tetrahymena and yeast to human cancer and aging. *Nature Medicine, 12*(10), 1133–1138. doi:10.1038/nm1006-1133

Blackburn, E. H., & Gall, J. G. (1978). A tandemly repeated sequence at the termini of the extrachromosomal ribosomal RNA genes in tetrahymena. *Journal of Molecular Biology, 120*(1), 33–53. doi:10.1016/0022-2836(78)90294-2

Brady, C. (2007). *Elizabeth Blackburn and the story of telomeres: Deciphering the ends of DNA.* Cambridge, MA: MIT Press.

Csikszentmihalyi, M. (1996). *Creativity: Flow and the psychology of discovery and invention* (1st ed.). New York: HarperCollins Publishers.

Epel, E. S., Lin, J., Dhabhar, F. S., Wolkowitz, O. M., Puterman, E., Karan, L., & Blackburn, E. H. (2010). Dynamics of telomerase activity in response to acute psychological stress. *Brain Behavior and Immunity, 24*(4), 531–539. doi:10.1016/j.bbi.2009.11.018.

Greider, C. W. (2009) Biographical. Retrieved on June 29, 2020 from https://www.nobelprize.org/prizes/medicine/2009/greider/biographical/.

Greider, C. W., & Blackburn, E. H. (1985). Identification of a specific telomere terminal transferase activity in tetrahymena extracts. *Cell: Part 1, 43*(2), 405–413. doi:10.1016/0092-8674(85)90170-9

Greider, C. W., & Blackburn, E. H. (1987). The telomere terminal transferase of tetrahymena is a ribonucleoprotein enzyme with two kinds of primer specificity. *Cell, 51*(6), 887–898. doi:10.1016/0092-8674(87)90576-9

Greider, C. W., & Blackburn, E. H. (1989). A telomeric sequence in the RNA of Tetrahymena telomerase required for telomere repeat synthesis. *Nature, 337*(6205), 331–337. doi: 10.1038/337331a0

Greider, C. W., & Blackburn, E. H. (1996). Telomeres, telomerase and cancer. *Scientific American, 274*(2), 92–97.

Mary, A., Yen-Pei, C. C., Anita, H., James, R. E., Chen, J.-L., Brodsky, R. A., … Greider, C. W. (2005). Haploinsufficiency of telomerase reverse transcriptase leads to anticipation in autosomal dominant dyskeratosis congenita. *Proceedings of the National Academy of Sciences of the United States of America, 102*(44), 15960–15964.

Sawyer, R. K., & DeZutter, S. (2009). Distributed creativity: How collective creations emerge from collaboration. *Psychology of Aesthetics, Creativity, and the Arts, 3*(2), 81–92. https://doi.org/10.1037/a0013282

Shampay, J., Szostak, J. W., & Blackburn, E. H. (1984). DNA sequences of telomeres maintained in yeast. *Nature, 310*(5973), 154–157.

Watson, J. D., & Crick, F. H. C. (1953). A structure for DNA. *Nature, 171,* 737–738.

CHAPTER 11

Ron Carter's Nonet

Inventing and Developing a New Sound

Ron Carter was already a legendary jazz bassist when he invented a new sound. He had previously been recognized as an exceptional musician, one often called to play bass on recordings. In fact, the *Guinness World Book of Records* (2015) acclaimed him as the most recorded bassist in the world. Jazz greats such as Randy Weston, Art Farmer, and Miles Davis sought out Carter to play bass in their bands. But he came to dream of leading his own bands and one of them turned to be a jazz group like no other: a nonet consisting of four classical cellists and five jazz musicians. How that dream was realized is this chapter's story. In the process we will see how many creative endeavors came together to produce the nonet's unique sound as well as the features that allowed musicians from such different traditions to collaborate in a rare musical adventure.

The clues to Carter's creative process came from several sources. A biography by Dan Ouellette (2015) provided background and also included quotes from extensive interviews with Carter and his players. Music reviews and other interviews, including two recent unpublished interviews, filled out the story (Carter, 2021, unpublished interview).

CARTER BEFORE THE NONET

As far back as Ron Carter can remember, music which he had heard came to play in his head. He calls it his inner FM radio. His sister remembers him leaving the dinner table for the piano to pick out some notes he was "hearing." His public school in Ferndale, Michigan, a suburb of Detroit, provided opportunity for him to make his own sounds in a different way. Students could choose from an array of instruments and the school would provide lessons for it. All eight Carter children did. Ron, aged ten, thought the cello had a nice sound and wondered what he could do with it. So cello it was.

He had learned discipline and tenacity from his father and, while attaining excellent grades in all his subjects, he spent many hours in cello practice. The first teacher who gave him lessons and his next teacher, a cellist from the Detroit Symphony Orchestra, told him that they had taught him all they could and that he needed a more advanced teacher. The medals he won at regional competitions, his admission to

DOI: 10.4324/9781003013860-17

youth orchestras, his being chosen as solo cellist at the Interlochen music camp, and winning a place at Cass Tech, a magnet high school in Detroit where he could major in music—all these told him: This was going to be his life. He would become a cellist in a major American orchestra.

Then, he realized something. Though he was commended by all his music teachers for his talent, he was missing out on opportunities. Cass Tech students often made extra money by being selected to play at conventions, parties, and PTA meetings. He rarely was chosen, though he felt equal to the cellists who were. Maybe if he switched instruments. The bass chair had just become vacant and there was only one. How different could that be from playing the cello? It turned out to be very different, but tenacious as always, he mastered it. And he discovered that the bass could open up a new source of earnings. A jazz band that played for parties needed a bassist and recruited Carter. He now had to learn a whole new library of tunes and to learn how the jazz bass functioned—working with the drums to set the beat that propels the music forward, improvising on melodies. Again, he was a fast learner. Still, his goal did not change—a career playing classical music in a major American orchestra.

He auditioned and won a scholarship to attend the Eastman School of Music in Rochester, New York. There, he again excelled and again earned extra money playing jazz. Rochester was a stop for well-known touring bands and Carter listened to and got to know major players. Still his goal did not change—a career playing classical music in a major American orchestra.

Outstanding orchestra conductors often visited Eastman, looking to recruit exceptional musicians. On his visit, Leopold Stokowski, then conductor of the Houston Symphony Orchestra told Carter, "Young man, you play wonderful bass. But I'm in Houston and I know that the board of directors is not ready for a colored man to be in its orchestra" (Carter, quoted in Ouellette, 2015, loc. 247).

Carter now came face to face with a realization. There were almost no black faces in major American orchestras. He had spent half of his life preparing for a goal that was closed to him because of the color of his skin. Still, he had another musical option. After graduation from Eastman, Carter came to New York to play jazz.

What a difference in reception. The jazz community recognized his gifts and welcomed him. Chico Hamilton hired him for a tour and when the tour ended, Carter worked steadily with outstanding groups as a sideman (a band member other than the leader).

He frequently was asked to play on recordings and became known both for his musical imagination and his ability to calm the waters when someone in the session was being difficult. At one session he knew the end of a song was not working. He said to the bandleader "Can we do something other than a C minor at the end, like an A-flat or something." The bandleader thought about it and then said, "I have an idea, how about if we end this on A-flat" (Ouellette, 2015, loc. 564). Another time a player was being obstinate, preventing the recording session from going forward. Carter took the player aside and convinced him to be more reasonable.

Four years after Carter came to New York, Miles Davis chose Carter and his bass to be part of the most admired quintet in jazz. Carter now played with four other premier musicians, each pushing the others to move in new directions. During this time

(1963–1968), he also wrote his first book (Carter, 1964) and composed music as well (Ouellette, 2015; Carter, 2021, unpublished interview).

PRECURSORS TO THE NONET

Becoming a Bandleader

Miles Davis became enamored of electronic music; Carter was less interested. The band was about to go on tour. Carter had two sons and wanted to stay home to be with them as they grew up. Above all, he was hearing different sounds and wanted to be in charge of realizing them. It was time to become a bandleader himself. Now he would choose the musicians. He would determine the band's arrangements and compose some of its songs. He did not give up being a sideman from time to time. For one session, he was asked to play the cello in a jazz band and he was intrigued to see how that would work. But leading his own bands became his major enterprise (Ouellette, 2015; Carter, unpublished interview).

Inventing the Piccolo Bass

Carter enjoyed and continues to enjoy playing the bass. He had attended to every aspect of his bass sound; for example, testing out various string types, till he found the kind that gave him what became his signature sound (Carter & McCoy, 2020). But he was hearing the possibility of a different string sound, one that could more often be a solo instrument, one that would put him in front of the band he was leading.

There were half basses, chiefly instruments for children before they were tall enough for the full-sized instrument. But he imagined an unusual tuning for the half bass, one strung to play sounds that were pitched higher than his bass. An instrument-maker friend worked with him and built what Carter asked for: a half bass whose strings were uniquely tuned to a higher range, one in between that of the standard bass and the cello. Carter called his new instrument the piccolo bass (Carter, 2021, unpublished interview).

Experiments in Sound with the Piccolo Bass

Now that he was a bandleader and had this new instrument to play with, what kind of group might he use it in? He formed, first a quartet, then a quintet each with two basses—someone else playing the full-sized bass and he playing his piccolo variant. He is still leading such ensembles.

Carter was still hearing strings. What could he do with a full string orchestra: nine violinists, three violists, and three cellists? Could the sound of strings work with a jazz quartet?

Carter has been quoted as saying "Trust your feelings." He explained that he meant, trust them enough to try them out. He could not tell whether the sounds in the head would work in the world until musicians, including himself, embodied them with their playing. He needed to hear and play in an ensemble made up of a string orchestra and a jazz quintet (Carter, 2021, unpublished interview).

There was no library of songs for such a group. So Carter did what he had been doing from the time he was in Miles Davis's band. He wrote original music, then arranged, and led such a group for all the tracks of a recording. The resulting album, *Pastels* (1976),[1] was a one-time experiment in sound which fused blues, bebop, pop, and classical music in an original mix, spiced with musical humor.

CREATING THE NONET

Carter wanted to continue to experiment with bringing the string sound into jazz. A group playing together, developing the sound over time, was his way of exploring possibilities. He knew he was taking a risk, but he said, "You have to take chances. The adventure is what it is all about" (Carter, quoted in Ouellette, 2015, loc. 1277).

He set out to form a jazz band that included strings, one that could play in clubs regularly. A full string orchestra was impractical. Besides, the string sounds he was now hearing were those of his childhood instrument, the cello. He imagined a jazz quintet accompanied by four classical cellists—convergence of a childhood musical stream and his ongoing jazz stream.[2]

His jazz friends discouraged him. Classical players can't swing, they told him. He was determined to prove them wrong.

Finding the Players

Part of the creative process of a bandleader is selecting the players. Choosing the jazz quintet members for the nonet was easy. He had worked with many players before. He knew that a key to a group's success was that the members respect and trust the leader and one another. He knew such players, ones who would listen when Carter gave a correction—knowing also that Carter would adapt to their needs, their impulses, and their ideas when they made the band sound better. He found jazz musicians who wanted to join him on the nonet adventure.

Next he needed to find cellists who were ready to explore, too. Carter had a network of colleagues across the musical spectrum. One was a classical viola player to whom Carter said, "Find me four cellists." The first name that came up was familiar to Carter, Kermit Moore. He had been in the group that played cello on the *Pastels* album. In addition to being a cellist, Moore was the founder of the Symphony of the New World, the first fully racially integrated classical orchestra. Moore had occasionally played in jazz bands himself. The prospect of being part of Carter's nonet adventure was exciting to him and he understood exactly the kind of cellist Carter needed. Moore found three other cellists fascinated by Carter's experiment. Before too long, the cellists were ready to meet Carter and his quintet for their first rehearsal (Ouellette, 2015; Carter, 2021, unpublished interview).

Learning as Needed along the Way

But what could the cellists play? The only way to find out was to try something, to learn from the success or failure. Carter had a motto that went something like this: The more mistakes you make, the more you learn.

Carter had some ideas. He spoke of musical "things" that came to him. When asked what the experience of getting ideas was, he said, "I hear. I hear." Ideas came to him in the form of sound, in a music world, whether he was arranging melodies or composing his own. Then he went to work with a group developing and revising till he was satisfied. This was always his composing process which he now applied to producing the first arrangement for the nonet.

The next question was how to communicate to the cellists so they could come to play what he wrote. He had never written a classical score. A new skill was needed—to learn how to write one. He found a copyist who became his teacher. Carter learned to write a score that cellists could read and to compose in a range in which cellists were comfortable playing.

Now came the test. Would they be able to read his score? Would they be able to play an unfamiliar jazz figure as written? Would they grasp the feel of the music? The first rehearsal told him, yes, yes. And yes, they could swing.

Next he wondered, could he find enough songs that would make the nonet "sound and feel valid to an audience unaccustomed to hearing an ensemble of this physical makeup?" (Carter, 2021, unpublished interview). He was curious to try.

There were new learning challenges for cellists, too. There was no conductor up front, arms prominently signaling the tempo. They had to hear it in the play of the other players.

With a classical piece, their playing was typically continuous from beginning to end of a composition. If they did cease playing for a period, the orchestra conductor cued them in a way they couldn't miss; here there was no conductor. As part of the nonet, they had to pay close attention even when they were not playing.

Carter did not expect the cellists to improvise. That was for the experienced jazz players, but gave another challenge to the cellists. So much varied with improvisation: which soloists played, when they played, how long they played, what they played. So to know when to resume playing, the cellists had to pick up the subtle cuing either from Carter or one of the other players who had been designated to do so. Then too, all the cellists had to come in at the same time.

The Nonet's First Recording

Another Carter challenge: He wanted to experiment with the nonet, and to do so he had to work with them in a series of performances. Club owners who usually booked jazz groups preferred to hire the smaller cheaper ones—trios or quartets. How could he convince them to take a chance on a group of nine, four of whom were inexperienced in the jazz medium? Carter's solution was to introduce the group sound by making a recording.

He needed a library of songs for them, chose some, and wrote some. He needed to arrange them all and copy the parts for the cellists in ways they were familiar with. He had to work with the engineer and mixer so that the sound of the record resembled the sound in his head. All this he did. His first nonet album, *A Song for You* came out in 1978 (Carter, 1978).

The recording did what Carter had hoped. Clubs such as Birdland booked his nonet to play for their audiences. Now he could continue to explore what the nonet could do.

DEVELOPING THE SOUND THROUGH PERFORMANCES

"I Go to School Every Night"

Carter has been quoted as saying this in several interviews including the recent one. When asked what he learned, he answered with a series of questions: What strengths and weaknesses were revealed by the players? How could he build on and develop their strengths? How could he shore up their weaknesses? Should the tempo be faster? Slower? Is the song in the right key? In general, what did he need to do to make the band sound better? Carter worked this way with all his bands and the nonet was no exception.

With the nonet, Carter learned what the cellists needed, too. He sent the arrangements to the band ahead of time allowing them to practice in their homes. Though with his other groups, Carter sometimes varied the order of tunes from night to night, the cellists found this unsettling, so he kept the same order throughout the week. He came to know which numbers and which keys they were most comfortable with. Their mistakes were his teachers, telling him what he needed to work on with them or what he had to change in the music.

Common Goals, Respect, and Trust

The nonet players, including the cellists, found their common task, making beautiful music together, fulfilling. Cellist Dorothy Lawson told Ouellette (2015, loc. 1266), "Musically this is as satisfying as anything I do."

Carter's way of working with the nonet was to be candid, at times complimentary, sometimes stern, always humane, always about the music, never personal attack. The cellists came to appreciate his honesty and responded to it. They, like the others, soon knew they could trust his judgment and his expertise, and his integrity won their respect (Lawson, quoted in Ouellette, 2015). Carter came to respect and trust the cellists as well. He found that "Whatever the arrangement, the cellos can play anything. Give the cellists the right notes and chords, and the results are mind-boggling" (Ouellette, 2015, loc. 1255). This was one more confirmation of the result that has emerged from the psychological study of other kinds of groups (e.g. Lee, Stajkovic, & Sergent, 2016): Common goals, mutual respect, and trust are keys to the creativity and effectiveness of a group. Humor also builds bonds (Francis, 1994) and all the players came to appreciate Carter's humor as well.

Telling Stories with Music

The nonet's typical engagement was playing at a club for at least a week. For a week of performances, he had to put together a program, choosing the tunes and their order for each of two sets each night. In planning a set, he saw it like a story, with a beginning, middle, and end. Sets were to have the shape of a narrative and a theme. The themes came to him, sometimes from the events of the day. For example, racial violence asked him to mourn, to protest, and to hope. So he might start and end a set with a hymn, the

African-American soundtrack to those feelings. Other possible themes might include a tribute to the variety in jazz or recalling its history.

Every Night Was Different

Every night was different, because the cellists became increasingly skilled and relaxed in playing their parts. Every night was different partly because the players had had an easy or difficult day. Carter wanted his band members to come early so that they could tell him how they were feeling. Were many of them tired? Should he adjust the tempos? And how did they feel about something he was thinking of telling the audience about his own feelings that day? For example, one day after reading the newspaper he wanted to protest the scant coverage given to current jazz performances compared to all other arts. (If any member objected, he would not talk about it to the audience. They rarely did.)

Every night was different because Carter was listening very closely to the music the nonet was playing. Before and after performances, he spoke to the musicians about what he had heard. He told them of adjustments he wanted them to make, some corrections, some change in arrangement—all ways to make the band sound better. And once the players understood where the music should be going, Carter welcomed their suggestions, too (Carter, unpublished interview, 2021).

The week was like a laboratory, researching what could be done to improve the performances.

> While early in the week, there may be problems, I expect by the last night of the week that everyone is in the zone of the music, with its different rhythms, the cues coming in different places, the arrangements changing every night.
>
> *(Ouellette, 2015, loc. 1270)*

Improvising. Every night was different because the jazz musicians were improvising on the tunes they were playing. Though Carter was responsible for all the notes in the arrangements, there were spaces for solos, allowing the quintet players to respond to the moment and to each other. Carter said, "they were adding what I couldn't" (Carter, 2021, unpublished interview).

The key was listening, listening closely. Carter kept using that word, listening. A good player he said, has to listen. And what he plays is contingent on what he heard. So the music was created in the moment, because what the other players played was unpredictable and a new sound emerged.

Carter, as one of the players, enjoyed being an improviser. Some of his memorable improvisations were when he on his piccolo bass was trading eights (exchanging improvised eight-bar phrases) with other players.

Speaking of trading eights with his nonet bassist, Boots Maleson, Carter said, "I like to step back, then play another phrase or develop what he played," he added. "He hears me play a phrase, then he may add in a different note. That's what's so important in this music: to take it somewhere else" (Ouellette, 2015, loc. 1279).

Maleson put it this way:

> It's fun and a challenge. Ron pushes me a little, and though we haven't talked about it, I think I may push him a little too. I play something. Ron picks up on it. You want it to be a conversation, not a mimicking back and forth. I don't really think too much about it when we do it. It just happens.
>
> *(Ouellette, 2015, loc. 1280)*

Maleson spoke to the essence of improvisation: the music just happens. The music flows without thinking. It happens because the players are listening closely. They can do it because they are so skilled in their understanding of music, they can spontaneously build on what they heard and take it somewhere else.

For Carter, too, the playing can just happen, his fingers finding the right notes. And he can be surprised by what he finds himself playing. Sometimes, though, Carter gave away a secret: Experienced players have a "bag," a suitcase full of musical ideas.

> Everyone who plays this music has what they do in their bag. And we all pull them out in times of desperation or emergency. Or we finally found out where this phrase really belongs—in this song and this key, at this tempo with this kind of sound.
>
> *(Carter, 2021, unpublished interview)*

The improvisations are in the moment, a spontaneous response to what was just heard, but that can mean a phrase that had come to the musicians earlier, but now fits here and advances the music.

Developing solos. Every night was different, because over a week of playing the same pieces with the same band, jazz players had an opportunity. The memory of last night's improvisation was still with them. They could develop what they started, develop and change it each night, according to how they felt, how the tempo might be different, how the audience was responding differently, what others have just played, how they could take it somewhere else.

Carter knew his jazz players each heard different music in their heads. He saw part of his mission to help his players by how he responded and how he accompanied them. He wanted them "to take the music they hear in their heads to a place that not only the audience can respond to (but to) help it do something else" (Carter, 2021, unpublished interview).

Group Flow

One of the pleasures of being in a jazz band is the moment when the music just flows.[3] Stephen Scott, a piano player in Carter's quartet and nonet, spoke of trust being a necessary ingredient.

> Once that trust is developed, that's when the fun and magic happen. If respect and trust is not there, it's hard to make magic, it's hard to do great things

together. It's when we mix everything together as a band, we experience our highest moments.

(Scott, quoted in Ouellette, 2015, loc. 1220)

When Carter was asked about when he experienced flow, he answered, "It's called a group. When you have a group, that's what happens...when everyone responds to the same impulse." And with the nonet, that included the cellists.

An example. The nonet was scheduled to play a rare one-night concert in Merkin Hall. In rehearsal that afternoon, the sound was off in all sorts of ways. The arrangements needed adjustment and Carter made changes the players had to write in. They flubbed some of them and missed some cues. Carter had to stop them several times as the band kept making mistakes in the same section over and over again. It was an occasion for being candid and stern. The tension was felt by everyone as the evening performance loomed. Tenacious as always, Carter kept the group working and improving till he was satisfied.

The performance that night was splendid, the nonet playing the music as just Carter had heard in his head. Ouellette described Carter at the performance this way:

he looked relaxed...and appreciative of how the group was finding all the right notes...filling the hall with a lyrical and mysterious sonority. Sitting on a tall stool and tapping his left foot to the rhythms...(he) led the swing, the glee, the romanticism.

(Ouellette, 2015, loc. 1275)

Late in the performance, Carter turned to the audience, introduced the eight other members of the band, and then said, "I'm hoping that you can see what is a bass player's dream" (Ouellette, 2015, loc. 1275).

CARTER'S CREATIVE PROCESS: SUMMARY AND REFLECTIONS

Ron Carter often lived in a world of music, hearing music in his mind's ear. His invention and development of his nonet led to creating of series of performances by a unique ensemble, a co-creation with his players—four classical cellists and five jazz musicians. Those performances were the culmination of a variety of Carter endeavors, many of them in and of themselves creative: hearing, imagining, composing, arranging, selecting players, adapting to the players, working with the band to improve the sound, performing, improvising while performing. Curiosity, a sense of adventure, listening, and learning were central to these endeavors. Though the performances were co-created with his band, the nonet's beginning was a private experience known to Carter alone.

The idea of the nonet began when Carter heard new sounds in his head. They harkened back to his early love of the cello. They incorporated his jazz quintet experience including the strains of the instrument he invented, the piccolo bass. The sounds that came to him told him that cellos could bring a new dimension to his music, an integration, bringing together two musical streams—the cello's classical sound and the syncopated rhythms and harmonies of jazz.

Curiosity propelled him into musical adventures. What could these new sounds develop into? To find out he needed to first embody them, assemble a band of players, listen closely.

Selection of the right musicians was critical to realizing and developing the sound. Choosing jazz sidemen was easy; he knew, played with, and led many of them before. One in his network of colleagues helped him find cellists.

There were no musical arrangements for this new kind of ensemble. Carter had to write them. He began by creating a single arrangement, curious especially about what the cellists could do. As he got to know their playing, part of his process was to write songs and arrangements for the specific musicians he was working with, building on their strengths, both the sidemen and the cellists, particularly adapting to the range and the keys the cellists were comfortable with.

Bringing eight disparate musicians together and forging them into a group who could play their parts to realize a shared goal was also a creative task. It involved modifying arrangements when his ear told him they needed change. It required winning the group's respect and trust in him as leader. The jazz players had worked with him before, so that was given. The cellists came to trust his keen musical ear as he made corrections and modified arrangements. He won that respect with his musical imagination and his honesty, complimenting them when they succeeded, being candid when something needed correction.

The rehearsals prepared the group for a multi-track recording; club and concert dates allowed the group to develop its sound over time. That meant selecting programs of songs, whether for sets to be played at a club or deciding the order that the tunes would appear on a recording. For Carter, putting together a program was also a creative task. He envisioned a series of songs as an organic whole, as telling a story with a beginning, middle, and end. Like the sounds that inspired him, story themes came to him, sometimes stimulated by national events.

A week of nonet performances was itself a process, in a way his laboratory, an opportunity to improve the performance of the night before. For Carter it was a chance to learn what was working, what changes needed to be made, and to talk to the group about them. For the cellists it was a time to become more comfortable with their parts so that they could adapt to changes in tempo, corrections in arrangements, variations in how the soloists improvised. For the soloists from set to set and night to night, it was an opportunity to develop their improvisations or change them completely depending on what they were hearing. And when everyone played, feeling the pulse of the music, there was the pleasure of group flow.

The creation of the nonet was a long process involving a variety of creative endeavors requiring different skills, but its realization consisted of co-created, partially improvised emergent performances, both bringing to fruition Carter's initial inspiration, yet new and surprising every night.

AFTER THE INVENTION OF THE NONET

Carter continued and continues to be curious about possibilities in sound. He had always admired Bach's bass lines. What could his basses do with Bach? He made a record in which he with his two different instruments, and overdubbing, played all the parts

(Carter, 1987). He recorded Bach's Brandenburg Concerto #3 with a string orchestra (Carter, 1991).

He got a call from the manager of a hip-hop group. Would he be available and interested in collaborating on a rap album? Carter was curious and checked out the group with his son Myles. Yes, A Tribe Called Quest was a serious, innovative group, so Carter went to the recording session and accompanied the group on his bass on one track. The resulting album, *The Low End Theory* (A Tribe Called Quest, 1991), has been called one of the 36 immortal rap albums (Ouellette, 2015).

Carter wrote the soundtracks for several films. As academia finally came to recognize jazz as serious music, Carter was hired to teach, first at City College of New York, then at Julliard. He has become an internationally beloved private teacher of the bass.

All the while, new chapters were being written for the nonet. One was the soundtrack Carter composed for a film. The music in *A Gathering of Old Men* (Schlondorff, 1987) was played by the nonet with the addition of a flute.

As the years went by, the musicians gradually changed as some players left to move in new directions. Each new group was a new challenge. There were new compositions to write, arrangements to try out, learning again how to build on each player's strengths (Ouellette, 2015).

Recently (except 2020 when all New York entertainment venues were shut down due to the Covid-19 pandemic), Birdland has been offering an annual celebration of Ron Carter. It is typically a four-week engagement, and Carter brings a different group he has been experimenting with to the stage for a week: in 2019, the first week featured Carter's 17-piece Great Big Band; the second, his Golden Striker trio, the third, his quartet. And capping the series of the performances, on the fourth week, Carter showcased the nonet (Birdland Jazz Club, 2019).

Each night the sounds Ron Carter heard in his head could once again be played and developed anew. He said, "Each night is my chance to find the right notes with some wonderful players...who are trusting me to help them do it" (Ibass Magazine, 2012, loc. 439).

CARTER LOOKING BACK

Carter was asked to look back on his long life in music: playing music, composing and arranging it, leading bands in live concerts and recordings, inventing an instrument, creating and developing the sound of an unusual ensemble never heard before in jazz. How did he feel now about the barriers that kept him from his high school dream—earning a regular chair in an American symphony orchestra? Was he resentful? His first answer was yes, because he was not given a choice. He quickly added with a half-suppressed smile, "but only for about 10 minutes a year." The rest of the time he was too busy finding fulfillment and pleasure in the many different ways he was making music—including adventure after adventure with his nonet (Carter, 2021, unpublished interview).

NOTES

1 All the Carter-led recordings mentioned in this chapter are available from youtube.com.
2 Streams and their convergence were introduced in Chapter 1.
3 The concept of flow was introduced in Chapter 1.

REFERENCES

A Tribe Called Quest (1991). Verses from the abstract (track). In *The low end theory*. Jive Records.

Birdland Jazz Club (2019). The Ron Carter Nonet. Retrieved January 20, 2021 from https://www.bir dlandjazz.com/e/ron-carter-nonet-64811840961/.

Carter, R. (1964). *Building jazz baselines*. Ron Carter Music Company.

Carter, R. (1976). *Pastels*. Milestone Recording.

Carter, R. (1978). *A Song for You*. Milestone Recording.

Carter, R. (1987). *Ron Carter Plays Bach*. Phillips Recording.

Carter, R. (1991). *Bach's Brandenburg Concerto #3*. Blue Note Recording. (Composed by J. S. Bach in 1719–1720.)

Carter, R., & McCoy, T. (2020). Ron Carter talks about his signature sound, Epifani bass amp, and strings. Retrieved January 18, 2021 from https://www.youtube.com/watch?v=cJPRxbVBOnM.

Francis, L. E. (1994). Laughter, the best mediation: Humor as emotion management in interaction. *Symbolic Interaction, 17*(2), 147–163. doi:10.1525/si.1994.17.2.147

Guinness World Book of Records (2015). Most recorded Jazz Bassist. Retrieved January 17, 2021 from https://www.guinnessworldrecords.com/world-records/387286-most-recorded-jazz-bassist.

IBass Magazine. (2012). Interview with Ron Carter. Retrieved January 20, 2021 from https://www.you tube.com/watch?v=gDp8SQyVSSs.

Lee, D., Stajkovic, A. D., & Sergent, K. (2016). A field examination of the moderating role of group trust in group efficacy formation. *Journal of Occupational and Organizational Psychology, 89*(4), 856–876. doi:10.1111/joop.12161

Ouellette, D. (2015). *Ron Carter: Finding the right notes*. New York: Retrac Productions. (e-book)

Schlondorff, V., director (1987). *A gathering of old men*. [film] Bioskop Films.

Epilogue

Reconstructing these creative episodes led me on intriguing, sometimes unexpected adventures. With an overall framework in the back of my mind, I still allowed each chapter to take its own shape. There were many surprises along the way. I had not thought that one of the pleasures of creating in science is akin to the pleasures of gambling—as Blackburn hinted and Darwin directly stated. That a set of early sketches that looked completely different from a final work could be seen as having the same theme—as Picasso's sketches suggested. That a major result in mathematics could appear spontaneously without intention or first posing a problem, as Poincaré reported. That a band leader could plan a jazz set to tell a story, as Carter did. That memory and imagination coming together in the creation of artistically acclaimed works can heal the wounds of childhood as well—revelations by Woolf and Biscardi.

Each episode was unique to its time, its culture, its era, the state of its domain, and the opportunities and obstacles provided by the field. Each was unique as the life history of each creator was unique. And even different episode chapters by the same creator were different from one another. My final task is looking back, noting the themes and variations that stood out to me…

ATTRACTION TO A DOMAIN

Each chapter began with a brief look at selected milestones in the creators' biographies. In many, there were early, pleasurable experiences in the domain as Franklin suggested—Blackburn's childhood collections from the beach, little Virginia Woolf already reading and writing, Ron Carter as a child already hearing music in his mind's ear, young Maurice Sendak, sketching the children below as he looked out his bedroom window, for example. But there were exceptions. Leon Addison Brown had never seen a live play or considered acting as a vocation till, almost by accident, he took a college course in theater. Carol Greider had not thought about science as a career till she found excitement and pleasure in carrying out experiments in her first year of college. What happened to both Brown and Greider is that their first experiences in creating in a domain were so satisfying that they set their lives on a new course. Opportunity to taste creative doing, earlier or later, was essential. Not all children have those opportunities.

IDENTITY AND COMMITMENT

Pleasure in working in a domain resulted in a commitment to doing that kind of creative work, an aspect of identity. Part of that commitment was learning the skills and prior contributions to the domain. Drawing on the knowledge gained was part of the preparation in later creative projects. Another aspect of that commitment was to make time and space in their lives for creative work. Darwin and Tolstoy were independently wealthy so that earning a living was not a consideration. Others needed financial support to do so. Carter was able to make a living in jazz performances and recordings, but later found additional work in teaching. Others found additional enterprises that paid them, brought satisfaction, and involved other forms of creativity thus buying time for their central work. For Biscardi, Blackburn, Greider, and the contemporary writers, it was teaching, grants, and awards; for Woolf, writing essays, translating, and editing, for Sendak, illustrating other authors' texts. For Paley, writing, teaching, and working for social justice were equally central to her identity. For Tolstoy, his work in education and his personal spiritual search were even more central to him than fiction writing. The place of the particular creative episode in the creator's identity varied. Still, all became committed to the specific creative episodes discussed in this book and were fortunate to find circumstances that enabled them to do so.

The very process of creating the works sometimes led to major changes in identity. With *Wild Things*, Sendak found his "voice" as a children's book artist. Darwin's process of creating evolution theory changed, as he knew it would, his social identity—lauded by some, condemned by others. DeMarse discovered new aspects of himself as he built his characters. Woolf's writing of *To the Lighthouse* and Biscardi's composing his quintet brought resolution to troubling emotions from the past.

THE CREATIVE PROCESS AS SOCIAL

Though much of this book focused on the work of individuals, the creative process always involved people other than the creators. The process was social in many different ways.

Significant Others

In many of the episodes, the support and enthusiasm of family and friends kept the creators at their projects. Woolf's husband, Darwin's wife, Blackburn's husband, Sendak's partner, and Tolstoy's wife and his critic-friend provided emotional support and other kinds of help as well.

Mentors, Gatekeepers, and Networks of Colleagues

Others opened up the opportunities for the creative episodes—Henslow for Darwin, grant givers for Biscardi, editor Nordstrom for Sendak. Evaluating the work, in progress or at the end, was typically shared, the creator and trusted others, reflecting together, with the developing work the shared ground—Tolstoy with Sofia and Strakov, Blackburn with mentors, the contemporary writers with literary colleagues, Sendak's peer and friend who gave him the word "rumpus."

Collaborative Projects

In some of the episodes, the making of the work itself was a shared undertaking. Sometimes it was centrally with peers. The actors in performance brought the drama world to life by listening closely to one another and reacting spontaneously. Blackburn could not have done a critical experiment without the expertise of Szostak, nor he without hers; their very experiment the result of conversation where each spontaneously responded to what the other said, allowing two streams of expertise to come together.

Collaboration with role differentiation. Sometimes the collaboration was constituted and directed by a leader. Though Blackburn felt that Greider was a complete collaborator in every phase of their work together, Blackburn was the mentor and she organized Greider's work, with Greider doing the bench work. In play rehearsals, the director as well as those that designed the set, the lighting, and the costumes, had different roles than the actors though they all contributed to what audiences experienced on the stage. Carter was the leader of the nonet, conceived the sound, chose the musicians, and designed the programs, and created arrangements.

The leaders, though, depended on the contributions of those they were leading. Blackburn and Greider played with possibilities for alternate explanations to their findings together, the ideas of each triggered by or built on by the other. Carter's music needed skilled musicians to develop his musical ideas and to add what he could not with their solos. As problems emerged, they too were solved through interaction, with each responding, to the suggestions of the others—Carter with his musicians, DeMarse with his director when an entrance didn't feel right. All these collaborative projects depended on mutual respect and trust among the collaborators. They depended on sensitive listening as well.

Even working alone. Badanes once said, "Writing is work you do in a room by yourself." Yet, even here, his creative work was imbued with sociality. He could not have done what he did without his schooling in reading and writing or his study of the work of the great writers of the past. His interviews with Holocaust victims impelled him to start his novel and gave him material to draw on. His editor's support sustained him; her critique of a scene sent him to engaging his wife to play the role of an angry wife. An early excerpt was accepted by a journal editor and gave him confidence in what he was doing. Even here, the creative process was in interaction with others.

THE EMERGENCE OF THE EPISODES' CREATIVE INTENTIONS

What about the creative episodes themselves? How did they start? Hill's statement could stand for all: by "a dive into the unknown," something unknown beckoning. In some episodes, what started that dive was clear: Grace Paley's puzzlement at meeting a known bigot with a young African-American boy in tow; Carter's hearing a musical idea that called him to develop it; commissions such as Biscardi's from the Music Library Association; Poincaré's decision to enter a contest about a specific class of functions; actors being cast in a play. These beginnings brought specific intentions.

For other episodes, the beginning was a gradual emergence of an intention. At first Darwin on the HMS Beagle was deeply involved with the geology of South America but also collected examples of the plants and fossil animals and occasionally raised questions about them. Then the finches of the Galápagos made him question whether a species can change a little over time. Finally, the analysis of his specimens by other experts convinced him of evolution. Only then did he form a specific intention; he started a notebook to discover how evolution worked, an account he demanded be supported by observations. Woolf's intention emerged gradually as well—a first glimpse of a possible story about her childhood at the seaside, then starting a story about her father. The project did not propel her into sustained writing till its structure came to her in a flow during a walk in the park. Sooner or later, conscious intentions typically brought about sustained work on a creative project.

NEXT STEPS

Variations in Initial Structure

Sometimes what to do next was very clear—the task was structured from the start. Actors knew they had to study their scripts. Blackburn knew to apply all the existent techniques for giving clues to telomere structure. Picasso decided to paint a new version of the artist and his model and he drew some sketches. Poincaré set out to prove Fuchs's assumption that a class of functions could not exist. Tolstoy's flow gave him the structure of a satiric adultery story; Carter knew he had to form a new kind of band. For others, embodied intuition-led trying was the next step. Biscardi sat down at the piano and allowed his fingers to go somewhere, already inhabiting the music world. LaChapelle wrote a sentence. Darwin wrote speculations in his notebook.

The Value of a Beginning: Promising or Not

Whatever the degree of initial structure, the creators plunged in. Sometimes the initial steps moved the project forward directly. For the first chapter of Blackburn's study of telomeres, a step-by-step process brought her clues to the answer she was looking for. Biscardi's first two chords felt right and became the first two chords of his piano work. By contrast, in several episodes, the creators deemed their first steps as unsatisfactory and discarded them: Darwin's theory of monads, Picasso's artist-and-model sketches, Sendak's attempts at his wild horses story, Poincaré's fruitless days. Yet those early, apparent missteps yielded elements that turned out to be generative. Darwin's sketch of the tree of life remained an important visualization. So did Sendak's picturing of a boy's room transforming into a garden. The features of the composition of Picasso's artist-model sketches were visible in his final mural. Poincaré's futile attempts to prove a class of functions could not exist brought him deeper understanding of mathematical relations. What appeared to be bad starts contained elements which often proved to be helpful.

Living in Worlds outside the Everyday and Embodied Creation

Sooner or later, the creative process involved leaving the everyday world and inhabiting one with distinctive features with respect to sense of self, taken-for-granted assumptions, typical activities, and sociality. The typical activities were embodied: actors moved in a drama world with self as characters; Darwin lived in a world of scientific theory where reasoning via writing or sketching in the light of empirical evidence was a taken-for-granted activity. Biscardi and Carter lived in music worlds, embodying sounds on the piano or with a band. Picasso, in an art world, thought visually by sketching.

Inhabiting these worlds took the creators out of their everyday concerns, their fears, their financial worries, the complexity of their interpersonal relationships, their self-doubts, even their ambitions at least for a while. They needed to return to the world of everyday life each day and often to the world of dreams at night.

So navigating among different psychological worlds recurrently was typical: the worlds of creation, a reflective world evaluating what had been created, and the everyday world. The different worlds affected one another successively. Reflection on an impasse could return thoughts to the everyday self, sometimes destructively as the inner critic. Everyday social support was frequently helpful in enhancing the pull to the creative world and its vividness. Reflection brought new intentions which affected the creative world; a satisfying trip to the world of creation enhanced the everyday sense of identity.

Figure-ground reversals. The different worlds also affected one another simultaneously as one world was the center of conscioiusness and another, explicitly or implicitly, was in the background. When on stage, the actor's everyday world—awareness of performing for an audience was in the background of the drama world. As in figure-ground reversals in perception, the actor's awareness of the audience may burst into the center of consciousness as a cell phone goes off or with a prop mishap.

The worlds of incubation. Several of the creators said in different ways, once you have been inhabiting a creative world that is important to you, it remains with you, though you may be consciously engaged in other modes of experience. Then the creative world may emerge, a figure-ground reversal of different psychological worlds. Sometimes what emerges is a creative visitation of the project so far and no more. Sometimes incubation ends with an insight into a creative problem, triggered by an event in the world—Picasso, jarred by the civilian bombing, allowed the political stream, formally kept apart from the painting stream, to converge with it. The creative world in the background of the everyday can emerge from the unconscious workings of the mind during incubation—such as the streams of two mathematical subdomains streams coming together for Poincaré or Paley's insight that the narrator of a story needed to change. Incubation leading to insight or flow can be understood in terms of one psychological world still active on the fringes of another, primed to become figure with the intimation that it is moving toward progress on a meaningful, but as yet incomplete project.

No Single Sequence of Stages

The episodes proceeded in different ways, and different chapters of the same episode differed as well. Poincaré had days of frustration trying to prove Fuchs's assumption till his sleepless night flow. In another chapter of the same episode, conscious heuristics guided him to a second result; the third chapter began with an insight that came to him without prior intention when two streams of mathematics came together.

Both intuitive and deliberate processes were part of creating, but when and how each entered the episode varied. Actors began by deliberately studying their scripts and continued to study them through rehearsal and performance; preparation never ended. Though entering other worlds of experience was also part of their independent preparation, the major work came during rehearsal as they analyzed together, got to know each other's everyday selves, and, most centrally, created intuition-led group flow in the drama world. These processes took place recurrently throughout rehearsal and performance. An emerging conscious intention could take hold after a flow which yielded a structure, as it did for Virginia Woolf and Tolstoy. Blackburn deliberately applied known methodologies to provide clues to telomere structure, but then allowed herself to play with possible visualizations till she recognized one that fit. Flow led to insight for Hill, insight to flow for Badanes.

Impasses. Experiencing an impasse was common and different creators dealt with it in different ways. Some, like Paley, Sendak, and Picasso chose incubation. Darwin formed a new intention. For Biscardi, impasses sometimes brought the deflating voice of the inner critic, sometimes led to seemingly giving up—followed by an intimation, an intuitive hunch that the solution was at hand (and literally in his hands).

Interruptions. Sometimes the episode was interrupted by events in the everyday world—Darwin's illness, Woolf's need to fill other commitments and her illnesses as well, Tolstoy grieving the deaths of loved ones. Then the pull of the work sometimes led to a difficult re-entry process (Badanes, Tolstoy). Sometimes the interruption served to be a useful incubation period as it did for Woolf.

Surprises. The creators often were surprised during their episodes. Surprise could happen during any phase. Sometimes the surprise came before an intention had taken hold—Tolstoy and Woolf both were surprised by a flow that gave them the starting outlines of their works. Insights were typically surprising, sometimes occurring during incubation—Poincaré stepping on a bus, Badanes getting an image of the protagonist's sister; sometimes during a flow—Sendak's relatives appearing on his sketch pad, Carter's fingers finding unexpected notes; sometimes, after a flow—Hill realizing the theme of her book after writing a paragraph. Surprises could come in the midst of reading—Biscardi recognizing a good composition title while reading a poem, Darwin seeing the significance of superfecundity while reading Malthus. In science, surprises could come from nature—to Darwin when he observed variations in birds on nearby islands—or from experimental outcomes, Blackburn when she discovered the unusual structure of telomeres.

Though the specific sequence varied, cycles of forming intentions, leaving the everyday world and entering a mode of experience outside the everyday, embodied flow allowing intuition to lead, consciously applying heuristics, playing with variations, incubation at times leading to insight and reflecting and evaluating were often phases of the creative episode. Which phases were part of a given episode varied as did the order in specific sequences. There was no template for how the creative process proceeded.

STRUCTURAL CHANGES OVER TIME: BROADENING AND REORGANIZING

The initial renderings often led to opening up to something more than the original intentions. For Blackburn and her collaborators, each result opened up new questions and new experiments. Paley felt impelled to write another story about a character, feeling the portrayal in the first had not done her justice. Woolf started out with a story centered on an avatar of her father; in the final novel her mother's avatar was even more central. Tolstoy started with an adultery story, broadened it to include other man–woman relationships, and then added a second plot which gave his novel a new theme that encompassed the earlier ones.

At times, the initial starts were totally transformed, sometimes even to their opposites. Poincaré proved the existence of functions whose very existence he set out to disprove. Tolstoy's first draft condemned an adulteress but he ended up writing her inner world with sensitivity and compassion. Badanes and Paley reversed the perspectives of their stories—from telling them from the viewpoint of their avatars to starting over with the perspective of another character. Picasso's first try had an artist in the center of the sketch painting a passive model; in the final mural, actively pleading victims took center stage pleading with his bull avatar in the upper left-hand corner.

Over time, new events could trigger major change. Picasso was deeply disturbed by the civilian bombing. Spontaneous insights could alter the structure of the work—Badanes's vision of the protagonist's dead sister required that she appear in already written sections and provided the narrative thrust of the rest of the book. New methods brought change as Blackburn and her colleagues found and Tolstoy discovered. Commitment to the project over time was the necessary ingredient that allowed these different changes to unfold.

WHAT BROUGHT THE CREATIVE EPISODES TO A CLOSE?

In some episodes the outer boundary of the creative episode was clear: a process was complete when writers submitted work for publication, when a play completed its performance run, when a musical composition was ready to be performed. In other cases, it was difficult to decide. Was a new experiment in Blackburn's lab a chapter in the telomere story or a new episode? Was each engagement or even each set of Carter's nonet band a new episode or was the development of the nonet sound over time a single story? Was each of Poincaré's insights a new episode or were the new supplements to his entry in the math competition simply different chapters of the same episode? Others may have made different decisions than I did. I let intuition be my guide as each story unfolded.

Nevertheless, one theme across many of the chapters and whole episodes was that the creative process was a search for a meaningful whole and the completion of a chapter or a whole episode, its construction. Evolution theory by natural selection captured the many different observations Darwin had been collecting. The making of Woolf's *To the Lighthouse* and Biscardi's quintet pointed the way to resolving unresolved issues from childhood and, at the same time, produced works that communicated universal meaning in form and content. Actors found new meaning in playwrights' words and brought them to life in performance. Blackburn, with her colleagues, kept working till they knew the story of how telomeres were formed. Sendak, through finding his way to "where the wild things are" and back, illuminated the developmental process children go through. Picasso found the form that challenged viewers to face the horror and devastation of war. Poincaré discovered the unity among first two, then three mathematical subdomains. Tolstoy found the overarching theme that brought together the tragedy of an adulteress and his own uncertainties.

One reason it was sometimes so difficult to determine when an episode was complete was that these episodes were part of a larger commitment. In diaries, memoirs, and interviews, various creators gave voice to what, in chapter after chapter, episode after episode, they were searching for: Paley spoke of "an absolute compulsion to tell the truth"; Darwin, of "an instinct for the truth." Biscardi wrote of wanting to discover "feelings below the conscious world" and "what it means to be human"; actors, of uncovering the deep layers of their characters, bringing to light "human possibilities." Poincaré wrote of revealing "mathematical beauty, the harmony of numbers and forms." Blackburn spoke of wanting to find out "how living things work"; writers, of discovering "how life is," "how we are."

My visit to the worlds of these scientists and artists at work has been a very moving experience.

Index

Note: 'n' after a page reference indicates the number of a note on that page.

acting 66–77; actors' independent work in 68–71; experiential worlds and interactions 76–77; performance 73–75; rehearsals 71–73; techniques 67
Actor's Studio 67, 68
adultery: *Anna Karenina* (Tolstoy) 109–120; theme in literature and culture 109–110
analogy, heuristics 13
Anna Karenina (Tolstoy) 109–120
apprenticeship, Sendak, Maurice 96–97
Arnheim, R. 37, 41–42, 48
artificial selection 28
association (as a mental process) 14, 69, 75, 96–97, 99
audience awareness, acting 74, 167
avatars 48; fictional avatars 61; in *To the Lighthouse* (Woolf) 130–131
Azbuka (Tolstoy) 110

Badanes, J. 53–54, 56–57, 59–60, 62, 64, 165
Bakhtin, M. M. 59
bandleading 152–158
Bartlett, R. 110
bass (instrument) 150, 151–158; piccolo bass 152, 157
Beagle voyage, Darwin, C. 24–26
beginnings 166; in specific chapters 10, 26, 29, 41, 55–56, 58, 68, 83, 110, 112, 138, 152, 158; value of bad 166; *see also* problem representation; seed incidents
biographers 1, 130
Birdland 154, 160

birth of an idea 12
Biscardi, C. 81–92
Blackburn, E. 137–147
Blaisdell, B. 111
Bloomsbury Group 123
Brady, C. 137
breeding 28
Brown, L. A. 66–67, 70-2, 75
Busch, W. 99

Carter, R. 150–160
catastrophism 24
cello 150–151, 153–155, 158
characters, fiction world 60–61
Chicken Soup with Rice (Sendak) 96–97
children's frameworks (Piaget) 24
Chipp, H. 39, 46
chromosomes 137–146
chronic stress (and telomere length) 146
Chrystie, F. 95
collaboration 165; in acting 71–72, 75; in music 87, 154, 156; in science 25, 141–144
commitment 56–57, 164
competition 11
composing music: classical 81–92; jazz 152–154, 158
A Confession (Tolstoy) 118
conjecture 115–116
convergence of streams 16–18, 130, 147n2, 157
courage 32
creationism 23
creative development 56, 104

creative visitations 85, 91, 129
Crick, F. H. C. 138
Cseh, G. M. 60
Csikszentmihalyi, M. 60
curiosity 34, 138, 144, 147, 158–159
Cuvier, G. 23

Darwin, C. 22–35; Beagle voyage 24–26;
    breeding 28; emotion 30–32; evolution
    26–30; monads 27–28; natural selection
    28–33
Darwin, E. 23
Davis, M. 151–152
DeMarse, J. 66–77
Die Leiden des jungen Werthers (The Sorrows of
    Young Werther) (Goethe) 110
directors, acting 71–72
discovery: in acting 71–72, 73; in art 49; in
    mathematics 12, 13, 16–17; in microbiology
    139, 146; in music 84, 88, 92; in writing 58,
    59, 63
divergent thinking 14, 97
DNA 138–146
domain 11; attraction to 163
drama world 71–73, 74–76
The Dream and Lie of Franco (Picasso) 39
dummy (for Sendak books) 96, 98–100
Duncker, K. 88

earthworms 33
Edmonstone, J. 23
effortless attention 13
embodied creation 68, 72, 84, 92, 100, 102,
    152, 159, 166, 167
emotions; in children's books 94, 102, 103, 104;
    in composing and music 84, 86, 89–90;
    conveyed in visual art 42; embodied by
    actors 67, 71, 74, 75; in mathematics and
    science 15, 30–32, 147; in writing 60, 62,
    121, 131
enzyme (telomerase) 142–147
errors, helpful 28, 71, 98, 153
evaluation 17, 58, 92, 98, 127; *see also*
    verification
everyday world 13, 34n3, 57, 62, 63, 74, 76,
    88, 167

evolution 23, 26–30
extrinsic motivation 10

Fascism 39
failure 16, 17, 86, 143
fathers: Biscardi 82, 86–87, 88, 89, 90; Carter,
    150; Darwin 22; Picasso 39; Sendak 94;
    Woolf 122–123, 125, 130, 131–132
fiction world 58–61, 97–98, 112
fictional avatars 61
field 11
fixity 88
flow 13, 60, 62, 86, 90, 112, 125, 129, 157–158
Frankl, V. 118
Franklin, M. 17, 56
Franklin, R. 138
Freud, S. 104n1, 129
Fuchs, L. 11, 13
Fuchsian functions 12

Gadamer, H. G. 56
Gall, J. 138
gatekeepers 11, 142, 144, 147, 164–165
Gedo, M. M. 37
Gestalt principle 85
Glynn, E. 95
Goethe, W. 110
Gould, J. 26
Grant, R. 23
Gray, J. J. 11, 18
Greider, C. 142–147
group flow (Carter, R.) 157–158
group trust 71, 153, 155, 157, 159
Gruber, H. E. 17, 22, 24, 27–28, 31–32, 132
Guernica (Picasso) 37–49

Hamilton, C. 151
Henslow, J. 23
heuristics 13
Hill, Kathleen 53–57, 59, 61–64
Hogarth Press 123
hypotheses 137, 139, 142, 146

identity 63, 74, 82, 164, 167
illumination 12; *see also* insight
impasses 58–59, 167, 168

Impressionism 38
improvisation: in acting 74; biochemical 147; in
    face-to-face conversation 147; jazz 151,
    154, 155, 156–157; narrative 59–60, 126,
    127, 128, 130
In Time's Unfolding (Biscardi) 85, 87, 91, 92
incomplete tasks, tension from 15, 19n1, 20n4, 86
incubation 12, 14–16, 19, 167–168; convergence
    of streams 16–18; Sendak, M. 96–97, 98;
    Woolf, V. 126; writers 59
influence vs resonance 83
initial structure, variations in 166; see also
    problem representation
inner critic 59
"inside-out" tradition, acting 67
insight 12, 13, 15–16, 17, 19, 31, 59, 89, 167,
    168, 169
intentions 60, 62, 72–73, 75, 76, 102, 125,
    165–166, 167, 169
intermittency, writers 61–62
interruptions 168
interview studies: with actors 66–77; with Biscardi
    81–91; with Carter 151–160; with writers
    53–63
intimation 12, 31, 89, 92, 168
intrinsic motivation 10, 124
intuition 19, 83, 84, 85, 87, 89, 91, 92, 92n, 96,
    98, 100, 101, 103, 139–140, 145, 146, 168

James, H. 130
James, W. 57
Jarrett, K. 83
jazz 150, 151–160; sets as stories 155–156
Johnson, C. 101

Kazan, E. 67
Kenny's Window (Sendak) 95
Kinnell, G. 85
Kunitz, S. 86

LaChapelle, M. 53, 55–59, 61, 63–64
Lamarck, J.-B. 23
Lamarckian theory 27
late modernism, music 82–83
Lawson, D. 155
Lee, H. 130

Lewin, K. 19n1
linear differential equations 11
listening: in acting 71, 72; in music 84, 88,
    156, 157
The Low End Theory (A Tribe Called Quest) 160
Lyell, C. 23–25, 27

Maar, D. 41
Mace, M. 60
Maleson, B. 156–157
Malthus, T. R. 29–30
manhood 87
The Meadow Bell (LaChapelle) 55
meaning: Guernica (Picasso) 48–49; Tolstoy, L.
    118–119
meaning-making 170
mentors 23, 24, 31, 138, 139, 147, 164–165
Mestiere (Biscardi) 88
metafictional statements 125
"The Method" 67
microbiology 138–146
mind-wandering 10
mishaps, acting 74
monads 27–28
Moore, K. 153
mothers, creators as: Blackburn 144, 147; writers
    54, 55
mothers of creators: Biscardi 82, 86; Sendak 94,
    98, 104; Tolstoy 116; Woolf 122–123, 126,
    130, 131, 132, 169
motivation 10, 124
Mrs. Dalloway (Woolf) 125, 130
multiple realities, writers 57
murder, adulterous wife 110
music, Biscardi, C. 81–92

narrative-phenomenological approach 1, 2;
    clues in 1, 2, 41, 66, 83, 94, 109, 122,
    137, 150
narrative voice 58–59, 115
natural selection 28–33
network of colleagues 25–26, 164–165
network of enterprises 17, 24, 33
nonet (Carter, R.) 153–159
Nordstrom, U. 95, 99
Nutshell Library (Sendak) 96–97

The Odyssey 86, 91
Ohio Ballet 87
The Orphans' Home Cycle (Foote) 68
Ouellette, D. 150, 158
"outside-in" tradition, acting 67, 70
Owen, R. 26

Paley, G. 53, 55–61, 64
Pastels (1976) 153
performances (theatrical) 73–75; audience
    awareness in 74; hazards in and avoiding
    them 74–75; preparation for (in the dressing
    room) 73–74
Peter the Great 110
Pevear, R. 117
phenomenologist: Schütz as 2, 53, 57, 63; Tolstoy
    as 120; Woolf as 129
Piaget, J. 24
*Piano Quintet, for piano and violin, with violin,
    viola and violoncello* (Biscardi) 91
Picasso, P., *Guernica* 37–49
piccolo bass 152
picture books 94
Pirogova, A. 111
plasmids 140
play with variations 84, 91, 92, 102, 143, 169
Poincaré, H. 9–19
point of creative frustration 58–59
preparation 12
problem representation: Darwin 26–27, 30;
    Poincaré 13
problem-solving 12, 56
psychoanalysis 1, 37, 95, 98, 103, 131
psychological worlds 13, 19n2, 30, 33, 57–62,
    63, 66, 68, 70–77, 77n2, 85, 88, 91,
    147, 147n, 154, 158, 167–168; figure-
    background relations in 72, 76; interactions
    among 76–77
publishing, writers 63

racism 151
reflection 17, 19, 42, 58, 59, 61, 62, 63, 68, 76,
    101, 83, 85, 88, 89, 97, 98, 100, 101, 103,
    125, 126, 167
rehearsals, acting 71–73
revisions 63, 99–102, 128

rhythm, children's books 97
RNA 145, 146
role differentiation, collaboration 165
The Russian Messenger 116–117

Sanger, F. 138
Schütz, A. 2, 3, 53, 57, 63, 66, 76,
    77n2, 147n1
scientific method 146
Sedat, J. 138
seed incidents: *Anna Karenina* 111; Biscardi 86,
    87; writers 56
self-doubt 85–86; *see also* inner critic
Sendak, M. 94–104
sense of direction 56, 60, 86, 126
Shampay, J. 140–141
shapes, meaning 42
sharing the work 63
Shinder, J. 86
The Sign on Rosie's Door (Sendak) 96
significant others 31–32, 95, 111, 112, 123, 164
sketches: for *Guernica* 39–40, 41–44; for *Where
    the Wild Things Are* 99–100
Smith, Lois 66–67, 69, 71–72, 74–75, 77
social aspects of creative process 31–32, 72, 76,
    111, 123, 124, 146–147, 164–166, 167;
    see also collaboration
A Song for You (Carter) 154
spheres of experience (Darwin) 31–32
spontaneous generation 27
spontaneous reorganization 19
stages (of the creative process) 12, 19, 168
Steinbeck, J. 59
Stokowski, L. 151
Strakhov, N. N. 111–112, 116
Strasberg, L. 67
stream of consciousness 123–133
streams 20n4
structure, vision of (at the beginning and
    changing) 33, 62, 73, 75, 84–85, 91, 125,
    132, 166, 169
suicide 110, 118
superfecundity 30–31
surprises 42, 61–62, 92, 119, 139, 157,
    168–169
Szostak, J. 140–142

Telemakhos project, Biscardi, C. 86–90
telomerase 144–146
telomeres 138–141
Tetrahymena thermophila 137–147
theta-Fuchsian 13
thinking: visual 27, 41–42, 47–49, 139; in
    words 26
titling 49, 85, 91, 94
To the Lighthouse (Woolf) 122–133
Tolstoy, L. 109–120
Tolstoy, S. 111–112, 116
Toulouse, E. 11, 16
The Train Driver 70
Traverso (Biscardi) 88
The Trip to Bountiful 69
twelve-tone music 82, 88

The Understanding (LaChapelle) 55
uniformism 24–25

value of a beginning 166–167
verification 12, 14, 17, 19
Very Far Away (Sendak) 96
visual thinking 27, 41–42, 47–49, 139

Wallace, A. R. 32
Wallace, D. 56–57, 124
Wallas, G. 12, 14, 17
Walter, S. A. 11, 18
War and Peace (Tolstoy) 111, 114
Ward, T. B. 1
Watson, J. D. 138
Wertheimer, M. 13
"When One Has Lived a Long Time Alone"
    (Kinnell) 85
whole-part relations 42. 43, 61 85, 91, 100,
    159, 170
Where the Wild Horses Are (Sendak) 94–95, 97–98
Where the Wild Things Are (Sendak) 94–104
Willie (Hill) 54, 61
woman question 110
Woolf, L. 123
Woolf, V. 122–133
writing places 57
writing realm 58–59

Zaidenshnur, E. E. 114
Zhdanov, V. A. 114
Zygarnik effect 19n1

network of enterprises : multiple interests
time away

mentorship, books
other ppls work : archive   NATURAL
personal archive   CONVO
current obsessions
fellow colleages
various ways of thinking
death + grief
emotion
attention / attending

obj vs subj